Knowing People

The Personal Use of Social Psychology

Michael J. Lovaglia

University of Iowa

 **McGraw-Hill**

Boston • Burr Ridge, IL • Dubuque, IA • Madison, WI • New York •
San Francisco • St. Louis • Bangkok • Bogotá • Caracas • Lisbon •
London • Madrid • Mexico City • Milan • New Delhi • Seoul •
Singapore • Sydney • Taipei • Toronto

McGraw-Hill Higher Education

A Division of The **McGraw-Hill** Companies

KNOWING PEOPLE: THE PERSONAL USE OF SOCIAL PSYCHOLOGY
Copyright © 2000 by The McGraw-Hill Companies, Inc. All rights reserved. Printed in the United States of America. Except as permitted under the United States Copyright Act of 1976, no part of this publication may be reproduced or distributed in any form or by any means, or stored in a data base or retrieval system, without the prior written permission of the publisher.

This book is printed on acid-free paper.

1 2 3 4 5 6 7 8 9 0 FGR/FGR 9 0 9 8 7 6 5 4 3 2 1 0 9

ISBN 0–07–303996–9

Editorial director: *Phillip A. Butcher*
Sponsoring editor: *Sally Constable*
Developmental editor: *Katherine Blake*
Marketing manager: *Leslie A. Kraham*
Senior project manager: *Jean Lou Hess*
Production supervisior: *Debra R. Benson*
Freelance design coordinator: *Pam Verros*
Supplement coordinator: *Rose M. Range*
Compositor: *ElectraGraphics, Inc.*
Typeface: *10.5/12 Times Roman*
Printer: *Quebecor Printing Book Group/Fairfield*

Library of Congress Cataloging-in-Publication Data

Lovaglia, Michael J.
   Knowing people: the personal use of social psychology/Michael
J. Lovaglia.
     p. cm.
   Includes bibliographical references and index.
   ISBN 0–07–303996–9
   1. Social perception.   2. Self-perception.   I. Title.
HM1041.L68   2000
302´.12—dc21
                                         99–33206
                                         CIP

http://www.mhhe.com

About the Author

H. HORAN

MICHAEL LOVAGLIA is an Associate Professor at the University of Iowa. He received his Master's and Ph.D. degrees in Sociology from Stanford University. Dr. Lovaglia's research on social power, status, and emotion has been supported by grants from the National Science Foundation. His articles have been published in *The American Journal of Sociology, American Sociological Review,* and *Social Psychology Quarterly.* He edits *Current Research in Social Psychology* and is Deputy Editor of *Sociological Quarterly.* In the spring of 1999 he became president-elect of the Iowa Sociological Association.

Dr. Lovaglia tries to incorporate social psychological research and teaching into other areas of his life. "Social psychology is important because you can use it to help people," he says. Over the years he has enjoyed the experience of having foster children live with him, his wife, Valarie, and two children, Kyle and Hannah. His older daughter, Domenica, lives in Seattle.

Before returning to college and eventually getting his Ph.D., he spent a number of years in a variety of occupations: food server, bartender, salesperson, waterbed and hot tub installer, janitor, and factory worker. He notes, "My general lack of success in these occupations led me back to school. Working through the difficulties in life gives people the raw material for social psychological insight."

Preface

My older daughter, Domenica, gave me the idea for this book. On a visit after she started college, she mentioned that she was thinking of majoring in sociology or psychology. I smiled with pride, thinking that her father might have inspired her interest in social psychology. Perhaps not noticing my reaction, she quickly added, "But not like anything you do, Dad. I want to study something interesting."

I wanted to argue that social psychology was interesting, but I didn't know how to convince her. I knew that when she dutifully tried to wade through one of my research papers, she would find it dry and abstract, maybe even useless. Academic research has a reputation for having little practical value. Of course, while most of us academic researchers are fascinated by what we study, we can also see how the rest of humanity might not share our interest. Why should I be surprised that my daughter had no interest in my research?

I wanted to tell her that social psychology is not only interesting but also useful—not just to me, but to everyone who has to get along with other people. I wanted to show her how social psychology had helped me solve the major problems that troubled me when I was her age: how to work with people, how to make friends, how to fit into a world that often seemed alien to me. It took a long time to do that. Instead of telling her directly, I wrote this book.

KNOWING PEOPLE

Social psychology is about knowing people. It is a scientific discipline as practical as a paycheck. Knowing people gives us the ability to cope with the tangled networks of human relationships in which we find ourselves. In turn, knowing people understand the beliefs, desires, and passions of the people they en-counter.

Knowledge of social psychology is power, to the extent that it lets us understand relationships among human beings. Understanding other people and ourselves allows us to turn our problems into opportunities. Knowing people can help us better fashion solutions to problems, solutions that benefit all concerned rather than one person or group at the expense of another.

Working out our relationships with others may be the central concern that we share as human beings. Some argue that the difficulty of people problems actually caused human intelligence to evolve (see Chapter 2). You will find that social psychology is not only an eminently useful science, but also interesting and at times fun. That is because human relationships are fascinating, troublesome, and funny.

USING SOCIAL PSYCHOLOGICAL RESEARCH

This book describes research in social psychology that has proven useful in my personal life. My goal is to present the highest quality research in plain language, then show how it was useful to me. Perhaps you can use it to improve your life. Along the way, I hope to give you the flavor—the fun and the adventure—of doing research. Conducting social psychological research inevitably means forming relationships with people. In my own research, I have formed relationships with many people whom I otherwise would not have gotten to know.

The studies discussed are real. They have been reviewed by experts in the field and published in the top scientific journals of psychology and sociology. They are mostly too new to be classics, yet almost all have stood up to years of research that has built on them and supported them. A few are so current that their conclusions have yet to be confirmed by further published work. Even the newest studies selected, however, are only those that have built directly on a solid foundation of valid earlier research.

Social psychology has blossomed as a scientific discipline during the last 50 years. Regrettably, I have been able to include only a small fraction of the relevant research. There are thousands of rigorous scientific studies that probably should have been included, but then the book would be impossibly long. I decided to focus on studies that were of the highest quality and had a personal impact on my life. That way I could describe them carefully rather than glossing over each study in a sentence or two.

At the end of each chapter, I have cited other supporting research and included additional references relating to both general reading and technical issues. Still, these added references make only a small dent in the body of social psychological research that has been left out. Serious students will want to study an introductory social psychology textbook as well.

You may decide that I have left out a study that is absolutely necessary for understanding the field. Should you think of an essential study or research area that is missing, please let me know. I would like to make this book as useful as possible. If readers will help me, I hope to improve future editions by using their suggestions. My e-mail address is michael-lovaglia@uiowa.edu.

THE STYLE OF THIS BOOK

I have tried to write in a friendly way. I have kept technical terminology to a minimum. Some technical terms are necessary, and I define them the first time they appear. I also try to remind readers of a technical term's meaning when it pops up again in another section.

This book is about my life and the lives of people around me as much as it is about science. Still, I have worked hard at the science that is my profession. When describing research, I stick closely to the practical details of what was done and what really happened. The results of the studies in this book are not opinions but represent knowledge you can count on. How these results have worked in my life and the lives of other people are interpretations. You will judge for yourself what is useful in your own life.

Sometimes careful scholarship gets in the way of easy reading. Readers who are interested in digging further into social psychology need to be able to find the original research publication in a library. To identify original sources, last names of authors of relevant works are given in parentheses followed by the date of publication: (Jones 1986), for example. Those interested in further reading on a topic can easily find relevant works by consulting the alphabetical listing of authors and their work in the reference section. If you are not accustomed to names and dates in the middle of sentences, then this may bother you at first. Please try to continue. You will soon read over them without noticing, until you decide you need to look up something; then they come in handy.

A FINAL NOTE TO THE INSTRUCTOR

Knowing People works as a supplemental text in social psychology and more general introductory social science courses. In the social psychology course, it works well in conjunction with a general social psychology text. It also may be used as one of several more specialized readings.

My main goal was to write a book that students would find useful and want to read. As it was being written, I used it in both my social psychology course and a large introductory course. Overall, students have given *Knowing People* high marks for readability and for making social psychological research relevant to their lives. The book is much better for students' suggestions and forthright criticism of earlier versions.

This book is also better because of comments and suggestions provided by a panel of reviewers. In closing, I would like to thank the following reviewers for their many helpful suggestions: Ann Branaman, Florida Atlantic University; J. David Knottnerus, Oklahoma State University; David Lundgren, University of Cincinnati; James Marshall, University of Northern Colorado; and Jane Sell, Texas A & M University. My father, Anthony R. Lovaglia, provided useful advice and editorial suggestions.

Michael Lovaglia
University of Iowa

Brief Contents

Contents

8. Why I'm Prejudiced 149

9. The Power In and Out of Love 180

CHAPTER 1

The Power of the Situation over You

Social psychology makes people uncomfortable. It shows us how little we know about ourselves and other people. And worse, it shows us that we do not have nearly as much control over our lives as we think. Why would anyone want to study such a science? Getting a true picture of our place in society, even if that picture disappoints us, is only a first step. Once we know how the social world works, we can find ways to change it, to make our social world a better place to live. Knowledge of social psychology gives us the power to shape our character and social circumstances in a way that is beneficial not only to us but to those around us. We study social psychology to improve people's lives. Social psychologists assume that good will come out of discovering how the social world really works, no matter how uncomfortable that knowledge makes us. We believe that knowledge will lead not only to a deeper understanding of ourselves as human beings but also to more tangible benefits. This book shows you how to use the knowledge discovered by research in social psychology.

The fundamental lesson of social psychology is that individual attitudes and decisions are less important in our lives than we think they are. The situation we are in limits our behavior much more than we think it does. For example, television news showed videotape of a teenager robbing an 80-year-old man in broad daylight. The attack occurred on a stretch of grass near a busy sidewalk and several stores. The teenager beat and kicked the man for a long time before taking his wallet and walking casually away. The man lay alone, a bloody heap on the ground. The announcer said that he had not regained consciousness. No one tried to intervene during the attack. No one called for help. The videotape showed people watching the attack from a safe distance. The videotape was filmed through a window from inside a nearby store. Most people are dismayed when they hear such stories. How can people be so unfeeling? Certainly we would have done something, at least yelled for help. There must be something wrong with people who just stood and watched. But not us. Certainly we would act differently.

Social psychology tells us that far from being callous and cowardly, bystanders in emergency situations are acting normally when they fail to respond. We, as normal people, would fail to respond as well. That social psychological insight makes us uncomfortable. We like to feel we would behave differently, better. The problem with bystanders, however, does not stem from defects in their character that prevent them from helping. Rather, the situation that bystanders find themselves in constrains their behavior more than we realize. For example, Darley and Latané (1968) found that the more bystanders there are, the less likely any one of them will intervene. They found that in an emergency, a single bystander would usually respond, just as we hope we would do. But when a number of bystanders witness an emergency, responsibility apparently diffuses among them. No one bystander feels enough personal responsibility to respond.

In many situations, no one helps because each bystander believes that with so many people around someone else is bound to help (Latané & Nida 1981). For example, think about how you would respond if you were driving on a deserted stretch of road. Quite a way ahead, you notice a car swerve off the road then flip over. You would stop to help the driver, wouldn't you? We would like to think we would, and most of the time in this situation, people do behave like the caring human beings they are. They stop and help. Now change the situation slightly. Imagine you are on a busy freeway instead of a deserted road. When the car up ahead flips over, would you still pull over to try to help? Probably not. Most people would continue past, assuming that other drivers would help. The point is that the situation, not our individual moral character, determines whether we stop to offer aid.

We are only as good as the situation we are in allows us to be. For example, Darley and Batson (1973) used seminary students to show how the situation can overshadow individual differences in whether people offer help. They chose seminary students because people studying for the priesthood are likely to be committed to helping other people. They would certainly be aware of the New Testament story about the Good Samaritan that described how people walked by a beaten man, ignoring his plight. Would seminary students walk past an apparently injured person?

Darley and Batson (1973) set up a situation in which seminary students on their way to make a brief speech had to walk past a groaning man slumped in a doorway. The researchers had told some of the students that they were late for the speech and should hurry. Only 10 percent of seminary students in a hurry stopped to help. Ten percent would seem to be a shockingly low percentage of seminary students who are willing to stop and help a person in obvious distress. However, the reason that so few stopped to help has little to do with the moral character of the students. Other students were not told they were late and so were not in a hurry to make their speech. Well over half the students who were not in a hurry stopped to help. The situation, some students being in a hurry and others not, determined whether they stopped to help. The religious convictions of the seminarians made little difference in whether they stopped to help. Darley and Batson tested the students' religious commitment. Those with greater religious commitment were no more likely to help than were those with less commitment. Yet we assume that people's character determines whether they stop to help. We ignore the power of the situation.

Ignoring situational causes of behavior and emphasizing the effects of individual character is a widespread human tendency, especially in modern Western cultures. Our overemphasis on individual character as the cause of behavior stems

Dilbert has less control than he thinks

from our dependence on other people. Hamilton (1980) suggests that attribution to an individual's character gives us someone to blame. We use guesses about the reasons for our own and others' behavior to help us navigate through a complex social world. That is, we make attributions for our own and others' behavior.

When we make an attribution for a person's behavior in a situation, the attribution helps us make sense of the social world. The attribution helps us to predict how that person will act in similar situations in the future. For example, suppose you and a group of friends are walking to lunch on a city street. A homeless person shuffles over and asks for spare change. All of your friends refuse or ignore him except one who pulls out his wallet and gives the beggar five dollars. To what do you attribute your friend's generosity? You might think he donated the money because he is a good-hearted, generous person, or because he is a soft touch. These would be dispositional attributions. You attribute your friend's generosity to relatively stable aspects of his character. Or you might look to the situation for an explanation. Maybe your friend recently got a raise at work. This is a situational attribution. The kind of attribution you make can determine how you behave toward your friend in the future. Suppose you go to lunch with the same group a month later. After you order, you notice with dismay that you have no money. Will your friend be as generous today as he was before? Had you made a dispositional attribution for your friend's generosity, you would feel confident in asking him for help. That is, if generosity is a stable part of his character, then he should be just as generous with you as he was with the homeless person.

Attribution research has become a major subfield in social psychology.[1] Much of that research investigates what Ross (1977) has labeled the *fundamental attribution error:* our tendency to attribute the cause of behavior to the stable disposition of persons rather than to situational factors. That is, we see ourselves and other people as more powerful and more consistent in our behavior than we actually are. In doing so, we ignore factors in our situation that significantly affect us.

[1]For more extensive overviews of research on attributions see Jones (1991) and Ross and Nisbett (1991).

INVESTIGATING THE FUNDAMENTAL ATTRIBUTION ERROR

The first studies to investigate the fundamental attribution error looked at the conclusions people draw when they watch another person's behavior. We use what people say and do as clues to discover what kind of person they are. However, we may attribute behavior to a person's character when that person had little or no control over what she did. Factors in a person's situation may have dictated her behavior. She may have had little choice but to act as she did, so her behavior would not really tell us much about the kind of person she is. Nonetheless, we will probably continue to assume that her beliefs and attitudes correspond to her behavior. Because we typically assume a correspondence between a person's behavior and attitude whether one exists or not, another term used almost interchangeably with the fundamental attribution error is *correspondence bias* (Jones 1986). Correspondence bias represents a different theoretical approach to the same research area. It helps to be familiar with both terms.

Jones and Harris (1967) set up a situation where people would judge a person's attitude based on an essay the person had written. People were asked to judge one of two essays about Fidel Castro's communist regime in Cuba. They were told that the essay they read had been written for a political science class. One essay supported Castro; the other essay attacked him. People read the essay then rated the author's true attitude toward Castro. Researchers predicted, as would most of us, that people would assume that authors of a pro-Castro essay had a pro-Castro attitude, whereas authors of an anti-Castro essay had an anti-Castro attitude. That is exactly what happened, to no one's great surprise.

When they repeated the study, Jones and Harris (1967) showed people the assignment that a teacher had given along with the essay that had been written to complete the assignment. People reading the pro-Castro essay saw that the assignment had been to "write a short cogent defense of Castro's Cuba." Similarly, people reading the anti-Castro essay saw that the assignment had been to "write a short cogent criticism of Castro's Cuba." People thus were aware that the author of the essay had little choice in the subject matter of the essay. The teacher's assignment dictated whether the essay would be pro-Castro or anti-Castro. Would people continue to assume that authors of pro-Castro essays had attitudes more favorable to Castro than did authors of anti-Castro essays? They did. Despite knowing that the essay author had little choice in the content of the essay, people continued to assume that authors of the pro-Castro essay were more pro-Castro than were authors of the anti-Castro essay. That is, despite direct evidence that a situational factor (the assignment) dictated the content of the essay, people assumed that the essay content *corresponded* to the true attitude of the writer. We now know that by ignoring the evidence of a situational cause for the essay's content, the students displayed *correspondence bias*. They committed the *fundamental attribution error.*

The scientific community did not immediately accept the existence of a widespread bias toward dispositional attributions, let alone a fundamental attribution error. Following Jones and Harris (1967), many studies were conducted that showed how correspondence bias persists in a variety of situations that restrict a person's behavior. In one study, students judged the attitude of a person reading an essay aloud. Students assumed the essay reader's attitude corresponded to the essay content even when they had been told that the speech had been written by someone else (Miller 1976).

In my social psychology classes, I demonstrate the pervasive effect of correspondence bias. Two students volunteer to present a short speech. I take them into the hallway and give each a handwritten speech on the abortion issue. One essay is prochoice, the other is prolife. The presenters then take five minutes to practice their speech. Meanwhile, in the classroom, I pass out index cards on which the students will rate their impressions of the true attitudes of the presenters toward abortion. Then the first presenter gives the prolife speech. Students rate the true attitude of the presenter on an index card and turn it in. The second presenter gives the prochoice speech. Again, students rate the true attitude of the presenter and hand in their ratings. In this situation, it is quite plausible that students rate the prochoice presenter as having a prochoice attitude and the prolife presenter as having a prolife attitude. Students, after all, may well assume that the presenters wrote the speech they were presenting, or that presenters had chosen to speak on the side of the issue that corresponded with their true attitude toward abortion.

The next part of the demonstration is more interesting. I ask for two more volunteers to give a speech. In front of the class, I ask the presenter of the prochoice speech to give the handwritten copy of the speech to the first new volunteer. I ask the presenter of the prolife speech to give the handwritten copy of that speech to the second new volunteer. It is clear to all students that I have assigned the new volunteers to speak on either the prochoice or prolife side of the issue. They had no choice in the matter. And, because students have just finished listening to the exact speeches, it is clear that the new volunteers will be reading material written by someone else. The new volunteers have a few minutes to practice their speeches. The first volunteer presents the prochoice speech and students hand in their ratings of the speaker's true attitude toward abortion. Then the second volunteer presents. Again, students rate the speaker's true attitude. In this situation, it is difficult to see how anyone would assume that speech content would necessarily correspond to the true attitudes of the speakers. After all, students had just heard another student reading the exact speech. Will students still assume that speech content corresponds to the true attitudes of the speakers? Will students rate the prochoice speaker as truly more prochoice than the prolife speaker?

Yes, students continue to display correspondence bias even when the situation dictates what the speaker will say and the students have just heard the exact words spoken by someone else. When we tally up the results in class, the pattern is the same for the second two speakers as it was for the first two speakers. The prochoice speakers are rated as having a prochoice attitude while the prolife speakers are rated as having a prolife attitude. The effect is not as dramatic for the second pair of speakers as for the first, but it is still apparent. Students assume that a person's spoken words correspond to the attitudes that person holds. That assumption proves very difficult to counteract.

In society, correspondence bias serves to maintain power and authority relationships among people. We give people credit for being competent when in fact their social position is responsible for their performance. One striking characteristic of modern social life is that some people have power and authority over others. Parents have power over their young children. Police detectives have power over suspected criminals. Teachers have power over students. When we deal with a person who has authority over us, it can often seem that the person is smarter and more competent than we are. Instead of attributing this power to the person's position in society, we make the fundamental attribution error. We assume the person is more competent than we are because the person has power over us. We ignore the fact that people have authority because of their social position, not necessarily because of any special expertise.

One way that society gives people power over others is by granting them authority to ask questions. When a person can ask you a question and require an answer, that person has power over you. For example, on TV police dramas, suspects often have higher social status than the detective does. The suspect might be a doctor, for example. When the detective tries to interview the doctor, the doctor usually asks a lot of questions: "What is this about, Detective?" or "Why are you interviewing me?" At some point, the detective gets serious and turns the tables, saying abruptly, "Here's how this works. I ask the questions. You answer them." Suddenly the social status of the two people has been reversed. The detective has asserted his authority, transforming the high-status doctor into a low-status suspect. Teachers demonstrate their authority by requiring students to answer questions on an exam. And children dread their parents' questions: "Why are you three hours late? Where have you been? What could you possibly have been thinking?" Anyone who has been trapped answering a five-year-old's questions for an hour knows just how much power the ability to question can give a person. Five-year-olds know it too. That is one reason they ask so many questions.

Ross, Amabile, and Steinmetz (1977) showed how questions work to cement the social position of those in authority. We think that people who ask questions are more knowledgeable than are people who have to answer them. Ross, Amabile, and Steinmetz set up a "quiz game" setting in which some students would try to answer questions as contestants. Some students would ask the questions as hosts, and other students would watch the game as the audience. It is easy to see how a questioner might have an advantage in such a situation. For example, the questioner can ask very difficult questions. Even people with little general knowledge know odd bits of information that others are not likely to know. Coming up with difficult questions is relatively easy. For example, in the study, questioners came up with questions such as "What do the initials W. H. in W. H. Auden's name stand for?" and "What is the longest glacier in the world?"

Beginning teachers soon discover a peculiar human trait. Anything we learn, no matter how complicated or difficult, seems obvious to us, even trivial, a short time after we have learned it. Because what teachers know seems obvious to them, novice teachers often make test questions too difficult for their students to answer. The teacher knows the answers, so the questions seem easy to her. The students do not know the answers and when they flunk the test, teacher and students may conclude that the class is not bright. For example, suppose you are a quiz game contestant and are asked "In what city did Sigmund Freud live and practice psycho-analysis during much of his career?" If you know the answer, it seems obvious—Vienna. You might be thinking "Everybody knows that," but you would be wrong. If you do not know the answer, the question seems impossibly difficult and even un-fair. However, the person who asked the question knows the answer. Unfair or not, the questioner will seem more knowledgeable than you.

In their quiz game study, Ross, Amabile, and Steinmetz (1977) made the ad-vantage given to questioners obvious to everyone. Students drew cards to determine who would be assigned to the various roles—questioner, answerer, or observer. Thus students realized that questioners had been chosen at random and not because they possessed any special qualification for the questioner role. Questioners were asked to come up with "challenging but not impossible" questions for the quiz game. They were asked to avoid easy questions and to create questions on topics in which they had the most knowledge. Answerers and observers also heard these in-structions given to questioners. Would students still rate questioners as more knowl-edgeable than answerers even though the advantage given by the answerer role was made obvious? Yes. Answerers consistently rated themselves as less knowledgeable than questioners. Neutral observers also rated questioners' general knowledge su-perior to that of answerers. Questioners, however, may have been more aware of the advantage their position gave them. Questioners themselves did not think they were much more knowledgeable than answerers. It may be true that those in positions of great power can sometimes more clearly see the effects of situational factors. Abra-ham Lincoln said, "I claim not to have controlled events, but confess plainly that events controlled me" (Lincoln 1965, p. 10). Being in a position of great power, Abraham Lincoln realized how limited his power actually was.

Results of the quiz game study imply that people in a low power position, who are required to answer the questions of a person with authority over them, will come to see the authority figure as having superior general knowledge. Our corre-spondence bias leads us to assume that the authority figure's apparent knowledge results from her personal abilities and general competence. We ignore evidence that the authority's position makes her appear competent. When questioners appear more knowledgeable because their position gives them the power to question, their authority seems more legitimate. We tend not to notice how big an advantage social position can be. Instead, we assume that those in positions of power must be as knowledgeable and expert as they appear. More generally, we fail to notice the situ-ational factors at work in our lives. Instead, we attribute outcomes to the personal abilities of individuals, whether to other people or ourselves. That is the fundamen-tal attribution error.

USING SOCIAL PSYCHOLOGY TO IMPROVE YOUR LIFE

Now that we know that we have less control over our lives than we had thought, how will social psychology help us? Research on the fundamental attribution error tells us that factors in our situation are more powerful than we think they are. If situational factors are so powerful, then changing them will change our lives. If you want your life to improve, then concentrate on changing your situation. Find ways to change your situation that will have the desired effect on you.

Recall that people are about as good as their situation allows them to be. If you want to be a good person, find a situation that supports your aspirations. For example, there is a saying among professional salespeople: "If you want to be an honest salesperson, then go to work for an honest boss." The sales game is highly competitive. Intense pressure to make a sale constantly tempts salespeople to cut corners, to lie to make a sale. Professional salespeople know that individual character is no match for the constant temptation to lie unless the organization they work for encourages honesty. They have found that an honest boss ensures that their own honesty will be supported. By changing their situation (finding an honest boss) salespeople can change a basic piece of their character (personal honesty). That insight empowers us to become better people.

Here is an example of our tendency to think we have more control over events than we actually do, and how understanding social psychology can change society. Consider this statement: "Meaningful social change must rise first in the hearts and minds of people." Most of us find it enormously appealing. We would not be surprised if a famous person had said it, perhaps Martin Luther King Jr. at the height of the civil rights movement. It conforms to personal experience. As you grow up, your ideas about who you are and what you want to do change, so you behave differently. It sounds right. Social psychology shows us that reality is much more complicated.

Successful leaders sometimes use the principles of social psychology although they may not be aware of it. Martin Luther King Jr. is a good example. During the civil rights movement in the 1950s—not so long ago—most Americans felt that African Americans should be treated differently than others. African Americans were required to use separate restrooms and drinking fountains. Facilities designated for African Americans were often unavailable. Few jobs were open to them. And while many Americans of all races believed in integration as an ideal, most of them felt that nothing could be done to change racial discrimination. Today, few people in the United States believe in or condone racial discrimination. How did such a profound change occur in the attitudes and beliefs of an entire nation?

Martin Luther King's strategy during the civil rights movement played a part in changing American's attitudes toward discrimination. At the time, popular wisdom held that you cannot legislate morality. According to popular opinion, legislation outlawing discrimination would not work unless people first came to believe that discrimination was wrong. It was commonly thought that people's hearts and minds had to change before their behavior would. Martin Luther King Jr. rejected the common wisdom in formulating a strategy for the civil rights movement (Branch 1988). While he spent much of his life trying to change people's attitudes, he did not wait for people to endorse social equality for African Americans. He saw that by changing the laws that limit people's behavior, not only would discrimination be reduced, but eventually hearts and minds would follow. He knew that long-held beliefs and attitudes, our feelings, are highly resistant to change. He also knew that most people will obey the law. His knowledge of people told him that over time attitudes and beliefs align with behavior. We now know there was a sound basis for his strategy in social psychological research. After civil rights legislation was passed and people grew accustomed to the new rules, attitudes toward racial discrimination changed rapidly. However, there is much work left to be done. Chapter 8 shows the progress that has been made in the social psychology of prejudice.

Social psychology teaches us that what we do, our behavior, has more impact over our attitudes and beliefs than we would have imagined. Common sense, after all, has told us that our attitudes and beliefs determine how we behave. However, the power of behavior to control deeply held beliefs was one of the earlier insights of the new discipline of social psychology. William James founded the first psychological laboratory in the United States at Harvard in the 1870s. In 1890, in the first American psychology textbook, he stated the principle that we can use our behavior to control our attitudes and beliefs. He said that while we cannot easily change our deeply held moral beliefs and emotionally charged attitudes,

> *we need only in cold blood ACT as if the thing in question were real, and keep acting as if it were real, and it will infallibly end by growing into such a connection with our life that it will become real.* (James 1890/1981, p. 949)

Behavior is easier to control than beliefs and attitudes. By consciously acting in certain ways, we will eventually come to justify and believe in the attitudes implied by our behavior. For example, when I was a freshman in college, foul language was the norm. It was cool. Speaking crudely was a badge of honor. Speaking politely was considered dishonest. That way of speaking became part of my identity. Swearing was who I was. Later, swearing caused problems for me. Children who heard me would use the same words I did. And I was working as a salesperson, so swearing was inappropriate on the job. I resolved to change the way I spoke. It was not particularly difficult. I reminded myself regularly not to swear and tried to think before speaking. My attitude toward swearing did not change so quickly. For a long time I felt like a phony. Blunt, coarse speech still seemed to me to be more honest and honorable. Those feelings faded the longer I went without swearing. Years later, swearing is awkward and I can make myself do it only with difficulty. My attitude toward swearing has also changed completely. It now seems unnecessary and

cathy®   **by Cathy Guisewite**

Action is sometimes more important than its immediate outcome

often destructive. My behavior changed first. My attitude toward that behavior followed.

"Bring the body, the mind will follow" is a slogan used by members of Alcoholics Anonymous. Problem drinkers often feel like phonies when they try to quit drinking. They feel they are being dishonest with other people and untrue to themselves. Deeply held attitudes may be difficult to change in normal people, but where the will has been damaged by alcohol or drug use, the conscious control of beliefs is virtually absent. Instead of trying to convince newcomers that drinking is a bad idea, AA members tell them to show up at AA meetings where no one drinks. "Bring the body" means show up, act like a sober person. Stop drinking one day at a time. Eventually, if a person does not drink for a long period, drinking comes to seem foreign, unnatural. The behavior change eventually produces an attitude change. The mind follows. Problem drinkers usually associate drinking with pleasant anticipation and exhilaration, but after quitting, they slowly come to realize and understand the problems that drinking caused them. The founders of AA had studied the psychology of William James. They knew that an effective program first must change the problem behavior. Healthier attitudes toward that behavior would follow.

The same principle that made the civil rights movement successful works to keep alcoholics sober. William James's idea that changing behavior can lead to improving personal character spurred the growth of a large self-help industry in the United States. Martin Luther King Jr. showed us that we need not be imprisoned by our history of prejudice. By changing our situation, changing the legal structure of society, racial prejudice is no longer predominant. It still exists and threatens to return full-force if we are not careful. But as long as we maintain our legal structure, our laws will allow us to be better people than our traditional fears and prejudices would suggest. The insights of social psychology can work on a more personal level as well.

PERSONAL SOCIAL PSYCHOLOGY TECHNIQUE: USING AFFIRMATION

Affirmations are positive statements about the person you want to be. By affirming the kind of person we want to become, we set ourselves up to change in that direction. The technique is not new. It has been used in crude form by teachers in the United States for about as long as there have been blackboards. Picture a whitewashed rural schoolhouse. A barefoot boy in pants too short for his legs stands at the blackboard writing laboriously "I will not stick Molly's braids in the inkwell," 100 times. We now think that positive statements make more effective affirmations than negative ones; so the boy wearing flashy athletic shoes and baggy jeans might write "I will respect Molly as a person." The idea is the same. All of that writing on the blackboard is supposed to change the boy's attitude toward tormenting the girl sitting in front of him, making him a better person.

The affirmation technique gained legitimacy with William James's insight that attitudes come to correspond to behavior. Affirmations are behavior. If you repeatedly behave as if you are a certain kind of person, you grow into that kind of person. Affirmations, then, are more effective the more active you make them. Affirmations should at least be spoken clearly aloud. Better yet, write them out laboriously in the best handwriting you can muster. Write so that someone else could easily read what you have written. It is not necessary to write an affirmation 100 times. A few times a day seems sufficient to produce noticeable results.

I first used the affirmation technique as a young man selling furniture. I had fallen into the habit of using little lies to make a sale. A customer might ask, "When can I get this sofa?" I would reply, "We have a shipment coming in next week. Let me reserve one for you. We only need a 20 percent deposit with your order." I would start to fill out the paperwork. The customer would start to write a check. It was another easy sale. I knew all along that the customer's sofa would not arrive the following week. It might take about a month, but the customer did not want to wait. If I told her it would be a month, then she might keep looking until she found a store that had what she wanted in stock.

I would rationalize that technically what I said was true. We would get a shipment the following week. The customer's sofa, however, would not be on it. It was a lie. Then I would lie again when the customer called to check on the order. "Yes, we did get the shipment. Let me check the warehouse. No, your sofa did not arrive. I don't know what could have happened. I will contact the factory and get back to you." After a series of postponements and excuses, more lies, the sofa would eventually arrive. The customer would usually be happy. Rarely did a customer cancel the order even after the third or fourth delay. By then they had become committed to their purchase. The social psychology of my selling approach was sound. The ethics were not.

I never felt good about lying. I dreaded hearing the phone ring. Which customer would it be? What would I tell them this time? What had I told them last time? It was a tumultuous period in my life. I had been drinking heavily for years. I quit suddenly. I started reading books that might help me find a better way to live. One of them suggested the affirmation technique. Here is the first affirmation I tried: "I, Michael Lovaglia, am an honest and sober person." I resolved to write the affirmation at least three times a day as clearly and legibly as possible. At first it was extremely difficult. The muscles in my forearm would knot up when I tried to write those few simple words. My stomach would feel queasy. Later I found out that meant the affirmation was on target. My unconscious mind was resisting the change suggested by the affirmation. Eventually it became easier to write. My lying steadily decreased. My sales volume did go down at first but then went back up. When the phone rang at work, my anxiety level would rise, tempting me to lie. I used another affirmation to remind myself what to do: "The truth is good enough." And it was. Lying turned out to be more of a crutch than a sales tool.

Affirmations are a standard technique of the self-help industry. *The Power of Positive Thinking* by Norman Vincent Peale uses it extensively and apparently successfully. My copy of the book has a red sticker on the cover that says, OVER 5 MILLION COPIES IN PRINT. Aside from being a popular idea, it would be nice to know that affirmations also have a sound basis in social psychology. One aim of this book is to help you identify such techniques. You can concentrate on techniques that have been demonstrated to be effective and avoid the more speculative ideas in the self-improvement literature.

Attribution research explains why affirmations change our attitudes. When we observe people behaving in a certain way, we assume that their attitudes correspond to their behavior. That is correspondence bias. Our own attitudes come to correspond to our behavior in a similar way. Just as we observe others' behavior, we also observe our own behavior, at least some of the time. In some situations we may be too busy or distracted to be very good observers of what we are doing. Bem (1965, 1967) pointed out that to the extent we observe our own behavior, we will assume our attitudes correspond to that behavior. When we observe a person giving a prolife speech on abortion, we assume that person's attitude is prolife. Correspondence bias operates when we observe our own behavior as well. Bem's proposition suggests that if we make a prolife speech for whatever reason, we will observe our own behavior and assume that our attitude must be prolife. We are, or at least become, what we do. Affirmations, whether spoken or written, constitute behavior. When we observe ourselves speaking or writing about the person we want to become, we assume that we are that person. Eventually, with repeated use of the affirmation technique, the assumption about who we are becomes belief. *Affirmations allow you to grow toward the person you want to become.*

Written affirmations are effective because written evidence is hard to deny. Writing has a permanence that thought and spoken words lack. It is relatively easy to take back what you have said. "Please forgive me, I spoke without thinking" usually works if you have said something inappropriate. It is more difficult to take back what you have written. We accept that people commonly speak without thinking. We are less likely to believe they have written without thinking. Thus, as observers of our own behavior, we find written affirmations more convincing. It is as if we say to ourselves "Look how carefully I wrote this. I must have meant it." Written confessions are a good example of the power of the written word. Criminal convictions based on a written confession are almost impossible to overturn. Convictions usually stand even when it has been proved that the person convicted was coerced and confused at the time of the confession and did not know what he was signing. Juries have been known to convict on the basis of a written confession even when evidence has proven conclusively that the person who confessed could not have committed the crime. We hold people responsible for what they have written. You will hold yourself responsible for what you write about yourself. That is what makes the written affirmation a powerful tool.

Social psychological research shows why a positive affirmation is preferred over a negative one. Tell yourself to do something positive rather than to *not* do something negative. It is better to write about the person that you want to become than about the person you want to stop being. Studies have shown that using a negative word in a sentence makes the sentence harder to understand (See for example Evans 1972; Leenars, Bringmann, & Balance 1978). The danger in using negative statements as affirmations is that they require more mental processing than do positive statements. The negative statement is first seen as true, then falsified by the negative word. When my toddler is concentrating fiercely on pouring herself a glass of milk, she will usually spill it if I call out "Don't spill the milk." She understands "spill the milk" first. If she had time she would then process the "don't." But she is concentrating on her task. Before she can fully process the negative sentence, she has reacted to it as if it was positive and spills the milk. In contrast, warning her to "Be careful" will not usually produce a spill. Positive questions are easier than negative ones. Teachers know that the test question "Which of the following is *not* one of Piaget's stages of cognitive development?" will be much harder than "Which of the following is one of Piaget's stages of cognitive development?" Affirmations work the same way. A negative affirmation will probably work. It just takes more mental processing. Why put the negative statement in your mind in the first place? Concentrate on who you want to become. Sometimes, it can be difficult to frame an affirmation positively. Suppose you want to stop biting your nails. What positive affirmation would you use? It takes some thought but can usually be done. ("I, Jennie Smith, have long, elegant nails" might work.) Whenever possible use positive statements for your affirmations.

Just as a positive statement makes a deeper impression than does a negative statement, a study by Gilbert, Krull, and Malone (1990) suggests that *true* statements make a deeper impression than do *false* statements. Researchers set up a situation to investigate how we process true and false information. By default, we accept statements as true. Then, if we have evidence that the statement was false, we reclassify the statement as false. Researchers had people read a number of statements. They then received information about which were true and which were false. When given time to think about it, people could correctly identify false statements about as often as true statements. However, researchers then tried the same experiment but added a distraction. A loud noise sounded after a statement. If the statement was initially accepted as true, then the distraction should have no effect on the accurate recall of true statements. However, the distraction should serve to decrease accurate recall of false statements by preventing people from reclassifying statements from true to false. That is exactly what happened. People were able to correctly identify true statements just as often whether distracted or not. However, false statements were misclassified as true almost twice as often when people were distracted. True statements are easier to handle mentally than false ones.

One reason that bad habits are hard to break is that *not* doing something is difficult. It is hard to build an identity in a vacuum. The problem is not really quitting nail biting or smoking or drinking or using credit cards or chocolate or coffee. The problem is what to do instead. When I first quit smoking, a day would stretch out before me forever. How could a person possibly fill up all those hours without a cigarette? What was I to do? I needed an activity to fill my time while not indulging my habit. Successful addiction recovery programs—whether Alcoholics Anonymous or hospital-based treatment—recognize that a positive activity has to be substituted for the addictive behavior. For example, Alcoholics Anonymous members go to meetings instead of bars. Writing affirmations is an activity you can substitute for the habit you are trying to break. Every time you get the urge to bite your nails, you could write an affirmation instead.

Make yourself write an affirmation at least three times a day, or more often if the mood strikes you. Pick one that you think will do you some good, one that will move you closer to the kind of person you want to become. Then keep at it. It may be difficult to remember at first. If I skipped writing my affirmations one day, then I made myself write extra ones the following day. Like me, you may find it difficult to make yourself write an affirmation that challenges long-held or unconscious beliefs about yourself. I would tell myself that I did not have the time to write. Then I figured out how long it took to write an affirmation three times. Writing in longhand, as carefully and clearly as possible, it took me about two minutes. Two minutes a day to change your life.[2]

Further Reading

Of General Interest

Branch, T. (1988). *Parting the waters: America in the King years, 1954–63.* New York: Simon & Schuster.

Jones, E. E. (1991). *Interpersonal perception.* New York: W. H. Freeman and Company.

Ross, L., & Nisbett, R. E. (1991). *The person and the situation: Perspectives of social psychology.* New York: McGraw-Hill.

Recent and Technical Issues

Fein, S. (1996). Effects of suspicion on attributional thinking and the correspondence bias. *Journal of Personality and Social Psychology, 70,* 1164–1184.

Gibbins, K., & Walker, I. (1996). Social roles, social norms, and self-presentation in the quiz effect of Ross, Amabile and Steinmetz. *Journal of Social Psychology, 136,* 625–634.

Gilbert, D. T., & Malone, P. S. (1995). The correspondence bias. *Psychological Bulletin, 117,* 21–38.

Hart, A. J., & Morry, M. M. (1996). Nonverbal behavior, race, and attitude attributions. *Journal of Experimental Social Psychology, 32,* 165–179.

Miller, A. G., Ashton, W., & Mishal, M. (1990). Beliefs concerning the features of constrained behavior: A basis for the fundamental attribution error. *Journal of Personality and Social Psychology, 59,* 635–650.

Webster, D. (1993). "Motivated augmentation and reduction of the overattribution bias. *Journal of Personality and Social Psychology, 65,* 261–271.

---

[2]Sounds simple, doesn't it? Simple but not easy. Chapter 3 describes some of the problems in trying to change our identities. Affirmations work but only if you keep at them.

CHAPTER 2

Knowing Yourself and Other People Too

Social situations are extremely complicated. Maintaining our social relations is probably the most difficult thing we do. People are not easy to get along with and they are all different. Figuring out how to behave in different situations with different people takes all the mental ability we have. There are three major areas of social competence for us to work on. First, we become more socially competent by seeing situations from another person's point of view as well as our own. Second, we can work on recognizing our personal biases in the way we look at social situations. And third, we can practice making more accurate social judgments.

The skill needed for social competence is easy to describe but difficult to put into practice. To succeed in social situations, *see situations from another person's point of view as well as your own.* Our failure to consider the point of view of other people creates many problems, from minor arguments between two drivers caught in traffic to war between countries. For example, what seems to Israelis to be the reasonable attempt to secure a tiny bit of land to call home, seems to Palestinians to be wanton aggression. Neither side is capable of considering the other's point of view. The result is recurring conflict. In everyday situations, seeing another person's point of view can help us to make accurate judgments.

Seeing situations from another person's point of view is not easy, even for a person who knows it is a good idea. Social situations develop quickly, suddenly. Emotional reactions can make it difficult to think clearly. For example, I get frightened and angry when another driver suddenly pulls out in front of me in traffic, making me brake hard to avoid a crash. From my point of view the other driver is a malicious lout with no regard for my safety. Blasting my horn and yelling insults would seem an appropriate response on my part, given the obviously intentional nature of the offense. After all, I need to let people know that they should not push me around.

Reacting with anger, attempting to warn or punish, is a common and even reasonable response when a person's wellbeing is threatened. That is the situation from my point of view. How does the other driver see it? Without knowing the other driver, I can get some idea of his point of view by imagining what I would feel in his place. There is good evidence for how I would feel because sometimes in traffic people blast their horn or gesture angrily at me. Usually this happens after I have innocently pulled into the flow of traffic. I may have realized that the driver I cut off would have to brake to let me in. A reasonable person would not mind. Would she? Or I may not have noticed the other car at all, an innocent mistake. It happens to everyone, and so the other driver's angry behavior seems not only rude but also puzzling.

The same social situation appears totally different to me depending on my position in it. When another driver cuts me off in traffic, a serious offense has occurred. My angry response is justified. Alternatively, when I pull into traffic, cutting off another driver, no offense has occurred. The angry driver behind me appears irrationally antisocial. My response to the situation in both positions has a common element. In deciding how to respond, I have failed to consider the point of view of the other driver. The failure to see a situation from another person's point of view as well as our own has serious consequences. Much human conflict is a direct result. For example, fist fights, collisions, and sometimes homicide result from minor traffic disputes. Many similar negative social consequences would not occur if drivers considered each others' point of view.

On one of my good days, I see the situation from the other driver's point of view as well as my own. When my social awareness is high, my response to a driver who cuts me off is quite different. Even though I may be startled, before I get angry, I will understand how I would feel in his place. I might shake my head at his inattentive driving but there seems no need to retaliate. And if someone I have cut off is angry at me, I would realize why. Instead of reacting to the other driver's anger with anger of my own, I might try to apologize by smiling sheepishly and mouthing "I'm sorry." Seeing social situations from another's point of view drastically reduces the chances of negative outcomes. It not only increases human understanding but encourages forgiveness. During the Civil War, when Abraham Lincoln's wife commented negatively about the Southern enemy, Lincoln said, "Don't criticize them; they are just what we would be under similar circumstances" (Carnegie 1932).

Social awareness makes possible extremely complicated networks of social relations. Human beings, when they are being most human, can see social situations from several different points of view simultaneously. Seeing situations from various points of view is the key to success in society.

THE SELF AND SOCIAL AWARENESS

How does the mental juggling act of social awareness, that most human of abilities, come about? How do we become aware of the various points of view held by those around us? The explanation comes from a branch of social psychology called *symbolic interactionism*. Symbolic interactionism is a way of looking at society, a perspective. From the symbolic interactionist perspective, people are social actors who create society by using symbols to communicate. Language is the main symbol system we use, but people also use gestures and other symbols. As we saw in Chapter

1, just about anything that a person does can be used by others to gain insight into the kind of person she is.

When people exchange symbols, they converse. For example, a new employee, Hanna, arrives at work and meets her new officemate, Toby. Toby says, "Hello, I'm Toby. Welcome to the company." The words are symbols that Toby has sent to Hanna. Hanna responds, "I'm Hanna. This is my first day." Hanna has interpreted the symbols sent by Toby and responded with symbols of her own. Toby then reaches out to shake hands, symbolically offering a nonhostile relationship (an open hand without a weapon). When Hanna responds by extending her own hand, the relationship has begun on a cooperative basis. The two coworkers have coordinated their behavior to accomplish their first collaborative task, shaking hands. Toby says, "Here is your desk. Let me show you where to put your coat. What did you do before joining us?" Hanna answers and the ongoing conversation between the two workers leads to a shared definition of the situation, a working relationship. Sometimes such social pleasantries can seem like a silly waste of time. But imagine how stiff Hanna and Toby's relationship would be for a while if they had not exchanged symbols of their willingness to cooperate. Through symbolic interaction, people come to agree, more or less, on a picture of the social world. Symbolic interactionists are fond of saying that reality is socially constructed.

Symbols have a peculiarly human property. They are capable of several meanings at once. When we use symbols, we must interpret the appropriate meaning given the context of the situation. Language, rather than making symbols less ambiguous, increases the need for interpretation. Words can mean many different things depending on the way they are used. For example, consider the question "How are you?" When two acquaintances meet it is common for one to ask "How are you?" and the other to answer "Fine." As long as both interpret the context of the question as a part of a greeting ritual, social interaction proceeds smoothly. The person who asked the question does not expect to hear a lengthy, or even accurate, description of the other person's health problems.

In another context, the same question requires a quite different answer. For example, if we see a person who looks ill or behaves oddly, we might ask "How are you?" hoping to find out if the person needs help. We want as much information as possible about the person's mental and physical state. How the person being asked interprets the question determines the answer. That interpretation depends on how the person sees the situation and himself. When I'm feeling good and a person asks me how I am, I interpret it as a friendly greeting. However, when things are not going so well, I can come to more troubling conclusions. Why did she ask me that? Do I look ill? Was I behaving inappropriately? I might interpret as a warning something that was meant as a friendly greeting. Further, I may start feeling worse having concluded that the other person found something wrong with me. Because symbols are ambiguous, when we use them we do not just describe reality. We also help create it.

The Interpretation of Symbols

The appearance of our socially created reality depends on our position in it. For example, the same situations often look different to women than they do to men. That is, women often interpret symbols differently than men do. One reason for this difference is that the everyday social world is more dangerous for women. For example, few men need to spend any time worrying about becoming the victim of a sexual assault. Women do not have that luxury. We are more observant when we feel threatened. At the same time, the awareness of danger alters a person's view of the world. The different interpretations of reality made by men and women were brought home to me while I was working my way through college selling furniture.

I worked for a chain of Scandinavian furniture stores. There were about 10 stores in the San Francisco Bay area at the time. Manufacturers' representatives would come around to the stores to show us the new products that the main office had ordered for our stores. A manufacturer's rep would demonstrate the product so we salespeople would know how to show it to our customers. One afternoon, a representative for a new line of mattresses came into my store. I was alone. There is relatively little foot traffic in furniture stores. During the week, fewer than 10 people might come in the store all day. If one of them bought a dining room set, then I would be happy. When the manufacturer's rep came in, I was the only salesperson on duty and no customers were in the store.

We had just put the new mattresses on the display beds in the store that week. The manufacturer's rep introduced himself and began showing me the features of his mattresses. He was like a lot of good salespeople. He was older than I was, perhaps in his midforties. Manufacturers' reps get paid more than retail salespeople, so they are often a little older. He smiled too much, looking me straight in the eye when he talked. He seemed sincere in a practiced way. Then, while he was showing me the mattress, a funny thing happened. He winked at me. He kept talking as if nothing had happened. Then a minute or so later, he winked again. I was confused. The social situation I was in had become difficult for me to interpret.

A wink is a symbol. It has a socially constructed meaning. Like most symbols, a wink has different meanings in different contexts. A wink can be conspiratorial, signaling a shared secret. In a group of people when one person winks at another, it can mean "You and I know what is really going on even if these others don't." When two people are alone and one of them winks, it can mean that something has been left unsaid. The person winking signals the other that he hopes what was left unsaid will nonetheless be understood.

I could not figure out what unspoken message the manufacturer's rep might be trying to send me. For one thing, a wink between two people who are alone often has a sexual connotation. Direct requests for sex are usually inappropriate. Rather than come out with a blunt proposition, a wink is one way for a person to signal interest in a sexual relationship. The manufacturer's rep winked at me then continued with his presentation as if nothing had happened. He asked me to lie down on his mattress to see how comfortable it was. I was not comfortable at all. As he demonstrated the features of the different mattresses, he winked again and again. By about the fifth wink, I realized that the rep had a facial tic that caused him to wink. It did not look like an involuntary spasm, however. He wore his salesperson's smile. He looked right at me and winked.

After I realized that the manufacturer's rep had a facial tic, the social situation changed. I no longer felt uncomfortable. The rep, sensing the change in my attitude toward him, relaxed as well. He finished his demonstration. I thanked him and he left to demonstrate his mattresses in the other stores in the chain. The demonstration had started normally enough. But the wink had caused me to reinterpret it. It forced me to consider other possible meanings that could create serious social problems. To overcome my confusion, the rep tried harder. He became friendlier, more sincere. He smiled more. But the rep's response to my anxiety only made it worse. Then when I realized that the wink had no intended meaning, it no longer worried me. Our interaction returned to normal. The rep went on to give his demonstration in the other stores in the chain during the next week or so.

A free phone line connected all the stores in the chain so that salespeople could locate furniture for their customers in other stores. To pass the time, we salespeople spent a lot of time on the phone and got to know each other. During the two weeks after the mattress demonstration, several salespeople told me about the manufacturer's rep. All were women and they were irate. Some were even a little scared. They thought the rep was a disgusting macho jerk. They thought he was leering at them. They called him sneaky and slimy for not making an honest if inappropriate proposition. They said things like "Can you believe this guy? He's showing me this mattress then winks at me and tells me to lie down on it." None of the other male salespeople mentioned the manufacturer's rep. When I asked if he had given them the mattress demonstration, they reported nothing unusual. Men had either not noticed the wink or ignored it.

Reality was very different for the women who interacted with the manufacturer's rep than it was for the other men or me. It is a useful lesson. However, the story about the manufacturer's rep can make people uncomfortable. Remember that we started off Chapter 1 with the idea that social psychology bothers people. In the different reactions of women and men to the manufacturer's rep, people see the stereotypes they deal with every day reflected back at them. According to gender stereotypes, women overreact and men are oblivious.[1] Might that be all that was happening? Probably not.

Stereotypes simplify and distort a more complicated reality. Research allows us to go beyond stereotypes. For example, it is likely that women were justifiably concerned with the behavior of the manufacturer's rep. In repeated studies, researchers have found that women are more accurate at reading nonverbal behavior and subtle emotional cues than are men.[2] Holtgraves (1991) found another factor that led people to see hidden meaning in a social situation. He found as other studies had that women were more likely to detect a hidden meaning than were men. Holtgraves also found that both women and men were more likely to detect a hidden meaning when a social situation was threatening. Women may be better observers of social behavior than are men because women live in a more threatening world than do men. Although the manufacturer's rep had a facial tic, his behavior may not have been innocent. He must have been aware of the effect his tic had on women. His

[1]Chapter 7 explains why women's opinions are given less weight than are men's in many work situations. It also provides techniques that help maximize your impact at work.
[2]See, for example, *Nonverbal Sex Differences: Communication Accuracy and Expressive Styles* by Judith A. Hall (1984). See also Ambady, Hallahan, and Rosenthal (1995), Card, Jackson, Stollak, and Ialongo (1986), and Rotter and Rotter (1988).

full-time job was to talk to furniture salespeople, many of whom were women. Yet he did nothing to reassure the women he met that he did not mean to threaten them. Why? He might have been embarrassed. Or he might have enjoyed his power to threaten women. Women may well have been able to detect the difference because they faced a serious threat.

With the manufacturer's rep, I felt uncomfortable and worried about being embarrassed, but I felt no serious threat. Usually men can afford to ignore the subtle meaning in others' behavior without fear of being attacked. However, men are pretty good at reading cues that signal danger for them. For example, men can accurately detect anger in the faces of other men (Rotter & Rotter 1988). As a social psychology student, I may have been more aware of other people's behavior than the other men were, but many women are better than I am at figuring out the meaning of subtle social behavior.

Men and women experience different social realities. If you realize that another person's reality, not just her or his opinion, is different from yours, then you can find out what that person's reality is. If you can visualize another person's reality and yours as well, then you are capable of acting in a way that will benefit both of you.

What's in a Name?

The power of symbols to create reality can be seen clearly in the importance we attach to names. Have you noticed how often a person's profession is related to his or her name? It seems too common to be coincidence. My dentist, for example, was Dr. Ivery. However, the effect of names can be less amusing. A recent newspaper account told of the conviction of Jesse James Smith for murder. All too often people live up to their names. It would be interesting to ask Jesse's mother what she had in mind when she named him. Did she think that he would grow up to be like the famous murderer and Old West outlaw? Human beings are social animals. We live in groups and conform to the expectations that members of our group have for us. People usually do about what is expected of them, good or bad. Group expectations are reflected in names given to people.

The power of names is an example of a more general process that social psychologists call *labeling*. Labels categorize an individual as belonging to a certain role or class of people. For example, a teenager in your neighborhood could be classified as a basically good kid or as a delinquent. Labeling theory proposes that an individual's behavior will come to conform to the label that he has been given (Becker 1963). It is easy to see how the process works. Suppose you learned that the teenager who does odd jobs for you was arrested for raping a young girl. Your behavior toward the teenager would probably change, wouldn't it? Although you might not be overtly hostile, you might at least avoid him and hire someone else to help you. If other people around him treated him the same way, then he might have trouble making money and turn to theft. If he felt that you had treated him shabbily, then he might retaliate. Whether or not he had committed the rape, the label that neighbors applied to him made his future antisocial behavior more likely. The self-fulfilling process by which a label encourages deviant behavior has been called *secondary deviance* (Lemert 1951).

cathy® by Cathy Guisewite

Cathy's fear produces the consequence she wanted to avoid

Lemert (1962) described the self-fulfilling process through which a paranoid personality creates the conditions that lead to paranoia. Full-blown paranoia is evident when a person has the delusion that others are conspiring against him. It is more common in men than women. Typical paranoid behavior includes threats and frequent litigation. We assume that the paranoid person has no rational basis for believing in a conspiracy. However, Lemert discovered a paranoid process that frequently begins with an actual social defeat. For example, a person susceptible to paranoia might be passed up for a promotion at work. Hostility, envy, and stubbornness characterize the paranoid personality. Lemert observed that coworkers described a person with paranoid personality as irritating, hypercritical, and thoroughly unlikable. As a result, they labeled him as difficult to work with and disloyal. This led them to consistently exclude the paranoid person from normal activities. For example, their whispered conversations around the water cooler suddenly stopped when he approached. Coworkers attempted to avoid him by coordinating work in informal meetings to which he had not been invited. When he confronted them on this, they denied it. Thus the paranoid person saw very real evidence of a conspiracy against him. Yet the attempts he made to be included at work, threatening to sue, for example, were seen as further reason to exclude him.

You can use a similar self-fulfilling process to your benefit. In a classic self-improvement book, *How to Win Friends and Influence People,* Dale Carnegie suggests that we "give a person a fine reputation to live up to." Research in social psychology demonstrates the power of this technique. Careful labeling can more effectively change a person's behavior than attempts at persuasion. For example, we want our children to be a little tidier than they usually are. Miller, Brickman, and Bolen (1975) tried different ways to teach fifth graders not to litter and to help clean up. They attempted to persuade some students with proven techniques such as repetition, explaining the benefits, and active role-playing. They made no attempt to persuade another group of students, instead labeling these students as responsible and neat. For example, the teacher complimented students on being "ecology-minded" and not dropping candy wrappers in the auditorium. Later, the teacher told students that a janitor mentioned that their classroom was one of the cleanest in the building. The principal sent a letter to the class complimenting them on their neatness. Results of the study showed that labeling had a bigger effect on fifth-grader's behavior than did persuasion. The labeled group was found to be less likely to litter and more likely to clean up after themselves than the persuasion group. Further, the positive behavior of the labeled students continued when measured two weeks later.

Labeling has also been shown to improve academic performance. Miller, Brickman, and Bolen (1975) tried to improve the mathematics scores of second graders. They labeled some students as having high ability at math and high motivation to work hard. Students in the labeled group were told that they were doing extremely well in math and that they were working very hard. Students in the persuasion group were told that they *should* be better at math and *should* work harder. The labeled students showed an immediate large increase in math scores. Their math scores continued to increase two weeks later. In contrast, persuaded students had a smaller immediate increase in their math scores, and this increase had disappeared two weeks later. To help your children grow, convince them that they are the people you would like them to become. We use symbols to socially construct reality. With the right techniques, we can construct a better reality.

The *social construction of reality* is a powerful idea that is easily misunderstood (Berger & Luckmann 1966). Money is a good example of the social construction of reality. We all depend on it. But what is it? A dollar bill is a nearly worthless piece of paper unless two people agree that it represents a dollar's worth of value—a cup of coffee, for example. The value of money is socially constructed. A common misconception is that if reality is socially constructed, then reality is anything an individual person believes to be real. That would more accurately be described as the *individual* construction of reality, something quite different from social construction. The social construction of reality refers to the shared definition of situations that we come to agree on through our interactions. An individual might reach the reasonable conclusion that because a 1-dollar bill and a 20-dollar bill are both the same size piece of paper, they should be equal in value. But no matter how long that person argued with a restaurant cashier, paying for a 20-dollar dinner with a 1-dollar bill would not work. Individuals who ignore the symbols of others and come to their own idiosyncratic definitions of social situations may be considered insane. Not coincidentally, treating psychological problems often requires the ability to see the world from different, sometimes bizarre, points of view as well as from a more conventional one. Psychotherapists try to see the world from the point of view of their patients in order to reintegrate the patient's point of view with the shared definition of the situation common in the patient's culture.

Acquiring a Self

George Herbert Mead's work is the foundation for the symbolic interactionist perspective. He taught social psychology in the philosophy department at the University of Chicago starting about 1900. Mead (1934) explains that human beings can learn to see situations from various points of view with the result that we can coordinate our behavior in more complicated ways than can other animals. Our extraordinary organizational power and adaptability come from that social skill, the ability to see ourselves as others see us. Mead proposed that to become socially aware,

cathy®

Using self-awareness, Cathy attempts to change

people must first acquire self-awareness. How does a person acquire a sense of self?

Self-awareness requires that a person recognize that she is distinct from other individuals around her. In distinguishing herself from those around her, similarities between herself and others also become apparent. Our ability to use language allows us to easily distinguish ourselves from others. Language provides convenient labels for the self, "I" and "me," for example. "I" can be used as the subject in a sentence; "me" can be used as an object. Mead noticed that one sentence can include both forms of self-reference. "I" can act to change "me." Our language, then, gives us the ability to think of ourselves as objects, to step outside ourselves. "Myself" explicitly combines the idea of "me" with the idea of "self" as an object that can be manipulated. For example, I can make myself more socially responsible by setting my alarm clock to wake myself up before an early class. By alternately labeling the self as subject and object, language allows us to distinguish ourselves from others and sets the stage for seeing ourselves from another's point of view.

With language, we can see ourselves as an object to be manipulated, as a goal. The self becomes a work in progress. But this raises an important question. Progress toward what? What should our goal be? Human beings are social animals. We look to others for guidance.

We judge our success, our competence, by how well we perform in social situations. We are the person we see mirrored in the eyes of the people around us. If they look on us with approval, we feel successful. In trying to improve ourselves, we can gain a sense of how well we are doing by imagining how other people will judge the changes we plan. For example, in nearly all cultures, young adults decorate their bodies to make themselves more attractive and interesting to their peers. Suppose that Betty is trying to decide on a tattoo. The tattoo she picks will depend on how she wants others to think of her. To make her decision, Betty can use language to have a conversation with herself about the possible effect of the new tattoo. She can ask herself what her friends would think of a colorful butterfly on her thigh. Would that have enough impact? How about something more exotic with a hint of danger? A spider on her neck? But what would her boss—or her mother—think about a spider tattooed on her neck?

In thinking about her mother's response, Betty might realize that people in general respond differently to a tattoo close to the face than to one farther down on a person's body. That is, she might see a negative reaction to the spider tattoo coming from what Mead called a *generalized other,* her impression of the general expectations that others hold for her. Betty's conversation with herself continues. She asks questions about the responses of different kinds of people in her life, then answers those questions by imagining how she would respond in their place. Symbolic interactionists call this *role taking,* mentally taking the role of another person. The more we use language to make decisions about ourselves as an object, the better our decisions will be at creating the response we want in others. Social awareness fosters social competence.

Mead proposed three basic requirements for an individual to achieve social competence: (1) A socially competent person has a self, a sense of herself as distinct from other people. (2) The sense of self is extended and formalized through the use of language for inner thought. (3) Through language, a person can learn to see herself as if through others' eyes (Michener & DeLamater 1994).

ACQUIRING SOCIAL AWARENESS FROM AN EVOLUTIONARY PERSPECTIVE

Social awareness is one of the greatest accomplishments of the human species. It is the foundation for the cooperative behavior on which civilization rests. Not only does social awareness require a large amount of intelligence, it may also be the reason that intelligence evolved so rapidly and to such a great extent in human beings. A major question in human evolutionary theory is, why do we have such enormous mental capacity? Most of us do not seem to use very much intelligence for most of what we do. In fact, most of us stretch our minds in play rather than work. We do crossword puzzles and play cards and videogames while our work is largely routine. Why would high intelligence evolve if we do not need it to live and raise children? The answer may be that high intelligence evolved because of the advantage that social awareness gives us.

Evolution works primarily through Darwin's process of natural selection. He noticed the way that dog breeders, for example, produced new breeds of dogs. Suppose a breeder wants to develop a breed of dogs with distinctive long noses. She starts by mating pairs of dogs that have noses that resemble the shape she has in mind. She then selects the offspring that have the best noses and destroys the rest. The selected dogs are mated together. Offspring with the desired noses are selected. The rest are destroyed. After many generations a breed of dog with a distinctively shaped nose results.

Darwin realized that nature will select individuals for different characteristics much like dog breeders do. For example, suppose a species of monkey lives under a particular fruit tree. The monkeys' diet is primarily fruit. Some monkeys are larger and heavier than others are. Large monkeys have difficulty climbing the trees and wait for the fruit to drop to the ground before eating it. Other monkeys are smaller and climb up to the fruit easily. As long as there is plenty of fruit, both large and small monkeys will continue to live and raise offspring. Now suppose there is a drought and fruit is not as plentiful. Smaller monkeys eat what fruit there is by climbing up to it. Little fruit remains to fall to the ground. Smaller monkeys continue to live and raise offspring. Larger monkeys face starvation, they have fewer offspring, and their offspring are more likely to die before reaching sexual maturity. Nature has selected small tree-climbing monkeys and destroyed larger ground dwellers. To the extent that small size and tree-climbing ability are inherited characteristics, future generations will more closely resemble small tree climbers than larger ground dwellers. In evolutionary terms, smaller monkeys were more successful, the only criteria for evolutionary success being population size and growth.

Intelligence may have evolved because it allows us to manipulate people and social situations rather than technology. Whiten and Byrne (1988) call this idea "Machiavellian intelligence." In the early 1500s, Machiavelli proposed that the cunning manipulation of people could produce better government (Machiavelli 1532/1940). Social situations are almost infinitely complicated. Understanding them requires all the mental capacity available and then some. For social animals like humans and chimpanzees, social situations determine who gets access to the most resources, the best food, and shelter, for example. Also important for evolutionary success, social competence determines who will have access to willing sexual partners. More resources and more sexual partners mean more children and more successful children. Thus mental capacity promotes evolutionary success by increasing social competence.

Language may be the key human evolutionary advantage. The ability to use language gives humans an advantage in dealing with social situations. The better you are at using language, the easier it is to manipulate other people to your advantage. Language, as Mead pointed out, facilitates self-awareness. We now know that self-awareness is not a uniquely human ability (Byrne 1995). Some other animals are self-aware to a certain degree. Not surprisingly, those animals that are most intelligent show signs of being the most self-aware: apes, especially chimpanzees, but also dolphins.

Detecting self-awareness in animals that cannot talk is an interesting problem, especially for dolphins, whose gestures are so limited by their body structure. Occasionally, though, evidence of self-awareness is unmistakable. For example, a human observer smoked a cigarette as he stood at the observation window of a dolphin tank. He blew a cloud of cigarette smoke at the window just as a baby dolphin approached. The baby dolphin immediately swam to its mother, obtained a mouthful of milk, and returned to the window. The baby dolphin then released the milk into the water, creating a cloud that looked very much like cigarette smoke (Byrne 1995). The dolphin had to realize it had a self as distinct from the person on the other side of the glass. Then it had to interpret that person's behavior (sucking on a cigarette and blowing out smoke) as analogous to its own (sucking milk from its mother and releasing it into the water). The dolphin also showed an attempt to communicate with the human observer because it returned to the observation window before releasing the milk.

Some animals recognize themselves in a mirror, but most do not. Most animals react to their image in a mirror as they would to a strange member of their own species. Monkeys learn to use mirrors to see around corners but react to their own reflection as if it were a stranger. Chimpanzees, however, use mirrors much the way we do, to groom themselves, for example.

Gallup (1970) set up a situation to test the self-awareness of monkeys and chimpanzees. When monkeys and chimpanzees notice a spot of paint on themselves, they immediately try to rub it off, the same way we would. Gallup put a spot of paint on the foreheads of unconscious monkeys. He put a mirror nearby, then waited for the monkeys to wake up. Monkeys who looked in the mirror and saw a spot of paint on their forehead had no reaction. They did not try to touch the spot or rub it off. They ignored the image in the mirror, showing no sign that they recognized it as themselves. In contrast, when chimpanzees woke up and looked in the mirror, they reacted with surprise on seeing the spot on their forehead. They immediately tried to touch the spot on their own forehead, not the image in the mirror, and immediately tried to rub it off. They were obviously aware that the image in the mirror represented themselves. Chimpanzees are aware of themselves as individuals in a group of chimpanzees like themselves.

Not all members of a given species are equally self-aware. For example, although adult chimpanzees show a high degree of self-awareness, young chimpanzees do not recognize themselves in the mirror. They have not yet developed the mental capacity required for self-awareness. Young human children may not react to themselves in a mirror either. However, they soon develop and then surpass the self-awareness of adult chimpanzees (Byrne 1995). Gorillas, although closely related to chimpanzees, often fail to recognize themselves. One captive gorilla, however, told researchers that she recognized herself in a mirror. Koko was raised around humans, treated like a human child, and taught the symbols of American sign language. When she looked in the mirror, she recognized the spot on her forehead; when asked what her reflection was, she signed, "Me, Koko" (Byrne 1995). Koko's unusual ability may have resulted from her use of sign language or from the rich social environment she experienced growing up. In any case, levels of self-awareness vary widely even among members of the same species. Humans, too, are more or less skillful at seeing themselves as a social object. Some more than others can see themselves from another person's point of view. Thus social competence comes more easily to some than to others. Self-awareness is not an unvarying human trait, but a skill to be practiced and honed.

Chimpanzees do not use mirrors in all the ways that humans do. They do not try to alter their appearance for social purposes. They may remove a smudge of paint from their face, but they do not try to rearrange their hair. In all societies humans change their appearance for the benefit of others. We arrange our hair, wear clothes and jewelry, paint our faces, and tattoo ourselves. We are aware that we can change ourselves to gain a social advantage. We know that by changing ourselves we can change the way others treat us.

Adornment and language are ways to use symbols to carry on a conversation. Symbol use implies an understanding that another person is as aware of us as we are of him or her. We understand that the other person is capable of understanding our symbols and altering her intentions toward us. We understand that when she responds with symbols of her own, we can interpret them and use that knowledge to adjust our behavior. We can converse. On our good days, we can imagine how she perceives us and arrange our behavior to everyone's mutual benefit. We have advanced beyond self-awareness to social awareness.

High intelligence can give individuals a reproductive advantage in everyday social interactions as well. Ape social organization is hierarchical. High-status males have access to the best food and more or less exclusive rights to mate with available females (Byrne 1995). Unlike other animals, however, status in ape society is not based primarily on size. Troop leaders are not always the best fighters. They maintain their position through alliances, selectively sharing their food and supporting others who they can count on to help them in the future. Here is the essence of Machiavellian intelligence. To succeed, an individual must maneuver others in such a way that more resources come to her or him. Machiavellian intelligence is using other members of your group as tools to secure your own ends. For example, to mate, low-status males have to outwit jealous high-status males. Females increase their chances of reproductive success by sneaking off to mate with low-status males. The more suitors a female can entertain without angering any of them, the more offspring she can produce. Juggling multiple lovers is certainly one of the most mentally demanding of human pursuits. The need to manipulate individuals as tools to gain a social advantage may have been the evolutionary push toward higher intelligence in apes and humans.

HOW WE SEE OTHER PEOPLE AND OURSELVES

The need to coordinate our behavior with many other people in complex social networks may have led to humans' large mental capacity as a species. Social relationships are so complicated that keeping them straight requires all the brainpower we can muster. We should not be surprised, then, that we make mistakes in how we see other people. The constant need to size up social situations, to see situations from the points of view of various other people at the same time, requires us to take mental shortcuts. We make assumptions about what ought to be, about how people should behave in situations. Sometimes those shortcuts prevent us from seeing how things really are. To get an accurate picture of social situations, we have to get beyond our feelings about how people should think and behave. Only then can we find out what they actually think and do. More accurate assessment of what others perceive in social situations can give us an advantage in devising creative solutions to difficult social situations.

When we look at a social situation, we assess it and the people in it in relation to what is on our mind at the time. For example, when students in medical school start to learn the symptoms of various diseases, they often find some of those symptoms in themselves. They may come to the conclusion that they have several different new diseases a week. "Do my eyes seem yellow to you? I could have hepatitis." Although medical school is stressful, medical students are not particularly prone to illness. Because students are concentrating on the symptoms of various diseases, they are primed to interpret aspects of their own health as symptomatic of those diseases.

Priming and First Impressions

Situations that we are in channel our thinking in specific directions. Social psychologists call this the *priming effect*. Studying diseases *primes* medical students to see evidence of disease. Higgins, Rholes, and Jones (1977) created a situation to study the priming effect. They first asked people to read a list of either positive or negative words, and then they read a paragraph about a person and gave their impressions of him. The paragraph was written so that a positive or negative impression of the person was about equally likely. For example, it told how the person tried exciting activities such as piloting a jet boat without knowing much about boats. Thus the person could be seen as adventuresome or reckless. The researchers wanted to find out if people who had read the list of negative words would judge the person more negatively than people who read the list of positive words. Only about 10 percent of people who had read the list of negative words formed a positive impression of the person. In contrast, about 70 percent of people who had read the list of positive words formed a positive impression. We see people and situations in light of what we have been thinking about at the time.

When we meet a person we already know in a new situation, our impression of that person is based on what we already know from previous meetings. Thus our impressions of people are relatively stable. In a given situation, the behavior of a person we know well will have little impact on our general assessment of that person. For example, when a friend you know to be responsible and reliable arrives at the restaurant late for your lunch date, you would not suddenly think of him as unreliable. Even if he failed to show up at all, your general assessment of him would change little, although you might be temporarily annoyed.

Because our assessment of people in new situations depends on our experience with them in the past, first impressions are important. A group of researchers (Jones, Rock, Shaver, Goethals, & Ward 1968) set up a situation to investigate the importance of first impressions. One group of people watched a student trying to answer multiple-choice questions on a test. They had been told that all questions were of equal difficulty. The student got most of the answers right on the first half of the test and most of them wrong on the second half. Another group of people watched the same student answering the same questions. The only difference was that this time the student got most of the answers wrong on the first half of the test and most of them right on the second half. In both cases, the student got the same score on the test.

For the people watching, everything was the same except their first impressions. In one group they began by watching the student get most questions right. The others began by watching the student get most questions wrong. Do first impressions make a difference? Would people rate the student as more intelligent when he started off answering questions correctly? Or would people pay more attention to the most recent information they have, the answers on the last half of the test? Would they therefore rate the student as more intelligent when he answered most questions correctly on the last half of the test?

First impressions had a powerful effect on the judgments of the people watching. Although the student always got the same score, 15 out of 30 correct, people who watched him get most questions right on the first half of the test rated him as more intelligent than people who watched him get most questions right on the last half of the test. Even more striking, first impressions have the power to alter the way people remember events. On average, people who had a positive first impression estimated that the student got more than 16 answers correct on the test. In contrast, people who had a negative first impression estimated that student got fewer than 13 correct on average. Putting effort into making a good first impression when you meet people is sound social strategy. Not only will they think more highly of you, but they may also see your future performance in a more favorable light.

Our impressions of people do change, but very slowly. Your opinion of your friend who left you waiting at the restaurant would change noticeably only after he repeatedly missed appointments and showed up late. Because our opinions of others change so slowly, the anxiety many people suffer in social situations is needless. Those of us who feel awkward in social situations and fear embarrassment can take comfort in the fact that our inappropriate behavior will not have a big effect on how our friends and associates see us. For example, after high school, I was sensitive and anxious around people. Social situations such as parties and weddings were especially difficult. I never knew what to say and worried that whatever I said would cause offense or seem foolish.

Drinking helped. It gave me something to do and the alcohol reduced my anxiety. That may be why I got a job in a nightclub. An older bartender taught me how to pour drinks and deal with people. One day, when he noticed my anxiety in dealing with a customer, he told me to stop worrying about what other people thought of me. He said that most people did not think about me at all and those that did had already made up their mind. I had thought that people's opinion of me seesawed wildly depending on my daily performance. In fact, our assessments of the people in our life change only slowly if at all. Our social missteps will be overlooked or forgiven and our triumphs will be discounted and forgotten. So relax. People form lasting first impressions that change only slowly over time.

Self-Serving Bias and Actor-Observer Differences in Attribution

The power of first impressions is common knowledge that turns out to be supported by research. Other assumptions commonly made about human social behavior are not as easy to demonstrate. For example, it is generally believed that people see their own behavior more positively than they do others' behavior. In many situations, our behavior seems to be biased in a self-serving way. We excuse or overlook our own failures while judging others more harshly. Recall my driving behavior when another driver cut me off in traffic and when I cut off another driver. The other driver and I have different points of view. I easily excuse myself for cutting someone off in traffic. I am more judgmental when someone cuts me off. My attributions for my own behavior differ from my attributions for someone else's behavior. I attribute the cause of the other driver's poor driving to some defect in his character. I attribute the cause of my driving errors to some temporary distraction or local obstruction. Perhaps a parked truck blocked my view of the other car. Attributions to stable dispositions, character traits, make it easy to place blame. Attributions to temporary factors in the environment make handy excuses. When we attribute our own behavior more to situational factors and others' behavior to dispositional factors, a self-serving bias can result. It turns out that in some situations people do not show any self-serving bias. They may in fact make attributions that show others in a more positive light than themselves. Human behavior is complicated. There are many reasons why we might make different attributions for our own behavior as opposed to others' behavior.

Our point of view determines the kind of attributions we make. Actors make different attributions for their behavior than do outside observers of that behavior. When using the term *actor,* social psychologists mean any person who does something. Storms (1973) set up a situation to investigate actor-observer differences in attribution. In the situation, two people would hold a brief "get-acquainted" conversation while two other people observed them. Here is how it worked. We will call the people holding the conversation actors A and B. The situation was set up so that only one observer, observer A, could see actor A. The other observer, observer B, could see only actor B. After the conversation, actors and observers rated the actors' behavior in terms of friendliness, talkativeness, nervousness, and dominance. They also rated the importance of situational factors and personal characteristics in determining the actors' behavior. For example, an actor might think his nervousness was caused by being in an experiment, a situational attribution. Or an observer might think that the actor's apparent nervousness was caused by his shyness, a personal attribution. Would observers attribute actor's behavior more to the actor's personal characteristics? Would actors attribute their own behavior more to situational factors?

In Storms's (1973) study, observers attributed actors' behavior to personal qualities of the actors much more often than did actors themselves. Actors were more likely to attribute their behavior to situational factors, such as the topic of conversation. Our assessment of actor-observer differences in attribution was correct. The different attributions made by actors and observers could well lead to a self-serving bias. Actors can easily forgive themselves for misbehavior they attribute to factors in the situation beyond their control. Observers, however, are more likely to hold actors responsible for misbehavior, attributing it to personal character flaws in the actor.

Storms (1973) then used videotape to demonstrate just how powerful our point of view is in determining how we attribute behavior. Two cameras were positioned to record what each observer saw. Camera A focused on actor A's face. Camera B focused on actor B's face. The use of videotape makes it possible to change a person's point of view from that of an actor to that of an observer. Storms had actors view themselves on videotape before they rated their own behavior. Actors now saw themselves from the point of view of observers. Would actors now make more dispositional attributions about their own behavior? They definitely did. After actors observed themselves holding a conversation, their attributions were to stable character traits, just as the observer's attributions had been. It is as if actors watched themselves in conversation and said to themselves, "Look how nervous I seem. I must be a really shy person." When they did not look at the videotape, they had an entirely different interpretation of the same behavior.

The picture we get of self-serving bias clouds when we look at how people attribute their own success and failure. A self-serving person would take credit for her successes while blaming her failures on outside factors beyond her control. A self-serving bias would suggest that people attribute their successes to stable character traits, such as ability. On the other hand, they might also attribute their successes to a less stable personal characteristic—effort, for example. Whether the attribution is to a stable or unstable personal characteristic, self-serving people would attribute their success to themselves and their failure to external causes, some aspect of their situation, rather than to themselves. Anyone who has watched children play a competitive game has seen evidence of a self-serving bias. A child who is tagged out complains of cheating or unfair rules. Never have I heard a child say that the rules helped him win. But a child who has just learned a new skill will eagerly tell you how she accomplished the feat, "all by herself."

Research, however, does not show a consistent tendency toward self-serving attributions in adults. Luginbuhl, Crowe, and Kahan (1975) set up a situation where people would either succeed or fail at a novel task. People in one group were told they had failed at 23 out of 30 attempts to identify similar geometric shapes while those in another group were told they succeeded on 23 out of 30 attempts. People who had succeeded attributed their success much more to their effort and ability than to luck or the kind of task involved. That is, people made internal attributions for success. They gave themselves credit. This supports the idea of a self-serving bias. The results for people who failed are not so clear. Those who had failed blamed their failure on stable causes, but not necessarily on external causes. Failure was attributed most to task difficulty, an external cause, which would support the idea of a self-serving bias. However, failure was attributed to lack of ability almost as much. In fact, people blamed their failure on their lack of ability more than people credited their success to their high ability. It seems that people who succeeded attributed their success to effort, a factor over which they had control. Those who failed attributed their failure to ability, a factor over which they had no control. While blaming failure on an uncontrollable factor would seem to relieve people of responsibility, they could also have blamed the difficulty of the task or luck, factors over which they had no control and which are external to themselves. The evidence supports the idea of a self-serving bias in some ways but not others.

A self-serving bias shows up more clearly in the college classroom. When Arkin and Maruyama (1979) asked students to account for their success or failure in a college psychology course, students who considered themselves successful attributed their performance more to personal characteristics, ability and effort. In contrast, students who considered themselves unsuccessful attributed their performance more to luck and the difficulty of the course.[3]

A self-serving bias could explain some of the troubling behavior of heavy drinkers. Some people, most often men, have a talent for getting drunk at exactly

---

[3]While these results are just what we would suspect if students were making self-serving attributions, there is another explanation that cannot be ruled out. What if students were simply reporting accurately the reasons for their success or failure? Maybe successful students succeeded because of their ability and effort, while unsuccessful students failed because the course was difficult and they were unlucky. Perhaps no bias occurred. Instead, successful and unsuccessful students may have performed the way they did for different reasons.

the wrong time. They may act responsibly and appropriately in most situations. But when they have something important to accomplish, an important business lunch, for example, they get drunk and blow the opportunity. I experienced my first hangover the morning I took the SAT test for college applicants. I was a little nervous and restless the night before. The idea occurred to me that my parents' brandy would help me sleep. I drank some brandy but did not fall asleep, so I drank more. The brandy eventually did make me sleep, but not before making me drunk. Why did drinking seem like such a good idea to me on that particular night?

Berglas and Jones (1978) explained that one way people handle failure is to set up a good reason for it in advance. A good excuse for failure would necessarily be one that reduced the effectiveness of performance, allowing a person to blame failure on the handicap rather than on himself. That is, a person could give himself a handicap that would excuse failure but also make failure more likely. In addition, succeeding in spite of a handicap is evidence of superior ability. The handicap also makes it easier to attribute success to himself, to his own ability. Thus self-handicapping is a strategy for enhancing self-esteem.

Berglas and Jones (1978) set up a situation that gave people the opportunity to choose a perfomance- enhancing or performance-inhibiting drug before taking a difficult mental ability test. They first had people attempt to solve impossibly difficult problems on a test of intellectual ability. The researchers then gave all the test takers high scores. Because people realized the test problems were beyond their ability and yet they were successful, it was difficult for them to attribute their success to their own ability. Researchers then gave people the opportunity to try again on a similar test after taking a drug that would either help or hinder their performance. Would people choose a drug that would hurt their performance, making it easier to attribute success to their own ability and failure to the drug? Some did, specifically, men. Men but not women consistently chose the drug that would hinder their performance on the test. We do not know why women might be less likely than men to self-handicap. Women in the study were more likely than men to attribute their performance to luck. Perhaps taking personal credit for success is less important to women, or was when the study took place. Men, however, showed a strong tendency to self-handicap.

In some situations, people may make attributions that are not self-serving at all. Ross, Bierbauer, and Polly (1974) set up a situation to investigate how teachers attribute the success or failure of their students. Teachers were given the assignment of attempting to teach an 11-year-old boy a list of commonly misspelled words. Afterward, teachers were told how the boy had done on a spelling test of those words. One group of teachers was told the boy had succeeded brilliantly. Another group was told he had failed badly. Would teachers attribute the success or failure of their students in a self-serving way? Would they take personal credit for their students' success and blame student failure on situational factors or the students themselves? They did not. Just the opposite occurred. Teachers blamed themselves when their students failed and credited their students' hard work and ability when they succeeded. When college students rather than professional teachers were given the same teaching assignment, the same pattern of results occurred. College student teachers also blamed themselves for the boy's failure to learn and attributed his success to his own hard work and ability.

In studies of self-serving bias taken as a whole, researchers have found less evidence of self-serving bias than had been expected. People seem to be less self-serving than is commonly believed, at least in some situations. When people were given the task of teaching a child, just the opposite of a self-serving bias was found. (See Pyszczynski and Greenberg [1987] for a literature review.)

A person's social position makes a difference in her attributions for success and failure. It is easier for people in dominant social positions, such as white men, to believe that success and failure are results of personal ability. Members of minority ethnic groups are more likely to believe that success and failure result from social position or luck (Kluegel & Smith 1986). Women are more likely than men to attribute their success to something other than themselves (Fox & Ferri 1992). In addition, Hispanic women are more likely to attribute job performance to something other than personal ability than are non-Hispanic women (Romero & Garza 1986). It is hard to tell whose view of success and failure is more accurate. As you will see in Chapter 4, sometimes the impact that a belief has on our behavior is more important than whether the belief is accurate. Chapter 7 describes how behavior and opportunity in the workplace depend on gender and other status characteristics. Chapter 7 also shows you what to do should you find yourself at a disadvantage in your job.

GAINING PERSPECTIVE

Keeping a Journal

How can we teach ourselves to be more effective in social situations? Social competence requires an immense amount of ability. We have to see social situations from other people's point of view as well as our own. We must learn to mentally take the role of various people around us, some of whom come from quite different backgrounds. We need to understand not only why they behave the way they do but also what they might think causes our behavior. To make good decisions and respond effectively to social situations, we must first compensate for our common perceptual biases. We have to estimate how much we may have misjudged the situation and in what direction.

As if that were not difficult enough, we must understand social situations quickly. Not only are social situations complicated, they also change rapidly. Rarely do we have the luxury of enough time to analyze a social situation carefully. When a coworker attacks you in a meeting with your boss, or your child throws a tantrum in the supermarket while shoppers glare, you have little time to think. The rules of social interaction require an immediate response. How can we gain confidence that we are doing what is best for ourselves and those around us?

Like any skill, social competence develops through practice. To be effective, practice must be separated from performance. In one sense, we practice our social skills every day as we interact with the people around us. However, professional performers know that they cannot get better through performance alone. During a performance, whether a concert or a play or a basketball game, performers concentrate totally on the immediate task. There is no time for self-awareness.

Self-awareness interferes with the automatic behavior learned through hours of practice. Because self-awareness is so limited during performances, it is difficult for performers to improve through performing alone. To get better, performers need practice sessions that allow them to self-consciously analyze their behavior. In the same way, we need to practice social awareness if we are going to improve our social competence.

A good way to practice social awareness is to keep a journal. Keeping a journal allows you to review the hectic encounters of a typical day. Alone, at the end of a day, you can assess what happened. You can think calmly about your performance. In what ways were you successful in dealing with other people? What could you have done better? You need not spend a lot of time working on your journal. Devote just 15 minutes a day to assessing your performance and you will see dramatic results. One advantage to keeping a journal is that results are easy to see. You have a written record of your progress. You can look back in your journal and see situations that used to baffle and upset you, situations you now handle easily.

Keeping a journal is easy. Starting a journal is hard. I remember trying to keep a diary once. Nothing that happened to me seemed interesting enough to put in it. You will not have that problem with your journal. A journal is a tool to practice your social skills. Every day we have social encounters, some only imaginary. You will use your encounters with people as material for your journal. This chapter will give you specific ways to analyze those encounters. As you get more comfortable with your journal, your analysis will become more insightful. First, however, you must start. Use whatever writing tools you like. It is convenient to have some way to hold the pages of your journal together, although some people just put the loose pages in a box, one on top of the other. Many people like bound blank books with attractive covers. I started with those but found it hard to write in them because they would not lie flat. Eventually I started using lined notebook paper with three holes, which I could put into a three-ring binder. Get something to write on and a pen or pencil to write with. Journals are especially easy to keep on a computer, especially now that a portable computer can go where you do. Start today. Put the date at the top of the page. That will help you assess your progress when you look back through your journal. Now what? Describe what happened to you today, whatever

cathy®   **by Cathy Guisewite**

Sometimes starting is enough

comes to mind. It might seem trivial. You might be embarrassed. What you write is not nearly as important as the fact that you write something. Pick something you said to someone else or something someone said to you. Write it down. You are done. You have started your journal and the rest of your life.

I started keeping a journal after my life had spun completely out of control. As a young person, I was sensitive and shy around people. I was afraid of social situations. Then I learned that alcohol could reduce my anxiety and help me to function socially. Sometimes, though, I would drink too much. The more I drank, the less control I had over my behavior. By the time I was 32 years old, it became clear even to me that my behavior had to change. Otherwise, jail or a mental hospital seemed inevitable. For example, I could not keep myself from driving while drunk. I tried going home early and drinking myself to sleep. But as I drank, my loneliness would become unbearable. I would stumble to the car and drive somewhere, anywhere, to try to get away from myself. My relations with other people became increasingly troublesome as they lost patience with my erratic behavior. Alcohol was no longer the solution to my social problems but their major cause.

When I quit drinking, all of my old social anxiety returned. I had never learned to deal with people and myself. I had used alcohol instead. Reading was a crutch I had used to avoid people before I discovered alcohol. After I quit drinking, I started reading again, trying to find a way out of my dilemma: needing people but being afraid to be around them. One of those books suggested keeping a journal. I resolved to start one, but what would I write? The idea of examining my life was terrifying. At the time, I tried to shave without using a mirror, afraid of what it might show me. I was too anxious even to write privately about other people or myself. So I wrote what I could. I began by writing down any trivial detail of my day. One sentence was enough. "I had a peanut butter sandwich for lunch today." No insight resulted but I had begun. Keeping a journal allowed me to capture insight when it eventually appeared. As my journal entries became more regular and elaborate, I began to examine other people and myself. Slowly, my social awareness and competence increased. Write one true sentence in your journal today.

How Your Journal Works

Your journal will help you accomplish several goals. First, you will gain social awareness, the ability to see social situations from another's point of view as well as your own. Second, you will learn to allow for the biases we all have in how we see other people. Third, you will learn to make more accurate social judgments and better decisions. Your investment of 15 minutes a day will be well rewarded.

When you sit down to write in your journal, take a minute or two to go over your day. Whom did you talk to? Could something that was said to you be understood in more than one way? We have seen how ambiguous language can be. Start by writing exactly what was said, as well as you can remember. Suppose that at work your boss told you to finish a project you had been working on for some time. You would write that your boss said "I want that project finished today." Good. Now that you know what was said, you can interpret it. Take a few more minutes to think about the situation that caused your boss to tell you to finish the project. You may have resented your boss's order. It was a difficult project. Did she think you had not been working hard enough? Maybe, maybe not. Doesn't she know how many different projects you are working on? Again maybe, maybe not.

Try to see the situation from her point of view. What is your boss's job like? How many different projects and people does she have to deal with? She might have no idea how many different projects you are working on. Why would she tell you to finish the project? If it wasn't past the deadline, maybe she didn't mean it as a criticism of your work. Maybe her boss asked her for a report on your project that she was unprepared to give. She might have reacted defensively by giving you the order to finish the project today. Or maybe a customer had called your boss asking about the project. Your boss may have forgotten the details of the project and assumed it was past deadline. At first you may find it difficult to see your boss's point of view. Put yourself in her place. Imagine you were doing her job. Soon you will be able to imagine several possible explanations for almost any situation. Write down any that seem plausible. If you have struggled to come up with one alternative explanation from the other person's point of view, then write it down. Even if it seems fanciful to you, you have made good progress.

Every day, use your journal to practice seeing a situation from another person's point of view as well as your own. Pick a social encounter you had during the day. Describe what happened. Then describe what you think another person thought happened. How do the two views differ?

You will also find that your resentments toward people will diminish as you write the alternative explanations for their behavior. Your boss probably does not see herself as domineering and critical. What looked to you like unfair criticism may have seemed to her to be a simple request for information. We all tend to justify and excuse our own behavior, even when it may have bothered someone else. When you look at a situation from another person's point of view, you will start to justify and excuse her behavior too.

Keep in mind the biases we have when we look at people's behavior. Remember the fundamental attribution error. We are biased to see behavior as corresponding to character traits of the person. We overlook situational factors that may have caused it. Think about the situation in which the behavior occurred. What details in the situation could have accounted for the behavior? Did your boss just have a meeting with her boss? Has she been overworked and distracted lately? Compensate for the tendency to fixate on personal character traits as causes of behavior. Seek out situational factors that may be important but overlooked.

Finally, use your journal to examine your own behavior from another person's point of view. This for me was the most difficult. After all, I was having trouble looking at myself in the mirror. For example, you see yourself as hardworking. Does your boss see you as just as hardworking as you do? Maybe not. Why might she come to the conclusion that you are not working hard enough?

A good technique to improve the accuracy of our social judgment is to consider the opposing point of view. No matter how obvious we think something is, our assessment of the situation will benefit from assuming that just the opposite is true. No matter how fair and unbiased we try to be, it is always possible that we will selectively look at evidence that supports what we already believe and ignore contradictory information. Lord, Lepper, and Preston (1984) set up a situation to investigate whether considering the opposite would result in more accurate social judgments. They asked people to try to find out, as accurately as possible, whether a person they were about to meet was an extrovert. Researchers gave subjects a profile of a typical extrovert to give them an idea of what to look for—outgoing, sociable, talkative, and so on. The researchers supplied a list of questions that people could ask to try to determine whether the other person was an extrovert. People then chose the questions they would ask. Some questions were biased toward confirming extroversion. For example, "In what situations are you most talkative?" Others were biased toward confirming the opposite, introversion. For example, "In what situations do you wish you were more outgoing?" Some questions were neutral. For example, "What are your career goals?" A good strategy to make an accurate judgment would be to pick neutral questions and about equal numbers of questions biased toward confirming extroversion and introversion. Picking a lot of questions biased to confirm extroversion is likely to produce the wrong answer. However, even though researchers had asked people to be as accurate and unbiased as possible in their judgments, most of the questions they picked were biased toward confirming that the person was in fact extroverted.

Lord, Lepper, and Preston (1984) asked another group of people to use the "consider the opposite" technique in the same situation. People tried to determine whether a person was in fact an extrovert. Instead of giving people a profile of a typical extrovert for them to use in making their assessments, the researchers gave them a profile of a typical introvert—shy, reserved, quiet, and the like. Researchers gave the explanation that since extroverts are just the opposite of introverts, the introvert profile should be just as useful to them. All people had to do was look for traits that were just the opposite of those in the profile. Would people still choose questions biased toward confirming extroversion? Or would considering the opposite of extroversion reduce their bias? The consider the opposite technique effectively eliminated people's bias toward asking questions that confirmed what they had set out to find. After people considered the introvert rather than the extrovert profile, the number of questions they chose that were biased toward confirming extroversion was about equal to the number of questions they chose that were biased toward confirming introversion. The consider the opposite technique is more effective in making accurate social judgments than attempts to be fair and unbiased. In your journal, practice considering the opposite, especially when you are certain you are right and another person is terribly wrong.

Use your journal to help you improve in the three major areas of social competence: (1) seeing situations from another person's point of view as well as your own, (2) compensating for biased perceptions of social situations, and (3) making more accurate social judgments. You probably will not have time to work on all three areas on any one day. On most days you may pick out only one or two incidents and analyze them in only one way. That is exactly as it should be. Starting a journal is hard. If you write a little bit each day, keeping it going is easy. Forgive yourself if you miss a day. Start again. Write at least one sentence in your journal. The little bit of progress you make each day will build up until you can see major differences in yourself as you flip back through the pages of your journal.

Further Reading

Of General Interest

Cook, K. S., Fine, G. A., & House, J. S. (1995). *Sociological perspectives on social psychology.* Boston: Allyn and Bacon.

De Waal, F. (1996). *Good natured.* Cambridge, MA: Harvard University Press.

Foschi, M., & Lawler, E. J. (1994). *Group processes: Sociological analyses.* Chicago: Nelson-Hall.

Fouts, R. (1997). *Next of kin.* New York: Morrow.

Savage-Rumbaugh, S., & Lewin, R. (1994). *Kanzi: The ape at the brink of the human mind.* New York: Wiley.

Tesser, A. (1995). *Advanced social psychology.* New York: McGraw-Hill.

Recent and Technical Issues

Deppe, R. K., & Harackiewicz, J. M. (1996). Self-handicapping and intrinsic motivation: Buffering intrinsic motivation from the threat of failure. *Journal of Personality and Social Psychology, 70,* 868–876.

Gallup, G. G., Jr. (1998). Self-awareness and the evolution of social intelligence. *Behavioral Processes, 42,* 239–247.

Leith, K. P., & Baumeister, R. F. (1996). Why do bad moods increase self-defeating behavior? Emotion, risk taking, and self-regulation. *Journal of Personality and Social Psychology, 71,* 1250–1267.

McDonald, H., & Hirt, E. R. (1997). When expectancy meets desire: Motivational effects in reconstructive memory. *Journal of Personality and Social Psychology, 72,* 5–23.

Midgley, C., Arunkumar, R., & Urdan, T. C. (1996). "If I don't do well tomorrow, there's a reason": Predictors of adolescents' use of academic self-handicapping strategies. *Journal of Educational Psychology, 88,* 423–434.

Rhodewalt, F., Sanbonmatsu, D. M., Tschanz, B., Feick, D. L., & Waller, A. (1995). Self-handicapping and interpersonal trade-offs: The effects of claimed self-handicaps on observers' performance evaluations and feedback. *Personality and Social Psychology Bulletin, 21,* 1042–1050.

CHAPTER 3

Who Are You?

Changing your life is not that easy, is it? If simple techniques like keeping a journal and using affirmations really work to help people grow, then why do so few people succeed? The techniques for personal growth that you will find in this book are both simple and effective. Yet changing yourself remains a difficult challenge. To understand our resistance to changing ourselves, we have to understand who we are. Social psychologists call our conception of who we are our *identity*. Research is sometimes similar to detective work. When social psychologists investigate identity, their goal is not so different from a police detective trying to establish a suspect's identity. Both investigators would like to establish who that person really is.

Establishing who a person is can be difficult. Just as criminals establish multiple identities to elude police, we behave quite differently in different situations, making it hard to identify just who we are. For example, I behave differently when I visit my parents than I usually do. It feels like I regress in age. Suddenly I'm enmeshed in the problems of growing up and separating from my parents. I compete with my brother and sister for my parents' attention. At my parents' house, I am a different person from the stuffy professor in a coat and tie that my students know. If we have several identities, multiple selves, does a core self really exist? If so, what might it look like?

Recall from Chapter 2 that a self emerges when a person becomes aware of herself as a person. A person has a self when she can mentally step outside herself, when she can see herself as she sees other people. To make an analogy with grammar, a person can think of herself as both subject and object, as *I* and *me*. Social psychologists call self-awareness a *reflexive* thought process. The *I* part of your mind considers—or reflects on—the *me* part. A person is an active being but also an object that is acted on. When people become self-aware, they can act to change themselves. For example, you can make yourself go to a job even when you don't want to. Rather than simply following your impulse to stay home from work, you reflect on the consequences, then push yourself out the door. Your *identity* is made up of the meanings attached to your self by you and by others. Psychologists also identify people in terms of their personality. You can think of personality as all the

cathy®   by Cathy Guisewite

Cathy's identity has to change when she realizes that others see her differently than she sees herself

psychological traits, urges, feelings, and thought patterns that make up a person. Self can be thought of as the conscious part of personality (Gecas & Burke 1995). Your identity, then, is what it means to be you.

MULTIPLE SELVES

Since the late 1970s social psychologists have increasingly focused on multiple selves and identities rather than on an underlying core self. Part of the reason for the focus on multiple selves is that a core self is harder and harder to find. Kenneth Gergen points out that postmodern society—society in the age of information—puts enormous demands on an individual's conception of her *self* (Gergen 1991). Recall from Chapter 2 George Herbert Mead's idea that we develop a unified picture of ourselves as we adopt the attitudes and prescriptions of the people around us concerning who we ought to be. Mead called this the "generalized other." As Cooley (1902) observed about what he called the "looking-glass self," we know who we are by seeing the opinions that other people hold of us. As an individual develops a conception of herself, she organizes a unified picture of what her community expects her *self* to be.

Gergen (1991) shows how postmodern society makes it difficult for an individual to maintain a unified conception of her self. Today, society puts us in situations where we constantly must adjust ourselves to a variety of people and social situations. In the course of a single hectic day, you can be a student, an employee, and a mother. You can sit in a small chair to talk to your child's teacher, supervise others on your job while being supervised by your boss, chat with friends at lunch, and entertain a lover over dinner. An observer following you around your day, observing you from a distance, would see several different patterns of behavior. You might seem to be a different person in each of those different situations. You might even feel like a different person. Which of those different people are you, really?

According to Gergen (1991), the more people we come into contact with, especially when those people are very different from each other, the harder it is for us to sort out who we really are. The self can become saturated or fragmented. The images of who we might or should be come at us from all directions, not just from meeting people face to face but also from television, from the car radio, from newspapers and store windows, and from all manner of advertising. It becomes easy for us to lose our social bearings, to lose our sense of self. Not knowing who you are can be highly disturbing. Some of the most severe mental disorders have to do with a damaged sense of self.

It may not be coincidental that cases of multiple personality disorder have increased along with the explosion in information technology. The *Diagnostic and Statistical Manual of Mental Disorders,* usually referred to as *DSM-IV* (American Psychiatric Association 1994), defines dissociative identity disorder (formerly multiple personality disorder) as a condition in which two or more distinct identities (or personalities) sometimes take control of a person's behavior. In addition, when one identity is in control, the person may not be able to recall behavior that occurred when another identity was in control.

Phillips (1995) writes about what it is like to live with dissociative identity disorder. Jane Phillips is the pen name of a college professor who suffered with dissociative identity disorder for years before finally being diagnosed as a multiple personality. She writes:

> Ever since junior high, I had been painfully conscious of the suspicion that something was profoundly wrong with me . . . Mostly I just never seemed to be who I really was— although I had no idea who that was. It seemed to me that I was no one; that when other people were around, I simply didn't exist—instead I assumed a role then performed it, often badly. Perhaps it was true that I *was* the dumb kid in the family: the crybaby who never understood, and who was ill, injured, or in tears . . .
>
> When alone, I often steadied myself by spending long hours staring into my mirror. I was far from vain, actually believing myself to be quite ugly, but when I stared into my mirror, I somehow slipped out of myself. The faces that looked back at me were not really mine. They all seemed related to me but they were sometimes young, sometimes very old, beautiful, wise, boyish, feminine, mischievous. . . . These faces were all very real to me, separate folks, it seemed to me, friends of a sort, and in the quiet of my bedroom I listened to them speak. My favorite, and the one I often sought, was beautiful, powerful, and wise. Was I crazy to believe she was there? Maybe. I was a little old for imaginary friends, but I could not live without her or the others, and I felt calmer, stronger, and safer after our visits in the glass . . .
>
> But during the past four or five months, I had begun sliding into trouble. The entire year had been rather stressful . . . I got through the days by sheer force of will, but by April I was suffering terrible headaches and, when my vacation started, I spent twenty hours a day in bed staring at the wall, an activity I found somehow reassuring, as I could not think, function, or control my emotions . . . In the kitchen, the knives seemed to call out to me to slit my wrists, and for long hours I would stand inside my closet weeping because none of the clothing there seemed to belong to me . . .
>
> I had made the alarming discovery that alcohol, a lot of alcohol, drunk alone in the privacy of my room, seemed to bring me a kind of peace and quiet I had not known for months. Then one afternoon, there were suddenly two of me: one Jane lay on the bed and watched the other Jane sitting at the desk and reading. One of us had the foresight to pause and write a note. It said: "Something is terribly wrong. See your doctor when you get home." (Phillips 1995, pp. 19–21)

Multiple personality as a mental disorder is both fascinating and controversial. The elements of playacting, the constant drama, the alcohol and drug abuse that frequently accompany it, all confuse the issue. Multiple personality has been used as a defense in high-profile murder cases, arousing suspicion that the disorder can be—and often is—faked. Ian Hacking, a philosopher who undertook a study of the historical and cultural development of multiple personality, concludes that it does exist (Hacking 1995). Patients diagnosed with multiple personality often have experienced years of real distress for which they are sincerely seeking help. However, some skepticism about multiple personality comes from accounts—such as the one by Jane Phillips—describing multiple personalities as the solution to the problems people face, rather than as the problem itself. If multiple personality is a disorder, why do sufferers seem so fond of their alternate personalities and even proud of their ability to dissociate?

Adopting a new identity is a common solution to problems that arise in a complicated social life. People in trouble have always been able to run away and start over, sometimes changing their identities. A complex postmodern society not only makes it more difficult to form a unified self, but technological advances provide more opportunity to create different selves.

An acquaintance told me how he had created for himself an entirely new identity, one that he preferred. By day he drove a local delivery truck, making routine stops at various businesses. But he had always wanted to be an airplane pilot. Instead of learning to fly in his spare time, he created social relationships that confirmed his identity as a pilot. He lived in a metropolitan area containing several million people. After work, he would go to his apartment, change clothes, then drive his car across the bay to a town about 30 minutes away. There he spent the evening in several bars where he became a regular. He was excited by the idea that the people who he met in the bars would be unlikely to see him in any other social situation. He lost his customary shyness and found he could meet people easily. He told them he was a pilot for a major airline. His stories of near collisions and adventures in the air entertained his new friends. They, in turn, would watch out for him, not letting him drink too much on nights when they knew he was scheduled to fly early the next morning. During the day, he would imagine what he would be doing if he were an airline pilot so that he could tell his friends about it after work. His job no longer bored and frustrated him because it seemed less real. His identity as a pilot became more satisfying and eventually more real to him than his daytime self.

In a complex society, it is easy to lose the sense that you have a core identity, what would commonly be called integrity. Instead, you feel yourself pushed around by circumstances, unable to orient yourself in a social kaleidoscope. Given the complexity of modern social life, investigating multiple selves makes sense. Similarly, clinical psychologists have seen a huge increase in cases of multiple personality disorder. The stresses of modern life seem to encourage multiple selves as a means to cope. One side effect of using multiple selves to cope with complex social situations is loss of integrity, a feeling of fragmentation. If you have too many selves, then does your true self continue to exist?

Relationships that begin on the Internet seem to encourage the formation of multiple selves. Mantovani (1995) tells the story of Julie, an early member of the

cathy®   **by Cathy Guisewite**

Cathy acquires a second identity. Who will she decide to be?

electronic community in the mid-1980s.[1] Julie was a totally disabled older woman who wrote with a headstick, tapping out messages on her keyboard. Many women who met her on the Internet were attracted to her. They found her compassionate and her advice valuable. They confided their most important secrets to Julie and sought her advice. However, one of her Internet friends was not satisfied with an electronic relationship and wanted to meet the real Julie in person. After several years, the persistent friend discovered that Julie was not a disabled older woman after all. Rather, she was in fact a middle-aged male psychiatrist.

Many of Julie's friends felt threatened and betrayed by this revelation. Women felt their privacy had been violated. A man masquerading a false identity had tricked them. Other women remained loyal to Julie. They were grateful for her good advice. To them Julie was still the person they knew and cared for. The male psychiatrist was a person whom they had never met. His identity was irrelevant to them. But just how real was Julie?

WHO YOU ARE DETERMINES WHAT YOU DO

Not only is it difficult to pin down a person's true identity, but the concept of *identity* itself is slippery. If identity is a real thing and not just a label for typical behavior, then identity must play a part when we choose our behaviors. Identity theory proposes that when we decide to do something, we first consider how closely the behavior we are considering coincides with our identity. Is it something that fits in with who we are? Then we try to shape our behavior to conform to our identity, our self-concept.

When your identity is positive, identity theory paints a commonsense picture of human behavior. Common sense tells us that people want what is best for themselves and the people they care about. If you want the best for yourself, then you will try your best to succeed. You will choose to associate with people who support you and enhance your self-esteem. However, suppose you have a negative view of yourself. Then you will try to shape your behavior so that it reinforces your

[1]Mantovani (1995) credits Stone (1991) with the original account.

negative self-concept. Negative identities explain much self-defeating and self-destructive human behavior, behavior that defies common sense.

If your identity shapes your stable patterns of behavior, then your identity must be stable as well. Identity theory sees the process of maintaining a stable identity as a *control system* (Burke 1991). Control systems are commonly used to keep environments stable, the way a furnace and thermostat work to control the temperature in a house, for example. In the theory, a person's identity is a set of beliefs held by a person about what it means to be that person. That identity, or set of beliefs, has developed slowly over time and becomes a standard that a person tries to maintain in the future. In a similar way, we set the thermostat on a standard temperature for the house. When a person with a negative identity gets positive feedback, she notices that the feedback is inconsistent with her identity. This new input is used as a tiny piece of evidence that may make her identity standard a bit more positive. However, her overall identity will continue to be negative. Because the new feedback is higher than her identity standard, she will behave in ways that confirm her negative identity. It is like the thermostat that compares the temperature of the house to the temperature standard that has been set. When the thermometer senses the house is too warm, the thermostat tells the furnace to stop until the house cools down below the standard. When a person with a negative identity feels that people are thinking too highly of her, she will do something to make herself look bad, confirming her negative identity. Identity theory proposes that people actively seek information that confirms their identities, whether positive or negative. People also avoid information that might disconfirm their identities. That is the theory. Will research confirm that people behave as the theory predicts?

Swann and Read (1981) wanted to find out if people would actually pay more money for information that confirmed their identities than they would pay for information that disconfirmed their identities. Swann and Read first gave people a questionnaire in which they rated how *assertive* or *restrained* they were. Researchers reasoned that if assertiveness (or lack of it) was part of people's identities, then they would seek out information that confirmed the amount of assertiveness they saw in themselves. A good way to test this would be to find out how much people would pay for confirming or disconfirming evidence. On the basis of their questionnaire responses, researchers could classify people as either assertive or restrained. Researchers then told people that they would be able to get feedback about their nonverbal behavior from another person who had observed them.

People in the study were given a list of questions that would tend to show whether a person was assertive or restrained. A typical assertive question would be "What makes you think that this is the type of person who will complain in a restaurant if the service is bad?" A typical restrained question would be "Why would this person not be likely to complain if someone cuts into line in front of them at a movie?" People could select those questions from the list that they most wanted to hear answered. However, they would have to pay 10 cents for each answer. Would people pay more for the answers to questions that would tend to confirm their preconceived views of themselves, that is, their identities? Yes, they did. Swann and Read (1981) found that people who had rated themselves as assertive would pay more money for the answers to questions they thought would make them seem assertive. Assertive people would pay substantially less money for the answers to questions that might make them appear less assertive. The results for restrained people also supported identity theory. Restrained people would pay more money for the answers to questions that might make them appear more restrained. They would pay less for the answers to questions they thought might disconfirm their restrained identities.

Identities are complicated. We have lots of them. Not only do we have different identities to cover different areas of our lives, but also identities can be positive or negative. In fact, we have some identities that are positive and some that are negative. For example, when I worked in a nightclub, I considered myself an excellent bartender but a terrible dancer. Remember that identities are supposed to determine our behavior. If they do, then my positive identity as a bartender would have produced behavior that made me a better bartender. At the same time, my negative identity as a dancer would have produced behavior that made me a worse dancer. That is, identities go beyond global conceptions of self-esteem. The positive identities that a person holds promote positive behaviors and the negative identities that a person holds promote negative behaviors, all at approximately the same time and for the same person. This is identity theory (Stryker 1980). Could researchers find evidence to support it?

Swann, Pelham, and Krull (1989) conducted a study that showed how a person could actively search for information supporting a positive identity in one area of her life and at the same time search for information supporting a negative identity in a different area. People in the study completed a questionnaire that asked them to assess their own ability in five areas of their lives. They rated themselves compared to others on intellectual ability, skill at sports, physical attractiveness, artistic talent, and social skills. As you might imagine, most people rated themselves fairly high in one area of ability but fairly low in one of the other areas. For example, a good student might rate herself high in intellectual ability but low in skill at sports. People also completed other questionnaires about themselves. Researchers then fed all of the information into a computer. They told people in the study that the computer would analyze their answers and give them feedback. People in the study could then choose which abilities or skills to get feedback on. To do so, they ranked the five ability and skill areas in order of how much they desired feedback in each area. For example, the good student might have ranked the areas as follows:

1. Intellectual ability   (*Most feedback desired*)
2. Artistic talent
3. Physical attractiveness
4. Social skills
5. Skill at sports   (*Least feedback desired*)

Researchers thought that most people would want to get feedback on their best feature rather than their worst feature. That is, people want to feel good about themselves and will seek out information that makes them look good. Swann, Pelham, and Krull (1989) found exactly that. However, it is not particularly surprising.

Researchers also made the more interesting proposal that people would seek positive feedback about their best feature while at the same time seeking negative feedback about their worst feature.

People could also pick particular questions to ask the computer about themselves. For each of the five ability areas, they could ask questions that would be likely to generate positive answers or others that would be likely to generate negative answers. For example, in the area of sports ability, a positive question would be "What is this person's greatest asset at sports and games?" In contrast, a negative question would be "In the area of sports, what is this person's largest problem?" People could pick from similar positive and negative questions for each of the five ability areas. Researchers wanted to know if people would pick the positive question in their best ability area while also picking the negative question in their worst ability area. Again researchers were correct. People were much more likely to pick the positive question for their best ability area than they were to pick the negative question. However, those same people were also much more likely to pick the negative question for their worst ability area than they were to pick the positive question. That is, Swann, Pelham, and Krull (1989) successfully showed that people seek different information about the different identities that they hold for themselves. When seeking information about a positive identity, people prefer positive information. In contrast, when seeking information about a negative identity, that same person is likely to prefer negative information. This result is important because it shows that even people with low self-esteem will seek positive information about their positive identities.

The discovery that identities change the way we seek information raises interesting questions. For example, there is ample evidence that people try to make themselves look good in many situations. In contrast, researchers found that people will seek out negative information about themselves if it supports a negative identity. How is it that a person wants to make herself look good while at the same time she wants to make herself look bad by confirming a negative identity? Swann, Griffin, Predmore, and Gaines (1987) came up with an explanation. They proposed that people try to obtain information that is consistent with their identities, whether they think of themselves positively or negatively. That is, they seek information that seems to them to be true. In contrast, positive information makes people *feel* good whether it is consistent with their identity or not. Emotionally, then, people want to look as good as possible. In their thoughts, however, people want information that is consistent with their identity, even if that information is derogatory about themselves. It is an interesting explanation that requires a test. Do our emotions push us toward positive information while our thoughts push us toward information we think is true?

Swann, Griffin, Predmore, and Gaines (1987) looked at the different cognitive and emotional reactions to feedback. Researchers gave college students a standard self-esteem questionnaire at the beginning of the semester. Later, students who participated in the study were asked to give a short speech. While the student gave the speech, another person observed through a one-way mirror. Students were then given a paragraph evaluating the speech. For some students the observer's evaluation was positive. For others the evaluation was negative. Researchers prepared the evaluations in advance. Students were randomly chosen to receive either positive or negative feedback. For example, a student picked to receive positive feedback would read that she seemed socially self-confident and probably felt at ease around people. In contrast, a student picked to receive negative feedback would read that she seemed to lack social self-confidence and probably felt somewhat uncomfortable and anxious around other people. After students had read the positive or negative feedback about themselves, they answered questions about their reactions to it. The questions asked how students felt about the feedback as well as what they thought about it. The students completed a standard test for depression, anxiety, and hostility. Researchers wanted to find out if students' *feelings* about the feedback were dramatically different from their *thoughts* about the feedback.

Just as researchers had predicted, students thought that feedback supporting their self-concept was more true than feedback negating their self-concept. That is, students who had scored high in self-esteem at the beginning of the semester thought the positive feedback was true and the evaluator competent. Meanwhile, students who had scored low in self-esteem thought the negative feedback was true and the evaluator competent. Students with low self-esteem thought the negative feedback was true, but would it still hurt?

Researchers had also predicted that low–self-esteem students would be just as distressed by negative feedback as high–self-esteem students. That is, students would feel bad about negative feedback whether their self-esteem was high or low. Again researchers were correct. For all students, those who received negative feedback were more depressed and hostile than were students who received positive feedback. In addition, students were more attracted to the person who gave them positive feedback than they were to the person who gave them negative feedback. Even though students with low self-esteem thought negative feedback was true and that the evaluator was competent, they were as emotionally distressed by negative feedback as were students with high self-esteem. In other words, although negative feedback about themselves may seem true to people with low self-esteem, they do not seek it out because it makes them feel better. In some ways, the thoughts and emotions of people with low self-esteem pull them in different directions (Swann, Griffin, Predmore, & Gaines 1987). People want information that seems true to them even if negative. They also want positive information that makes them feel good about themselves.

Swann and his colleagues discovered something important. They showed that people do more than label their typical behavior patterns. Identities are self-concepts that have the power to shape people's behavior in ways that tend to confirm their identities. Identities, then, are self-fulfilling. A positive identity can be expected to produce positive behavior. That idea is neither new nor startling. But can a negative identity produce self-defeating and self-destructive behavior?

NEGATIVE ASPECTS OF IDENTITY

Dawn Robinson, then at Stanford University and now a professor at Louisiana State University, and Lynn Smith-Lovin of the University of Arizona wanted to find out if a negative self-concept would produce negative behavior. These social psychologists work with one of the most mathematically precise theories in the social sciences, *affect control theory* (Heise 1979). Affect control theory explains how thoughts, feelings, and behavior work together to maintain stable identities. The theory predicts that people will behave in ways that maintain their identities, even when that behavior has painful consequences.

Robinson and Smith-Lovin (1992) proposed that people with a negative self-concept would actually choose to associate with people who reinforced their poor self-image. Would people with a negative self-concept choose partners who would criticize them rather than partners who would praise them? To find out, researchers first gave people a standard test that measures self-esteem. Then, just as in earlier identity research, people gave a short speech and received feedback about their performance. Robinson and Smith-Lovin, however, gave people feedback from two observers. The feedback from one of the observers was positive while the feedback from the other observers was negative. After reading the feedback, people chose which observer they would like to work with on another project. As we might expect, people with a positive self-concept (high self-esteem) chose to work with the observer who had praised their speech. More surprisingly, people with a negative self-concept chose to work with the partner who had criticized them. As in the earlier identity studies, people with a negative self-concept felt as bad about criticism as did others. Nonetheless, they chose to work with someone they believed would criticize them. By their choices, people with a negative self-concept work to ensure that they will continue to feel bad about themselves in the future.

Swann, Wenzlaff, and Tafarodi (1992) conducted a related study with depressed and nondepressed people. They found that depressed people would choose to interact with a partner who had criticized them rather than go on to another activity. How negative self-concept deteriorates into depression is not understood. Studies by identity researchers do show that both negative self-concept and depression encourage behaviors that maintain negative thoughts and feelings.

We can now see that while the techniques explained in Chapters 1 and 2 are simple and effective, they are not easy. You can change your life and how you feel by changing the way you behave. However, if your behavior opposes a negative self-concept, your mind will tell you something is wrong. Even if the behavior is making you feel better, you will think that what you are doing must be wrong. It will feel like a betrayal. Who we are is important to us, even when it hurts. You can expect the techniques for change and growth suggested in this book to produce some resistance. The message is not that change is easy. Rather, change is possible. You can become the person you wish to be if you work at it and don't give up.

MULTIPLE IDENTITIES AS THERAPY FOR A TROUBLESOME ONE

As Jane Phillips's description of multiple personality earlier in this chapter suggests, one way to cope with a negative identity is to become someone else for a while. Sherry Turkle is both a sociologist and a clinical psychologist who studies the development of multiple identities on the Internet. She finds that developing multiple identities creates both benefits and risks for Internet users. The Internet provides a variety of interactive role-playing games called multiuser domains. People log onto the game and create characters that then form relationships with other users and develop virtual societies. Commonly in multiuser domains, people adopt identities that are far removed from the people they are in real life (Turkle 1995).

Women, for example, sometimes practice being assertive by becoming a man in a multiuser domain. One woman who benefited from practice as a man said: "As a woman, standing firm and drawing the line has always made me feel like a bitch and, actually, I feel that people saw me as one, too. As a man I was liberated from all that. I learned from my mistakes. I got better at being firm but not rigid. I practiced, safe from criticism" (Turkle 1995, p. 221).

Becoming different people in multiuser domains also allows people to escape from difficult problems in their real lives. Turkle (1995) describes how Gordon, who was an unpopular misfit in school, used multiuser domains to get a fresh start with people who did not know that he was unpopular. Multiuser domains can be addictive as well when creating new identities is used only as a means of escape. Some people create many characters and run from one to the other as problems arise in their Internet relationships. Real-life problems develop as some people devote 70 or more hours a week to multiuser domains.

Turkle (1995) describes how Robert first used multiuser domains for escape. After a childhood with an abusive father, Robert went away to college. Cut off from his mother and friends, he felt lost and lonely. He spent nearly all of his waking hours at the computer, sometimes 120 hours a week. While he was someone else on the computer, he did not have to worry about his own problems. He was addicted. He would tell himself that he was going to stop and go to class, but he could not.

Although Robert's addiction to multiuser domains eventually led to his leaving college, he got more out of his experience than temporary escape. Robert thinks that had he not spent all his time on the Internet, he would likely have started drinking abusively like his father. Instead, Robert became an administrator developing a new multiuser domain. His duties required him to work out the disagreements that people have just as they do in real life. He had to allocate resources, recruit people, and assign jobs (Turkle 1995). People depended on him for a secure virtual world. By the time he left school, Robert had acquired the secure sense of self he needed to function on his own. Robert had solved many of his own problems by helping other people in a multiuser domain. Chapter 4 explains in more detail how effective helping other people can be as a technique for solving our own problems.

Further Reading

Of General Interest

Baumeister, R. F. (1986). *Identity: Cultural change and the struggle for self.* New York: Oxford University Press.

Gecas, V., & Burke, P. J. (1995). Self and identity. In K. S. Cook, G. A. Fine, & J. S. House (Eds.), *Sociological perspectives on social psychology* (pp. 41–67). Boston: Allyn and Bacon.

Gergen, K. J. (1991). *The saturated self.* New York: Basic Books.

Hacking, I. (1995). *Rewriting the soul: Multiple personality and the sciences of memory.* Princeton, NJ: Princeton University Press.

Phillips, J. (1995). *The magic daughter.* New York: Viking.

Swann, W. B., Jr. (1997) The trouble with change: Self-verification and allegiance to the self. *Psychological Science, 8,* 177–180.

Turkle, S. (1995). *Life on the screen: Identity in the age of the Internet.* New York: Touchstone.

Recent and Technical Issues

Burke, P. J. (1997). An identity model for network exchange. *American Sociological Review, 62,* 134–150.

Burke, P. J., & Reitzes, D. C. (1991). An identity theory approach to commitment. *Social Psychology Quarterly, 54,* 239–251.

Geisler, R. B., Josephs, R. A., & Swann, W. B. Jr. (1996). Self-verification in clinical depression: The desire for negative evaluation. *Journal of Abnormal Psychology, 105,* 358–368.

Joiner, T. E., Jr. (1995). The price of soliciting and receiving negative feedback: Self-verification theory as a vulnerability to depression theory. *Journal of Abnormal Psychology, 104,* 364–372.

Riley, A., & Burke, P. J. (1995). Identities and self-verification in the small group. *Social Psychology Quarterly, 58,* 61–73.

Swann, W. B., Jr., Stein-Seroussi, A., & McNulty, S. E. (1992). Outcasts in a white-lie society: The enigmatic worlds of people with negative self-conceptions. *Journal of Personality and Social Psychology, 62,* 618–624.

CHAPTER 4

Of Sound Mind

Trying to solve other people's problems is good mental exercise and, as will eventually become clear, more effective than trying to solve your own. There have been times in my life when nothing seemed to go right, when I lost a job and a dog, got sick, wrecked a car, broke up with a woman, all more or less at once. My problems would pile one on top of the other. Working hard to solve one problem seemed to create several new ones. What could I do? All of my time was spent trying to organize and manage my problems that only got worse. In the middle of one of these crises, a very wise person said something I did not appreciate at the time. She said that my problems were none of my business. It will take the rest of the chapter to explain that strange idea.

In trying to solve another person's problem, you start by imagining what you would do in her place. Imagine yourself in the following predicament. Suppose that after a series of weird coincidences you awake one morning to find yourself in a hospital psychiatric ward. When you hesitantly begin to explore your surroundings, you find that the door at the end of the hallway is locked. When you ask a staff person why, she explains with some sympathy and obvious condescension that the doors to the psychiatric ward are locked for your own protection. You try to explain that you are not sure how you came to be in a locked psychiatric ward, but you are fine now. Could you please go home or at least make a phone call? The staff person makes a note of your comment then continues with her duties without replying. Left alone, you try to strike a balance between confusion and rising panic as you consider your problem. What would you do to show people that you are sane? A sane person might become upset and protest loudly about being locked up by mistake. But consider the point of view of the psychiatric staff. Might they see your distress and arguments as paranoid or delusional, as symptoms of some mental disorder?

"YOU PROBABLY THINK I'M CRAZY"

Stress, fatigue, alcohol, various combinations of prescription and nonprescription drugs, and many types of physical illness can produce behavior that temporarily mimics a mental disorder. While the chance is small that you will find yourself a patient in a psychiatric ward, it could happen for a number of reasons. Surely, the doctors would soon notice your obvious sanity and correct the mistake. Wouldn't they?

A famous study suggests otherwise (Rosenhan 1973). Doctors in psychiatric hospitals may have difficulty sorting out perfectly sane people from legitimate mental patients. Social psychology explains the problem. Doctors base their clinical judgment, their *attributions* for patients' behavior, on the context in which that behavior occurs (Rosenhan 1975). Knowing that a person is on a psychiatric ward can lead doctors to interpret her behavior as symptomatic of a mental disorder. The context of the situation leads doctors to expect mental problems. What would be considered normal behavior elsewhere is then interpreted as abnormal.

The fundamental attribution error plays a role. Recall from Chapter 1 that human beings (at least in Western cultures) tend to attribute behavior to stable character traits rather than to circumstances of the situation in which the behavior occurred. The tendency to attribute to a person rather than to elements of the situation is so widespread that it has been labeled the fundamental attribution error by some researchers (Ross 1977). Doctors are human too. A doctor would note your anxiety and distress at being confined to a psychiatric ward. However, instead of attributing your behavior to discomfort caused by a confusing and threatening situation, she might well attribute it to some underlying mental disease. The doctor might be more likely to discover your sanity if she considered your point of view. How might the doctor feel if she were in your predicament? However, we are more likely to be able to consider another person's point of view if we see her as similar to ourselves, as like us. Unfortunately, seeing themselves as similar to a mental patient makes doctors uncomfortable. Most of us want to feel safely different from people who become mental patients. So we avoid imagining what it would be like to be in their situation. Doctors also avoid seeing the hospital situation from a patient's point of view. (See Chapter 8 on prejudice for more on how we treat people who are different from us.) The context of a mental hospital makes it difficult for doctors to discover the absence of a mental disorder.

David Rosenhan's study was as simple and dramatic as a social psychology experiment can be. He and seven of his associates checked themselves into various mental hospitals around the United States. They then waited to see how long doctors would keep them in the hospital.

The people that Rosenhan (1973) picked to masquerade as mental patients had no history of mental problems whatsoever. Other than that, they were a variety of people: psychologists, a medical doctor, a painter, a homemaker. Three of them were women. Some deception was necessary for Rosenhan and his associates to gain admittance to the mental hospitals. False names and employers were used. Those who worked in the mental health field gave false occupations to preclude doctors giving them special privileges. When researchers presented themselves for admission to mental hospitals, all complained of the same symptom. They had been hearing voices. The voices were unfamiliar, often unclear. The voices said specific words including "empty," "hollow," and "thud." These words were picked specifically because they had *not* been associated in psychiatric research with any typical psychiatric disorder. Thus there was no compelling reason to label the symptoms with any specific psychiatric diagnosis. Other than hearing voices, Rosenhan and his associates gave accurate histories of their mental health to hospital personnel. None of them suffered from any sort of mental disorder, and they never had.

At the time, the researchers worried that hospital personnel would immediately recognize them as imposters and embarrass them. After all, most of us expect that our sanity is apparent to those around us. Yet the researchers' need not have worried about being discovered. At every hospital, the researcher was admitted and diagnosed with a serious mental illness. In one case the diagnosis was manic depression. In the rest it was schizophrenia. Having initially expected to have their sanity discovered before gaining admittance, the researchers entered mental hospitals as patients expecting doctors to soon discover their sanity, correct the mistaken diagnosis, and send them home. Again their expectations were not met.

Like most patients in mental hospitals, the researchers were admitted with no estimate of how long their stay might be. They had been committed to a mental hospital and would remain until doctors decided to discharge them. They had all been told that they would get out when doctors were convinced of their sanity. Imagine how that must have felt. Not knowing when they were going to get out of the mental hospital caused researchers considerable anxiety during the first few days of their stay. All but one wanted to be discharged very soon after admission (Rosenhan 1975). Of course, hospital staff interpreted their symptoms of nervousness as indications of mental problems. However, as soon as researchers were admitted, they acted as normally and as cooperatively as possible at all times. When asked, they said they no longer heard voices and now felt fine. Wouldn't doctors discover the mistaken diagnosis after extended observation of normal people trying hard to show how sane they are?

No, doctors did not discover that any of the patients were sane. Not one of the mistaken diagnoses was reversed. Researchers remained hospitalized from 7 to 52 days. "In remission," "improved," or "asymptomatic" was added to the diagnosis upon discharge, but the schizophrenic or manic depressive label remained. Doctors continued to believe that patients had a serious mental disorder but had improved. That is very different from discovering that no mental disorder existed.

Although not one doctor gave any indication that the researchers might not have a mental illness, many legitimate mental patients could tell that the researchers were sane. All researchers took extensive notes during their stay in the hospital. Note taking seemed to be a giveaway to other mental patients that the researchers did not belong, although doctors paid little notice. Patients would comment, "You're not crazy. You're a journalist or a professor. You're checking up on the hospital" (Rosenhan 1973, p. 252). Hospital staff gave seemingly normal behavior a very different interpretation. For example, one researcher was observed pacing the long hospital corridor. "Are you nervous?" he was asked. "No, bored," he replied (p. 253). Hospital life is boring. Patients looked forward to meals as a bright spot in a dreary day. They would sit outside the cafeteria for half an hour waiting for lunch. A psychiatrist noticed patients waiting for lunch and commented on it to a group of young residents he was training. He said that such behavior was characteristic of the patients' mental disorder. It did not occur to him that the patients might have been bored. Behavior caused by circumstances of the situation was invariably attributed to the mental characteristics of the patients. Attendants sometimes mistreated patients, often unwittingly, sometimes provoking angry outbursts from the patients. However, nurses assumed such behavior always resulted from a patient's mental problems. Further, staff members increased the probability of such attributional errors by interacting with patients as little as possible (Rosenhan 1973).

Patients became depersonalized to the point where hospital staff paid them little attention. Here is a typical exchange between a doctor and a patient. "Pardon me, Doctor. Could you tell me when I am eligible for grounds privileges?" The doctor replied, "Good morning, Dave. How are you today?" Then the doctor walked away without waiting for a response (Rosenhan 1973, p. 255). Such depersonalization makes it unlikely that doctors will be able to take the role of their patients and see situations from their patients' point of view. It is not that determining whether someone is sane is impossible. After all, other mental patients in the hospitals could do it. Rather, the context of a mental hospital makes it difficult for doctors to determine whether a patient is sane.

How would you go about proving your sanity? Many of us would fall back on the reasonable idea that sane people have a good grasp of reality. In contrast, mental problems make reality difficult to distinguish from fantasy. Hallucinations and delusions often accompany serious mental disorders. Hallucinations are false images or sensations that seem real. Delusions are persistent false beliefs. Common sense tells us that sane people should be able to make more accurate judgments about the world around them than can people suffering from a mental disorder.

DEPRESSION AND SOCIAL PSYCHOLOGY

In the 1970s, the accepted view held by mental health professionals was that sane people judged reality more accurately than did those with mental problems. For example, cognitive theories of depression proposed that depressed people overestimated the likelihood of bad things happening. In contrast, nondepressed people would more accurately estimate the likelihood of events, both good and bad. It was thought that depressed people misjudged how much control they had over their lives. The idea that depressed people's judgment of reality might be *more* accurate in certain situations was not considered. Before describing the famous study that dared to suggest that depressed people more accurately judge some situations than do nondepressed people, it will be helpful to describe the social psychological background of depression.

Depression is one of the most common mental problems people face (Shulman, Tohen, & Kutcher 1996). Its symptoms include prolonged periods of sadness or negative mood, loss of interest and pleasure in life's activities, sleeping too much or too little, appetite disturbances leading to weight loss or gain, fatigue, feelings of worthlessness and guilt, poor concentration, and sometimes thoughts of suicide. Especially in adolescents and young adults, episodes of depression are related to eating disorders, alcohol and substance abuse, and suicide. In any given month between 1 percent and 2 percent of adults suffer from serious depression. More than 10 percent of people may suffer an episode of depression during their lives. Depression is nearly twice as common in women as in men. Children have traditionally had less trouble with depression than adults have. However, depression among adolescents and young adults has been rising steadily since at least 1950 (Shulman, Tohen, & Kutcher 1996).

Depression creates profound problems in the social functioning of those who suffer from it, more so than some other psychiatric disorders (Gotlib & Lee 1989). Thus it is no surprise that social psychologists have been interested in understanding depression. The symptoms of some mental problems produce reactions in other people that can make the problem worse. In Chapter 2 we saw how people reacted to a person with a paranoid personality in ways that convinced him that his paranoid view was correct. In short, they actively conspired against him. So it is not surprising that his paranoia grew. Social interaction, then, is an active part of the mental disorder. The reactions of other people to the symptoms of depression produce a similar self-fulfilling process. That is where social psychology can contribute.

Strack and Coyne (1983) studied how people respond to depressed persons. They proposed that depressed people behave in ways that produce negative reactions from those around them. Depressed people may then feel rejected and isolated, reinforcing their negative thoughts. Strack and Coyne wanted to find out how people in a depressed mood would affect those around them. In addition, they wanted to find out whether people would actively reject another person who was in a depressed mood.

Strack and Coyne (1983) set up a situation where people would meet and talk casually with another person during a 15-minute "get-acquainted" conversation. Before people got together to meet their partners, they were given a standard test for depression. After their get-acquainted conversation, people gave researchers their impressions of their partner. They were asked how willing they would be to talk to their partner again. Would people who talked with a depressed person be more depressed, anxious, and hostile than would people who talked with a nondepressed person? Also, would people who talked to a depressed person be less willing to talk to that person again than would people who talked to a nondepressed person?

The answer to both questions was yes. People who talked with a depressed person became more depressed, more anxious, and more hostile than did those who talked with a nondepressed person. Talking with a depressed person produces negative reactions in people. Also, those negative reactions can lead to rejection of the depressed person. Strack and Coyne (1983) found that people who had talked to a depressed person were less willing to talk to that person again than were people who talked with a nondepressed person. The results were clear. Depressed people behave in ways that can produce social rejection. Depressed people often have feelings of worthlessness. If, as a result of being rejected, depressed people feel low self-worth, then other people's response to depression may prolong a period of depression.

Depressed people may be attracted to people who will view them negatively. That is, depressed people may actively seek out negative feedback. Swann, Wenzlaff, Krull, and Pelham (1992) proposed that depressed people seek out rejection because rejection has become familiar to them. They are more comfortable with rejection than with acceptance from those around them. That is, depressed people acquire an identity as a person who is rejected by others. Recall from the discussion of identity in Chapter 3, people seek out situations that verify their conceptions of themselves. Even a bad familiar environment may be seen as comfortable because it seems predictable. Familiarity increases our sense of control over our situation.

Swann and colleagues (1992) used students in psychology classes to set up a situation where people had the opportunity to choose a partner who had rated their personality positively or negatively. Early in the semester, students were given a personality test. Students were told that if they volunteered for a study, several people would be evaluating their personality based on their responses to the test. Later, when some of the students volunteered for the study, they were given a standard test for depression.

During the study, researchers showed students the evaluations made of their personality by three different people. The same evaluations were shown to all students in the study. One of the evaluations was positive, one was neutral, and one was negative. Students were then asked how much they wanted to meet each of the evaluators. Researchers expected, as most of us would, that nondepressed students would want to meet the positive evaluator much more than they would want to meet the negative evaluator (Swann, Wenzlaff, Krull, & Pelham 1992). That turned out to be true. Nondepressed students were much more eager to meet the positive evaluator. They had little interest in meeting someone who negatively evaluated their personality.

Researchers also made the surprising proposal that depressed people would prefer to meet the *negative* evaluator rather than the positive evaluator. Researchers thought that depressed people would actively choose to meet a person who had negatively evaluated their personality. That is, someone they thought would reject them. Again researchers were correct. Depressed students wanted to meet the person who had negatively evaluated their personality much more than they wanted to meet a person who had positively evaluated their personality. In some situations, then, depressed people do actively seek out negative feedback, actually preferring to meet people who they know are likely to reject them.

Some of the negative reactions that people have to a depressed person suggest that depression may be in some sense contagious. Joiner (1994) wanted to find out whether living with a depressed person could make a roommate more depressed. He studied college roommates over a three-week period to see if those roommates who lived with a depressed person would become more depressed themselves by the end of the study. Using standard tests for depression, Joiner found that roommates became more depressed while they lived with a depressed person. However, the extent to which roommates became more depressed was not severe.

The studies just described show that depression is a complicated mental disorder with important social aspects. Depressed people have difficulty coping with social situations and social duties. The way others respond to depression may play a part in the severity and duration of a depressive episode. Depressed people may actively seek out the company of people who will confirm their negative self-image. Also, depression may be contagious to the extent that living with a depressed person increased a roommate's depressive symptoms. Other social psychologists have sought ways to relieve some of the problems caused by depression.

SADDER BUT WISER

In the 1970s, cognitive theories of depression proposed that depressed people made errors in judging situations that led them to feel hopeless, helpless, and out of control. If depressed people habitually made errors in judgment that caused them problems, then correcting those errors might help. It was taken for granted that people suffering from a mental disorder must distort reality. Recall that the accurate perception of reality was considered the main characteristic of sanity.

Meyers (1996) describes how commonsense ideas about sanity and the treatment of depression were turned upside down. Two graduate students in psychology agreed that social psychology could be used to understand depression. However, they were shocked that nobody really knew whether depressed people distorted reality. They decided to find out. What they found was surprising. Depressed people see reality *more* accurately than nondepressed people do in important ways. The work of those two graduate students, Lauren Alloy and Lyn Abramson, profoundly changed the way we understand depression and mental health in general. Both went on to the top of their profession. They are now among the most influential social psychologists. Lauren Alloy is a professor at Temple University. Lyn Abramson is a professor at the University of Wisconsin. They succeeded by maintaining a skeptical attitude toward what "everyone knows to be true" and working hard to find good evidence.

Alloy and Abramson (1979) set up a simple situation to find out whether nondepressed people would distort reality and whether depressed people would judge reality more accurately. People in the study were asked to judge how much control they had over a positive event. They would each be given 25 cents every time a green light came on. The goal was for people to judge how much control they had over whether the green light came on.

In the study, people faced a green light. In front of them was a box with a button to be pushed. During a trial period lasting a few seconds, they decided whether to push the button, then watched to see if the green light came on. Then the second trial period started. They again decided whether to push the button and watched to see whether the green light came on. This continued for 40 trial periods. Could people accurately judge how much control they had over whether the green light came on? If the green light came on after every push of the button but never came on when they decided not to push it, they could be confident that by pushing the button they had control over the green light. The green light coming on was a positive event. Every time it came on they earned 25 cents. If the green light came on sometimes after they pushed the button and sometimes after they did not push the button, then they might not have much control at all over the green light.

Before people in the study went to work with the green light, Alloy and Abramson (1979) gave them two standard psychological tests to determine whether they were depressed. If both tests showed a person to be depressed, that person was considered depressed. If both tests showed the person to be free of depressive symptoms, that person was considered nondepressed. Thus the study included only people who were clearly depressed or people who were clearly nondepressed. Now Alloy and Abramson were prepared to answer their surprising research question: Would people in the depressed group more accurately judge their control over the green light than would people in the nondepressed group?

Alloy and Abramson (1979) then set up their situation so that people actually had no control at all over the green light. Half the time when they pushed the button the green light came on. And half the time when they decided not to push the button the green light came on. It was pure chance. The button and the light had nothing to do with each other. People had no control over whether the positive event occurred. Would people be able to figure that out? Would depressed people correctly judge that they had no control over the green light, while nondepressed people wrongly judged that they had considerable control over it? Do normal people maintain an illusion of control over their lives while depressed people view the world accurately? That is, are depressed people "sadder but wiser"?

In some ways, yes. Alloy and Abramson's (1979) results supported the strange idea that depressed people insist on accurately judging their situation when they are powerless over positive events. In contrast, nondepressed people maintain an illusion of control over events, giving themselves credit for events over which they have no control. On average, nondepressed people in Alloy and Abramson's study judged they had 60 percent control over a positive event, the green light coming on. In contrast, depressed people accurately judged their lack of control over a positive event.

Finding out that only nondepressed people maintain an illusion of control over positive events had profound implications for our understanding of depression. Could normal people derive some benefit from being optimistic even to the point of distorting reality? If so, then the illusion of control should disappear when normal people judged their control over negative events. Alloy and Abramson (1979) also conducted their study using negative events instead of positive ones. People lost money when the green light failed to come on instead of gaining money when it did. Does the illusion of control in normal people disappear when the event is negative? It should if optimism is somehow beneficial. After all, believing you controlled the bad things that happen to you would not be very optimistic. Alloy and Abramson's results showed that the illusion of control occurs when normal people judge positive events but not when they judge negative ones. When people lost money in the experiment, both depressed and nondepressed people accurately judged their lack of control over the light.

A single study, even a very good one, can never conclusively prove a scientific idea. Before Alloy and Abramson could be confident in their conclusions about the illusion of control, they had to close a loophole in their study's design. Recall that they divided up the people in their experiment into those who were depressed and those who were not. The illusion of control showed up in nondepressed people. But we cannot be confident that depression *caused* people to more accurately judge their lack of control. Maybe something else about that particular group of depressed people caused them to be especially accurate judges of control. Researchers cannot be aware of everything about the people they study. (The appendix discusses this and other problems in interpreting research results.) How can we be sure that it is depression or lack of it that made the difference?

Alloy, Abramson, and Viscusi (1981) did a follow-up study to determine whether the negative mood accompanying depression was responsible for people accurately judging their lack of control. Essentially, they repeated the same study where people judged their control over a green light but added a new wrinkle, a process that scientists call *replication*.[1] This time researchers first put people in a positive or negative mood before they judged their control over the green light. When researchers can control the situation, when they can make people sad or happy rather than just separating out depressed and nondepressed people from a group, then we can be more confident that a person's mood causes the illusion of control. Because Alloy and Abramson (1973) did not control people's moods, something other than depression may have been responsible for the results in that study.

The trick is to find a way to put people in an elated or depressed mood that works reliably without causing them harm. Velten (1968) did just that. His technique uses a series of 60 statements that people read aloud slowly to themselves. The statements start out emotionally neutral. For example, "Today is neither better nor worse than any other day." To induce elation, the statements become progressively more positive. For example, "Things will be better and better today." From the discussion of affirmations in Chapter 1, you probably recognize these as affirmations that Velten used to put people in either an elated or depressed mood. To induce a depressed mood, the affirmations start out neutral then become progressively more negative. For example, "I want to go to sleep and never wake up." Velten's affirmation technique has been used in many studies that show its power to change behavior.[2] As you read Chapter 1, you may have been skeptical when I suggested the use of affirmations to change your life. Affirmations really do work.

Alloy, Abramson, and Viscusi (1981) set out to discover what would happen to the judgment of control in depressed people placed in an elated mood and nondepressed people placed in a depressed mood. Would elation induce the illusion of control found in nondepressed people? And would a depressed mood in otherwise nondepressed people eliminate their illusion of control?

The answer to both questions was yes. When depressed people were elated, they had an illusion of control similar to that of nondepressed people. When nondepressed people were placed in a depressed mood, their illusion of control disappeared. These dramatic results supported the idea that normal people distort reality.

Evidence for the illusion of control in healthy people is not limited to laboratory studies. Glass, McKnight, and Valdimasdottir (1993) studied the relationship between depression, job burnout, and perceived control that nurses had over their job. Nurses working in a major university hospital were tested for depression and

---

[1] See the appendix for a discussion of how replication works in practice and the various other techniques researchers use to test their ideas.
[2] Some studies using Velten's mood-altering technique include Aderman (1972), Hale and Strickland (1976), Natale (1977), Raps, Reinhard, and Seligman (1980), and Strickland, Hale, and Anderson (1975).

job burnout. Symptoms of job burnout included feeling helpless, low energy and motivation, and negative attitudes. Not surprisingly, depression was frequently present in nurses suffering from burnout. Those suffering from both burnout and depression were especially likely to feel a lack of personal accomplishment. Would the illusion of control fail to occur in nurses suffering from depression and burnout?

Glass, McKnight, and Valdimasdottir (1993) tested nurses for depression and burnout, then asked them how much control they thought they had over their job. Researchers also made objective ratings of how much control nurses actually had. Nurses' beliefs about how much control they had could then be compared to objective ratings of job control. Would nurses suffering from depression and burnout accurately judge their control over their job? Would nondepressed and non–burned-out nurses believe they had more control than they actually had?

Again, the answer to both questions was yes. Nurses suffering from depression and burnout estimated their job control accurately compared to the objective criteria. In contrast, nondepressed nurses who also were not suffering from burnout substantially overestimated their control over their jobs (Glass, McKnight, & Valdimasdottir 1993). Also, nurses suffering from burnout accurately estimated their control over their jobs even if they were not depressed. Thus the illusion of control was found to be present in normal people with respect to an important area of their lives, the control over work. Depressed and burned-out nurses more accurately judged their control at work. However, depression and burnout cause major life problems. Thus in the case of depression and burnout, accurate judgment of reality seems to provide no personal or social benefit. In contrast, an illusion of control may give people some protection against these mental problems.

Normal people believe they somehow cause good things to happen even when they really have no control at all over them. For example, people who win the lottery might think they really know in advance which numbers will come up. In contrast, depressed people much more accurately judge their lack of control. If normal, healthy people maintain illusions and people suffering from a serious mental illness judge reality accurately, then it seems to follow that those illusions might be beneficial. How can distorting reality help?

CAN ILLUSION BE BENEFICIAL?

When I look back over the troubled period in my life, I realize that I was depressed for the most part of about 10 years. Certainly I showed the destructive behavior that often accompanies depression, especially heavy drinking. Perhaps most striking was my attitude toward reality during those years. I was a committed realist, no fairy-tale illusions for me. I used harsh words to describe a harsh reality. If that offended people who were too weak to see things as they really were, so be it.

The morning of my last drink showed me how optimistic most people are. I had gotten drunk again the night before. It was a Saturday night at a bar not far from my house. Other cars had parked so close to my truck that I could not move it. I had broken a headlight trying to inch back and forth to angle an escape. I gave up and went back into the bar wanting to scream in frustration. How else would I find the idiots who had blocked in my truck? But I could not stay there any longer. I walked home through snow piled high from a recent storm as more snow began to fall.

I woke early that Sunday morning. While I did not feel at all well, I could not stay in bed either. Alcohol is well known for its short-term sedative effects. After a few hours, though, it also produces anxiety, a major component of most hangovers. I felt too bad about myself to stay in bed. I got up and decided to drive to Spokane, Washington, 30 miles away, for a Sunday *New York Times*. The *Times* was not available in the small northern Idaho town where I lived. My anxiety increased when I noticed my truck was not in the driveway. My mind raced. Where was it? What had happened? Had I blacked out again?

I calmed down some and remembered that my truck was in the parking lot of the bar about half a mile away. As I walked through the snow to retrieve it, the frigid air helped clear my mind a little. After driving to the city for a newspaper, I drove back to town, through an unfamiliar neighborhood, past a church. The Sunday church service was about to start. People were arriving, greeting each other, standing around talking in the unshoveled snow. They stood out in the cold, cheeks rosy, talking animatedly to each other. They were smiling. Their eyes were bright. They were happy. I was miserable. I wondered how they could be so happy with winter coming and snow already knee deep? Unemployment was high and rising. The economy was terrible. They must be fools, unaware of how bad things were. Then another thought occurred to me: Maybe they knew something that I had missed.

I got home that morning, unfolded the newspaper, and opened a bottle of white wine. I rationalized that wine, after all, was traditional with Sunday brunch. With one of the curious mental twists common to heavy drinkers, I had decided that alcoholics drank domestic beer and wine from bottles with screw caps. So, not wanting to be an alcoholic, my refrigerator contained a couple of bottles of good wine with corks, some Canadian beer, and no food. Usually a little wine or beer did wonders for my hangovers. A good working definition of addiction is activity that relieves its own side effects. But that Sunday my anxiety increased as I drank the wine. Alcohol was not working. I put the cork back in the wine bottle and have not had a drink since. I did not realize at the time that it was going to be my last drink. If I had, I probably would have had another. Who knows what the consequences of that would have been?

My gloomy outlook did not disappear immediately. I prided myself on my hardheaded realism. It had become part of my identity. I wanted to see reality as it was, without the sugarcoating. What I saw was not encouraging. Yet, as the days passed and alcohol leached out of my system, the image of those churchgoers in the parking lot stayed with me. Still today, I see them as clearly as I did then, 15 years ago. They were happy. How could that possibly be? Might it someday be possible for me to be happy too? First I had to develop a tolerance for certain kinds of illusions.

Mental health requires more than a valid interpretation of reality. Recent conceptions of mental health include a positive self-image, the ability to be happy, to care about other people, to work, and to grow in a sometimes threatening environment (Taylor 1989, p. 48). As long as an illusion does not interfere with safety, relations with other people, happiness, and personal growth, it need not be a sign of mental distress.

The illusion of control over positive events might benefit people by giving them hope. If a person feels she has no control over what happens to her, then why go on? Why work to accomplish anything? Instilling hope is a major component of many religions. Hope is thought to keep people going through hard times. Might the illusion of control actually be beneficial to people's health?

Ellen Langer and Judith Rodin (1976) thought that the perception of control might help elderly people stay healthy in a nursing home. Their study took place in a nursing home rated highly for its fine medical, recreational, and residential facilities. The home had four floors. Residents on two of the floors were similar to each other. Thus, by giving nursing home residents on one floor increased control over their lives, Langer and Rodin could compare two similar groups, one with increased control and one without increased control.

To increase the perception of control for residents on one of the floors, residents were told they had to make decisions. They were given responsibility to decide how their rooms would be arranged and how they would spend their time. They were also given the opportunity to select a plant they could care for themselves.

On the other floor, residents were not given increased responsibility and control. The nursing home staff provided them with all of the same activities as residents on the increased-control floor. They were all given plants that nurses would water and care for. Residents on both floors received the same amount of attention. Thus the main difference between the two floors was that residents on the increased-control floor had to make daily decisions about the course of their lives, whereas virtually everything was provided for residents on the other floor without their having to make decisions or take responsibility. For example, residents on both floors had the opportunity to see a movie. Those on the increased-control floor decided on which night the movie would be shown, whereas the night the movie would be shown was simply announced to residents on the other floor.

Residents completed questionnaires a week before the study started and three weeks after it began. The questionnaires included questions about how happy and active they felt. Nurses also completed questionnaires rating patients' physical improvement or lack of improvement, as well as their happiness, alertness, activity level, and social skills. Attendance records were also kept on the night the movie was shown.

Results of the questionnaire given one week before the study began showed that residents on the two floors were very similar. No significant differences were found between residents on the two floors. However, large differences emerged between residents on the two floors on the second questionnaire given three weeks after the study began. The reports of residents on the increased-control floor indicated that they were happier and more active than residents on the other floor were. At the same time, nurses also rated the improvement or lack of improvement of residents during the study. Nurses' ratings showed *improving* health for 93 percent of patients on the increased-control floor. In contrast, nurses' ratings showed *declining* health for 79 percent of patients on the other floor, and increasing health for only 21 percent. The differences were highly significant and dramatic. In addition, attendance was higher at the movie on the increased-control floor. Thus we can conclude that an increased perception of control and responsibility had the effect of making residents healthier, happier, and more active.

The effects of perceived control for nursing home residents were even more dramatic in a follow-up study conducted by Rodin and Langer (1977). Eighteen months after the original study, residents who had lived on the increased-control floor continued to be more active, sociable, and vigorous than residents who had lived on the other floor during the original study. Rodin and Langer used residents' medical records to estimate their general health at the time of the original study and again 18 months later. On average, the general health of the residents from the increased-control floor improved during the 18 months following the original study. In contrast, average general health declined for residents from the other floor who had not experienced increased control. Thus we can conclude that residents' increased perception of control provided them with real health benefits.

Perhaps more dramatic was a comparison of death rates between the two groups. Rodin and Langer (1977) found that, overall, 25 percent of patients in the nursing home died during a typical 18-month period. During the 18 months following the original study, a much smaller percentage of residents from the increased-control floor died, only 15 percent. In contrast, an alarming 30 percent of residents from the other floor, who had not experienced increased control, died. The death rate was cut in half when patients were given increased control and responsibility. Thus the perception of control can actually keep you alive.

Rodin and Langer (1977) showed how powerful social psychological research can be. It sometimes makes the difference between life and death. But was the study ethical? If researchers had given all patients in the study increased control over their lives, some people would have lived longer. When the study started, however, researchers had no way to know that. Research produces new knowledge that we can use to help people. But when we start research, we really do not know what will happen. (See the appendix on methods for more on ethical problems in research.)

When the original Langer and Rodin (1976) study started, researchers had to be careful that what they were doing to people in the nursing home would not harm them. They tried to increase patients' control over their lives without putting them in danger. Researchers did not change the way that people on the other floor were treated. Patients on the floor who did not get increased control continued to receive the same care they had before the study. Thus researchers knew that they were not harming the patients who did not get increased control. While researchers were confident that increased control would not harm patients, they did not yet know that it would help them. If researchers had known that increased control was keeping patients alive, then they would have had the duty to stop the study and promote increased control for all patients. But researchers did not know. They did not have the results showing that increased control kept patients alive until 18 months after the first study ended. Then the follow-up study showed that patients with increased control were less likely to die than were patients whose treatment had not been changed. Social psychological research can have a big impact. When Rodin and

Langer's (1977) study was published, the results were dramatic enough to produce changes in the way that nursing homes are run.

OPTIMISM AND ILLUSION

The illusion of control is a persistent belief that we have control over good things that happen to us, despite evidence to the contrary. The illusion of control is one aspect of a more general thought pattern usually referred to as optimism. Optimists look at the bright side. They see the world through rose-colored glasses. Their cups are forever half-full, never half-empty. The many references our language has to the different ways that optimists and pessimists see the world reflects the importance of the issue. Whether a person is an optimist or a pessimist makes a difference not just in how that person lives but in the world that person inhabits.

What kind of world do you live in? Is it a jungle where the strong and vigilant survive, where the weak and unwary perish at the hands of lurking predators? Or do you live in a world where people support each other, where people cooperate to accomplish goals no one person could achieve alone? If you have personal difficulties that prevent you from fulfilling your responsibilities, will other people pitch in to cover for you? People have widely differing views on the basic features of the world they live in. Sometimes there are good reasons for thinking the world is a jungle. Poor people, for example, are less trusting of other people than are people comfortably in the middle class. It makes sense. If you live in a poor neighborhood with a high crime rate, you are probably more worried about being victimized than if you live in an exclusive suburb with little crime. Women are more worried about being attacked and victimized than are men, and with good reason. Criminals see women as easier targets and sexual aggression almost always involves an attack on a woman by a man. The world is more dangerous for some of us than others. However, it often seems that a person's view of the world has little to do with the world itself and more to do with her feelings about herself and others. Two people living next door to each other, similar in many ways, can see the world entirely differently. One locks her doors not only when she leaves the house but also when she is at home in the daytime. The other often leaves her doors unlocked and her keys in the car. Both have had similar life experiences, but they see the world entirely differently. One sees predators lurking outside her door; the other cannot imagine that anyone would do her harm.

Are pessimists right about the world? Optimism certainly can be dangerous. Recently, a young man was murdered in his cheap apartment in New York City. The young man was unusual in that his family controlled a great fortune. He wanted to help others less fortunate than himself, so he taught at a high school in inner-city New York. He worked hard at teaching. His students admired him because he took time to help them. He cared. The police found no evidence that someone had broken into the apartment. In fact, the attacker seemed to have been invited to dinner. The police arrested the teacher's former student, a disturbed young man, who had come to the teacher for money. Knowing the teacher's wealthy background, the murderer was convinced that the teacher must have a lot of money and valuables in the apartment. The murderer took the little that was actually there.

The teacher from a rich family had brought his optimistic view of the world with him to a very different world. Where he grew up, students did not kill their favorite teachers for a few hundred dollars. He did not take the precautions that other residents of the area would take if they had money. His worldview proved to be fatally naive. Pessimists are convinced by stories such as this one that their view of the world is correct. Pessimists usually see themselves not as pessimists, but as realists. Given that optimism can be dangerous, why are so many of us optimistic?

Lauren Alloy and Anthony Ahrens (1987) found that depressed people were pessimistic about the future. Nondepressed people were optimistic. In the study, depressed people predicted they would be more likely to fail than would other people similar to them. In contrast, nondepressed people predicted they would be more likely to succeed than would other people similar to them. Alloy and Ahrens suggest that optimism may have evolved because it maintains hope, motivating people to persevere. In contrast, pessimism may lead to hopelessness, lack of effort, and failure.[3] Over the last several thousand years, techniques have been developed to help people condition their thoughts in ways that lead to success. The goal here is to identify ways of thinking that will help you.

HEALTHY THOUGHTS

The nursing home patients in Langer and Rodin's (1976) study were really given increased control over their lives. They got to choose their activities and when they would have them. They took responsibility for the care of a plant. Would the same benefits result if they merely thought they had increased control? Social psychologists have found that certain thought patterns or ways of thinking are better for you than others. Using techniques to discipline your thoughts can make a big difference for you as you navigate your social world. It is probably not true that your thoughts create the world you live in. However, your thoughts are part of the social world. And, as we saw in Chapter 2, reality is socially constructed. Techniques are available that allow us to shape our thoughts, even those thoughts that are deep-seated and troubling. Through shaping our thoughts we can shape our relations with other people in ways that improve our own lives and the lives of the people around us. Most techniques for training our thoughts have been around a long time. They have been used and advocated by religious leaders and philosophers for thousands of years. Now these same techniques and many new ones are often promoted in self-help books and sales training seminars. Some are effective and beneficial. Others are not. Social psychology can show us which techniques are effective and why.

My thought patterns are completely different depending on how I feel. During the time when I was depressed, living in Idaho, I would often be late to work. Either I had been up late the night before or I just could not drag myself out of bed in the morning. When I realized how late it was, I would throw my clothes on in a panic

[3]For more on the evolutionary arguments favoring optimism see Taylor (1983, 1989) and Tiger (1979).

cathy®

by Cathy Guisewite

Cathy is overwhelmed by too many small problems

and rush out the door. Sometimes my old car would not start. Why does this always happen to me? I would wonder. I guessed the old junker needed at least a new battery, probably a starter, and maybe an entire electrical system. Not that it mattered. I did not have enough money to buy a battery, let alone the rest. The real problem was the crummy job I was stuck in that did not pay enough to live. Getting a better job was impossible because I had dropped out of school and had no experience. Being late to work again, I would probably lose this job anyway. The chance was slim of my being able to find another job, even a bad one. The economy was terrible. You can imagine how negative my mood was by the time this train of thought had run through my head.

My usual response was to climb back into bed, pretend to be sick, and wait for someone from work to call and yell at me. The car did not get fixed. Worse, as I rehearsed what I would tell people at work about being sick, I really began to feel sick. At least I was convincing myself. Other mornings, feeling a little better, I could make myself call work and tell someone my car wouldn't start. Usually, a woman named Vicki would answer the phone and say something like this: "A lot of cars won't start this morning. Did you know it is 10 degrees below zero out there? Kelly, the new delivery guy, is making a delivery near your neighborhood. I will tell him to stop by to jump start your car." A nondepressed person confronting the same situation saw no catastrophe at all, only a routine problem easily solved.

The person who talked to me on the phone saw the situation in a healthy way. I did not. My thoughts did not produce a solution to my problem because I had attributed the dead battery to factors that were enduring, general, and my fault. Notice I did not say "Why do these things *sometimes* happen to me." I identified the problem not simply as a dead battery but ultimately as the result of my general failure in life. Ultimately, I was a failure because I had messed up by dropping out of school. In other words, the dead battery was my fault. My attributions for bad events happening to me reflected my hopelessness and resulted in helplessness. My preferred response was to crawl into bed rather than try to solve the problem. In contrast, the person I called, Vicki, saw the problem from the perspective of a nondepressed person. She saw the problem specifically as a car that would not start. She saw it as temporary, caused by unusually cold weather and not my fault at all. Of course, it wasn't her problem. She might have responded differently had her own car not started. Our different attitudes toward our own and other people's problems suggest techniques for warding off depression and maintaining good mental health. Later in the chapter you will find specific ways to help keep your mind healthy.

Martin Seligman developed the theory of learned helplessness to explain some kinds of depression (1975). Briefly, the theory of learned helplessness says that when people see that their responses have no effect on a problem, they can learn not to respond to problems in their lives. They become helpless. People who feel helpless can easily lose hope and become depressed. In testing his theory, Seligman and his colleagues discovered the importance of the attributions people made for problems in their lives. Some attributions seemed to lead to helplessness and negative outcomes, whereas other attributions protected against helplessness and seemed to lead to positive outcomes (Seligman, Abramson, Semmel, & von Baeyer 1979).

The attributions we make for the problems in our lives determine how we respond to them. For example, I made one set of attributions for my car not starting that did not lead to a solution. My *pessimistic attributional style* failed to help me. In contrast, the woman I called made another set of attributions for the same problem. Her *optimistic attributional style* led to a quick solution. The work of Seligman and his colleagues shows us why optimism and the perception of control help people solve their problems even when that optimism is misplaced, even when the perception of control is merely an illusion.

If a problem is going to last indefinitely, if it generalizes to several areas of your life, then it is easy to become overwhelmed by the magnitude of the problem. My depressed thinking would lead to the conclusion that fixing my dead battery required first finishing school then getting a good job so that I could buy a new car. It's hopeless, I thought, so why even start? And if the problem is your fault, then you might feel you deserve the problem and should not be rewarded by solving it. Thus the three factors in a pessimistic attributional style—permanence, stability, and self-blame—lead to helplessness and prevent people from solving their problems. Those pessimistic attributions get in our way even if they are entirely accurate. It might be true that my old junker car needs a whole new electrical system and I need to go back to school, get a better job, and buy a new car. Still, my going back to bed only makes matters worse. In contrast, optimistic attributions would lead me to try to solve my problems even if my original assessment of a problem were wrong. If I maintained my optimistic outlook and kept working, then chances are my life would eventually improve.

Martin Seligman (1991) has written a fascinating book called *Learned Optimism.* Not only does it explain the history and development of his work in a highly readable way, it also lets you measure your own attributional style. Seligman's research so far leads to the tantalizing implication that changing a person's attributional style can have a major effect on her outlook on life as well as her success. *Learned Optimism* also suggests techniques to change your attributional style. Research is currently being conducted to test how effective those techniques are. At this point, they appear promising. I found from reading *Learned Optimism* that my own attributional style remains extremely pessimistic. Maybe now I will be able to do something about it.

Self-Blame

It is common for rape victims to blame themselves. As many as 74 percent of rape victims blame themselves, at least in part, for the assault (Janoff-Bulman 1979). Rape victims often go over and over their behavior preceding the rape, trying to pinpoint what they did to trigger the attack. The common occurrence of self-blame experienced by rape victims has led to the idea that self-blame might actually help them recover. In contrast, the work of Seligman and his colleagues (1979) suggests otherwise. Self-blame is a component of a pessimistic attributional style. Thus self-blame should hinder recovery.

Patricia Frazier (1990) studied how rape victims recovered from their traumatic experiences. She wanted to find out whether self-blame helped or hindered their recovery. Her study included women participating in a rape crisis program at a metropolitan county hospital. Frazier (1990) designed a questionnaire to find out how much each rape victim blamed herself for the attack. In addition, rape victims in Frazier's study completed a standard test for depression. Would rape victims who blamed themselves be less depressed than rape victims who did not blame themselves? If so, then self-blame might somehow be beneficial to recovery. In contrast, if rape victims who blamed themselves were more depressed, then that would support the idea that self-blame is harmful to recovery.

Frazier's (1990) results showed clearly that rape victims who blamed themselves were more depressed than rape victims who did not blame themselves. Thus it is unlikely that self-blame plays a positive role in the recovery of rape victims. Rather, it is possible that self-blame somehow perpetuates the depressive symptoms that rape victims suffer after the assault. Also, because self-blame is part of a pessimistic attributional style, Frazier's results also support the idea that a negative attributional style has negative consequences.

Peterson, Seligman, and Vaillant (1988) wanted to find out if people who had a pessimistic attributional style as young adults would later develop more health problems than would people who had an optimistic attributional style. The researchers analyzed statements that young men had made in response to a questionnaire given them in 1946. From the men's statements, researchers could tell whether they expressed an optimistic or pessimistic attributional style. These men had participated in a study of adult development conducted at Harvard University. For a period of 35 years, the study kept track of the health and medical care of all the men who filled out the original questionnaire. Peterson, Seligman, and Vaillant could then compare the attributional style that men expressed at about age 25 with their general health up to 35 years later. Would men with an optimistic attributional style be healthier in the long run than would men with a negative attributional style? If so, then an optimistic attributional style might be beneficial in keeping people healthy.

Peterson, Seligman, and Vaillant (1988) found that men who had an optimistic attributional style and men who had a negative attributional style started out with about the same level of general health. That was not surprising because the men in the study were generally healthy, as are most young adults. However, a big difference showed up when the men reached age 45. At age 45, those men who began the study with a pessimistic attributional style had much poorer health than did men who began with an optimistic attributional style. When men explained bad events in permanent, general, and stable ways, they suffered significantly more health problems *three decades later.* Frazier's 1990 study of rape victims suggested that a pessimistic attributional style might be harmful to mental health. Peterson, Seligman, and Vaillant's study of men over the course of 35 years suggests that a negative attributional style might be harmful to physical health.

Self-Focused Attention

Self-blame is a specific kind of thought pattern that social psychologists call self-focused attention. When people are self-focused, they ruminate. That is, they repeatedly evaluate themselves, going over in their minds what has recently happened, trying to decide how well or poorly they did. Too much self-focus can lead people to analyze and reanalyze their problems to the point where they can do little to solve them. They are effectively trapped by their thoughts, unable to act, helpless. It is not surprising, then, that self-focus has been linked to depression.

When nondepressed people suffer a setback, they bounce back quickly, not dwelling on the defeat. They go on to new activities, expecting to be successful. Nondepressed people forget failure quickly. They blame defeat on specific, temporary factors. They avoid self-blame. In contrast, depressed people actually prefer to focus on the defeat. They ruminate about the general implications of the defeat. Depressed people blame defeat on general, permanent factors, especially their own inadequacy.

Pyszczynski and Greenberg (1985) found that depressed people preferred to self-focus after a defeat, whereas nondepressed people avoided self-focus after a defeat. In their studies, social psychologists induce self-focus in simple ways. Rather than trying to get people to self-evaluate and ruminate, social psychologists often simply place a mirror where people can see themselves in it. Seeing yourself in a mirror makes you self-aware. Seeing yourself encourages you to think about yourself, producing self-focused attention. Pyszczynski and Greenberg gave people two word puzzles from a test of verbal ability.

Researchers gave some people two easy puzzles that they solved successfully. Other people worked on two difficult puzzles that they could not solve. On one of the puzzles, everyone worked in front of a mirror that created self-focused attention. On the other puzzle, everyone worked in a different room without a mirror, so they would not self-focus. Then researchers asked people which puzzle they liked more. Both puzzles were identical in difficulty. People either worked on two hard puzzles or two easy ones. The difference was that some people worked on the puzzles in a room with a mirror, inducing self-focus. Others worked on the puzzles in a room without a mirror and so they were not as self-focused. Would depressed people prefer to be self-focused when they failed to solve the puzzles? Would nondepressed people dislike self-focus when they failed to solve the puzzles?

The answer to both questions was yes. Depressed people actually prefer to self-focus after a defeat. In contrast, nondepressed people avoid self-focus after a defeat. Pyszczynski and Greenberg (1985) had given people a standard psychological test for depression before they worked on the word puzzles. Researchers found that when depressed people failed, they preferred the self-focusing puzzle (the one in the room with the mirror). Depressed people did not prefer the self-focusing puzzle when they succeeded. They wanted to dwell on their failure and move on quickly from their success. In contrast, nondepressed people preferred the self-focusing puzzle more when they had succeeded than when they had failed. Further, nondepressed people were found to attribute their failure to luck or to an invalid test more than did depressed people. Nondepressed people showed an optimistic attributional style. They attributed their failure to temporary, specific, and external factors. In contrast, depressed people showed a pessimistic attributional style. They attributed their failure to their lack of intelligence. In addition, failure reduced self-esteem for depressed people but not for nondepressed people. Thus the optimistic attributional style of nondepressed people may have protected their self-esteem following failure.

In a follow-up study, Pyszczynski, Holt, and Greenberg (1987) tried to get depressed people to focus externally. Remember that self-focused people ruminate about their problems. Rumination, then, leads to pessimism. If depressed people did not self-focus, would they be less pessimistic? For this study, researchers induced self-focus with a more elaborate technique. They asked people to write a short story using as many words as possible from a list. In the self-focus condition, the list contained words such as *I, mirror, alone,* and *me.* In the external-focus condition, the list contained words such as *he, picture, together,* and *him.* People in the external-focus condition were also asked to write about someone other than themselves, specifically Abraham Lincoln. This story-writing technique produces self-focus perhaps more effectively than does a mirror.[4] Researchers could then compare the predictions for their future success made by depressed people and nondepressed people. Would inducing depressed people to focus externally reduce their pessimism?

Pyszczynski, Holt, and Greenberg (1987) found that depressed people whose attention had been self-focused thought that bad things were just as likely to happen to them as they were to happen to other people. Thus depressed people whose attention had been self-focused judged the situation accurately but negatively. Recall that accuracy about negative outcomes is typical of depressed people, whereas nondepressed people often maintain optimistic illusions. Researchers also found that depressed people whose attention was externally focused thought that bad things were *less* likely to happen to them than to other people. Thus depressed people who focused externally maintained an optimistic illusion typical of nondepressed people. If people could somehow focus their attention away from themselves, they might become more optimistic. Greater optimism might then alleviate hopelessness and other symptoms of depression. First, however, researchers needed to find the link between depression and self-focus.

Wood, Saltzberg, and Goldsamt (1990) wanted to find out if the negative mood that accompanies depression could trigger self-focused attention. Researchers first

---

[4]Fenigstein and Levine (1984) and Greenberg (1992) show the effectiveness of the story-writing technique to induce self-focus.

put people in either a happy or sad mood. People were asked to recall or imagine personal events that were sad, neutral, or happy. When people start thinking sad thoughts they get sadder. When they think happy thoughts they get happier. Researchers then measured how self-focused people were. People were asked to complete a number of sentences using one of three words provided for each sentence. One of the words provided always referred to the self. For example, people might complete a sentence by choosing from *I, they, we* or from *my, their, our*. Researchers could then judge how self-focused a person was by how many self-focused pronouns that person used to complete sentences. When people were put in a sad mood, would they choose more self-focused pronouns than would people put in a neutral mood?

They did. People placed in a sad mood became more self-focused than did people in a neutral mood. Wood, Saltzberg, and Goldsamt (1990) also found that people in a happy mood were no more self-focused than were people in a neutral mood. It appears, then, that sad mood does produce self-focus. Also, it is not any kind of emotion that produces self-focus. Rather, the negative emotion that accompanies depression has a self-focusing effect.

One more step is necessary before we can use what we know about self-focus to help people. We know that depressed people are more self-focused than are nondepressed people. We also know that the bad mood that accompanies depression produces self-focus. Next we would like to find out if self-focus produces some of the problems associated with depression. If self-focus is responsible for some of the problems associated with depression, then changing a person's focus of attention might help with those problems.

Sonja Lyubomirsky and Susan Nolen-Hoeksema (1995) at Stanford University tried to find out if self-focused attention could reduce the pessimism associated with depression. Researchers first gave people a standard psychological test for depression. Then researchers got people to self-focus or to focus on external things. To get people to self-focus, researchers asked them to think about 45 statements about themselves. For example, people were asked to think about "your current level of energy" and "what your feelings might mean." To get people to focus externally, researchers asked people to think about something other than themselves, for example, "a boat slowly crossing the Atlantic." Then, to measure how pessimistic people were, researchers asked them to imagine themselves in a story and to pick their likely response to that situation. Responses ranged from optimistic to pessimistic. For example, in one story people ran for president of an organization and lost. A pessimistic response would be to "feel bad and imagine I've lost by a landslide." People who picked more pessimistic responses were considered more pessimistic. Would depressed people who focused externally be less pessimistic than depressed people would who self-focused?

As expected, depressed people who focused on themselves were much more pessimistic than were nondepressed people. More important, depressed people who focused externally were no more pessimistic than nondepressed people were. Thus focusing attention externally can help depressed people become more optimistic.

Lyubomirsky and Nolen-Hoeksema (1995) also asked people how they would go about solving several interpersonal problems. Remember that difficulty dealing with others is a problem for depressed people. Researchers wanted to find out whether getting depressed people to focus externally would improve their social skills. To measure social effectiveness, researchers gave people problems to solve. For example, people were asked what they would do when a friend seems to be avoiding them. Independent judges then rated people's answers for effectiveness. For example, an effective solution would be for a person to go see the friend in person, tactfully approach the issue, and let the friend know she or he is still a friend. In contrast, examples of ineffective solutions would be to avoid the friend or to criticize the friend when discussing the issue. After judges had rated people's problem-solving effectiveness, it was then possible for researchers to see whether depressed people who focused externally would be more effective problem solvers than would depressed people who self-focused.

As expected, the solutions given by depressed people who self-focused were less effective than were solutions given by nondepressed people (Lyubomirsky & Nolen-Hoeksema 1995). In contrast, solutions given by depressed people who focused externally were just as effective as solutions given by nondepressed people. Thus focusing attention externally can improve the social skills of depressed people in addition to making them more optimistic.

Nix, Watson, Pyszczynski, and Greenberg (1995) tried to find out if getting depressed people to focus externally could actually relieve their depression. Before the study, researchers gave people a standard psychological test for depression. Then researchers got people either to self-focus or to focus externally. After their attention was focused either on themselves or externally, people took a different standard psychological test for depression. Would depressed people who focused externally become less depressed? Yes, depressed people who focused externally became less depressed than did depressed people who focused on themselves.

When depressed people focused externally they became more optimistic. Their social skills improved. They actually became less depressed. Here is hard evidence that the thought patterns of depressed people, their pessimistic attributional style and their self-focused thoughts, contribute to their problems dealing with other people and to their depression. Such thoughts are hard to change in part because pessimism expressed by depressed people may be more realistic in many situations than the optimistic illusions of nondepressed people. Thus depressed people may feel they are being asked to give up reality before they can get better. However, the research we have reviewed shows that changing a depressed person's focus of attention can change her attributional style. If depressed people focus less on themselves, then they become more optimistic and more socially adept. In addition, the benefit comes without requiring depressed people to consciously try to distort reality.

CHANGING YOUR MIND

The knowledge that social psychologists have gained about healthy and unhealthy thought patterns can benefit us all. Depression is common. While most of us will not suffer a depressive episode severe enough to require treatment, most of us slip into depressed moods that cause us problems. Even people who are socially adept go through periods where they cannot seem to connect with the people around them. Sometimes we feel helpless. We cannot motivate ourselves to get our work done. If you are extremely insightful, you may have realized that your thoughts contribute to these down periods. Your thoughts become difficult to organize. You realize that situations you otherwise would handle in stride seem ominous. You expect things to get worse, not better as you usually would. Trying to channel thoughts in a healthy way has been an important human endeavor at least since people invented writing.

"Your Problems Are None of Your Business"

The benefits of focusing your attention outside yourself explain why focusing on our own problems is so ineffective. Remember that at one point when my problems were overwhelming me, I was given some very strange advice. I was told that my problems were none of my business. At the time it did not seem like advice at all. How could ignoring my problems help? Now we know that self-focused attention, mulling over our problems, ruminating, can lead to common symptoms of depression such as feelings of helplessness and inadequacy. Problems can overwhelm us *because* we focus on them. Focusing your attention outside yourself increases optimism. Optimism, then, makes it more likely that you will engage in behavior that will lead to a solution.

Now that we know the benefits of focusing attention outside ourselves, what should we focus our attention on? If my problems are none of my business, then what is my business? Many of our most serious personal problems are social. Human beings are social by nature. We live and work in groups. Maintaining strong relationships within a social network of acquaintances, friends, and relatives is important to a successful life. Similarly, cooperation is the key to a successful social group. Helping other people solve their problems is an excellent way to cement social relationships. Other people's problems are my business. When people help to solve each other's problems everyone benefits.

Recall that when my car would not start, in my depressed state, I blamed myself for the problem. I focused my attention on my problems and ultimately on my own inadequacy. However, when my coworker helped me fix my car, she was not likely to blame herself for the problem. After all, it was not her problem. Because self-blame is less likely when dealing with other people's problems, it is easier to maintain a positive outlook toward other people's problems than our own problems. Thus efforts to solve other people's problems are often more effective than are efforts to solve our own problems. When we help to solve other people's problems our status and feelings of self-worth increase. People tend to think highly of those who help them. People who help others gain prestige. Knowing that others think highly of us increases our self-esteem. Helping others, then, is a technique for warding off depression and maintaining good mental health in general.

Of course, the advice to help others is not new. Helping others is a major focus of many philosophies and religions. Social psychology shows us why helping others is beneficial to us. You might worry that your problems will still be there after you get home from a hard day of helping others. You need not worry. While you are helping others with their problems, others will be helping you. Cooperation in a successful social group requires faith that the group will help solve your problems. When we self-focus it is easy to become isolated, to think that no one else cares. That reinforces our focus on ourselves. We think that we better concentrate on our problems because no one else will. We begin to feel helpless, overwhelmed. Self-focus is a trap that not only makes it harder to solve our problems but also makes us feel that more intense self-focus is needed.

Social psychology shows us how to avoid the self-focus trap. We now know that focusing on our problems actually interferes with finding solutions to them. An external focus will help us solve our own problems, even if nobody helps us at all. So we have little to lose by helping other people. Believing that others will help us while we are helping someone else still requires a leap of faith. But the leap required is not nearly as large as we had thought. Spending your time helping other people is a good way to solve your own problems. No surer way to a successful life exists.

My experience with higher education shows how trying to help other people can help you. I was dissatisfied with college when I enrolled right after high school. I knew that college would get me a good job and a secure place in society. But I did not care. It just seemed like too much work. Why couldn't I have a good job without going to college? I soon dropped out. I went back several times over the next 14 years, but never stayed. Often I failed to even enroll. I once drove to San Jose State University determined to enroll, go back to school, and change my life. When I got there, I couldn't find a parking place. After driving around the campus for 10 minutes, I gave up and went home. Why couldn't I overcome such a trivial obstacle as finding a parking place? Why didn't I try again later, or go early in the morning the next day? I had been out in the working world long enough to know that good jobs usually require a college degree. I wanted a better job and I knew a college degree would help me get one. Yet I could not make myself go. The self-focused goal of future personal reward simply wasn't enough incentive to keep me in school.

My attitude toward higher education was much different when I returned to college at age 34. I enrolled in a couple of classes at a community college thinking that an education might increase my ability to help other people. Instead of selling furniture, maybe I could become a counselor of some kind. I went back to school to find out what I could contribute to society rather than what I could get out of it. That change in attitude made all the difference. I found myself eager to get to school. Before my attitude changed from a focus on myself to a focus on other people, the cost of education had seemed exorbitant; afterward it seemed amazingly cheap. Once my focus of attention changed from myself to other people, my life improved. Before, I *thought about* writing books because I wanted to be a successful author but I never actually wrote anything. Now I *am* writing a book because I think people might find it useful. That is the difference between focusing on myself and focusing on other people. Self-focused attention is debilitating. It prevented me from accomplishing anything useful. Externally focused attention, especially when attention is focused on helping other people, will allow you to accomplish more than you think possible.

Managing Your Problems by Writing about Them

Another technique for managing your problems is to write about them. This approach might seem to contradict what we have learned about self-focused attention. Wouldn't writing about your problems serve to focus your attention on them? Writing about your problems does focus your attention on them but only temporarily. Once you have written about your problems, you can more easily put them aside. Some of the negative effects of self-focused attention are due to the rumination that goes with them. When people self-focus they chew over their problems, worrying about them without ever coming to grips with them. Problems seem to grow out of control as people continually rethink and reevaluate them. Self-focused rumination actually prevents people from dealing effectively with the daily realities of life.

Concentrating on other people's problems rather than our own is one way to reduce the anxiety and self-blame that come with self-focused attention. Still, we have to cope with the details of daily life. Perhaps there are saints or spiritual gurus who live only for others, completely disregarding the personal details of their lives. Few of us are capable of that kind of life. Most of us would not want it. That means we have to find a balance. While we set out to help others and do good in the world, we have to take care of our own daily lives as well. After all, if you do not pay the phone bill, then a person who needs your help will not be able to call you. And there are so many details involved in modern life. It is impossible to keep them all straight in your mind. They float around, in and out of your conscious thoughts, bumping into each other, growing and multiplying. Writing about personal problems helps to stop the self-focused rumination that creates so much mental distress and prevents people from acting to solve their problems.

Pennebaker, Colder, and Sharp (1990) wanted to find out whether getting people to write about their experiences could help them cope. Young people who first go off to college are under considerable pressure. The transition to college life causes great stress. Young adults in college have to cope with many new details and responsibilities in their lives. Researchers asked one group of first-year college students to write about their deepest thoughts and feelings as they coped with adjusting to college life. Students in a second group also wrote, but not about their problems. Instead, students in the second group wrote about minor details. For example, "Describe in detail what you have done since you woke up this morning . . . Do not mention your own emotions, feelings, or opinions." All students wrote for 20 minutes on each of three consecutive days. Then, at the end of their freshman year, researchers checked to see how well the students had coped. Would students who wrote about their problems have fewer health problems? Also, would students who wrote about their problems do better in school?

The answer to both questions was yes. Writing about your problems does help. Pennebaker, Colder, and Sharp (1990) found that students who wrote about their problems needed less medical care than did other students. Also, students who wrote about their problems had higher grade point averages at the end of their first year than did other students. While the difference in grade point averages was not large, remember that students wrote daily for only three days. The effects of regularly writing about your problems might be even more beneficial. The study clearly demonstrated that writing about your problems is an effective way to cope.

Recall that Chapter 2 gave you reasons to start keeping a journal. Now we see that keeping a journal in a specific way can have added benefits. In your journal, you practice seeing social situations from the point of view of other people. You put your problems in a broader perspective. You get outside yourself. Use your journal to write about the serious problems and issues in your life. Write about your deepest thoughts and feelings. You will soon see real improvement. Over three-quarters of the students in the Pennebaker, Colder, and Sharp (1990, p. 534) study reported gaining insight from writing about their problems. For example, one student wrote, "It made me think things out and really realize what my problem is." Another wrote, "It helped me to look at myself from the outside."

"HONESTLY, DOCTOR, I FEEL FINE, REALLY"

Before closing, we should complete the exercise started at the beginning of this chapter. Recall that, as a way to help solve other peoples' problems, we tried seeing a situation from the point of view of a person in trouble. What would you do if you were committed to a mental hospital by mistake? We found that showing hospital staff that we had a good grasp of reality probably would not work. In a mental hospital, doctors might interpret normal actions as evidence of mental illness. Also, we found that normal people sometimes maintain illusions while depressed people sometimes see reality more clearly. Rosenhan's study of mental hospitals showed that it was no easy task for a perfectly healthy person to gain release from a mental hospital. What could you do to demonstrate that you were sane? Real patients in Rosenhan's (1973) study could answer that question based on their actual experience. Should any of us have the misfortune to find ourselves mistakenly admitted to a mental hospital, we might try their advice: "Don't tell them you're well. They won't believe you. Tell them you're sick, but getting better. That's called insight, and they'll discharge you!" (Rosenhan 1973, p. 472).

Further Reading

Of General Interest

Peterson, C., & Bossio, L. M. (1991). *Health and optimism.* New York: Free Press.
Seligman, M. E. P. (1991). *Learned optimism: How to change your mind and your life.* New York: Pocket Books.
Taylor, S. E. (1989). *Positive illusions: Creative self-deception and the healthy mind.* New York: Basic Books.

Recent and Technical Issues

Anderson, C. A., Miller, R. S., Riger, A. L., Dill, J. C., & Sedikides, C. (1994). Behavioral and characterological attributional styles as predictors of depression and loneliness: Review, refinement, and test. *Journal of Personality and Social Psychology, 66,* 549–558.

Berkowitz, L. (1987). Mood, self-awareness, and willingness to help. *Journal of Personality and Social Psychology, 52,* 721–729.

Bootzin, R. R. (1997). Examining the theory and clinical utility of writing about emotional experiences. *Psychological Science, 8,* 167–169.

Hirt, E. R., Zillman, D., Erickson, G. A., & Kennedy, C. (1992). Costs and benefits of allegiance: Changes in fans' self-ascribed competencies after team victory versus defeat. *Journal of Personality and Social Psychology, 63,* 724–738.

Metalsky, G. I., Joiner, T. E. Jr., Hardin, T. S., & Abramson, L. Y. (1993). Depressive reactions to failure in a naturalistic setting: A test of the hopelessness and self-esteem theories of depression. *Journal of Abnormal Psychology, 102,* 101–109.

Pennebaker, J. W. (1997). Writing about emotional experiences as a therapeutic process. *Psychological Science, 8,* 162–166.

Pyszczynski, T., Hamilton, J. C., Herring, F. H., & Greenberg, J. (1989). Depression, self-focused attention, and the negative memory bias. *Journal of Personality and Social Psychology, 57,* 351–357.

Wiedenfeld, S. A., O'Leary, A., Bandura, A., Brown, S., Levine, S., & Raska, K. (1990). Impact of perceived self-efficacy in coping with stressors on components of the immune system. *Journal of Personality and Social Psychology, 59,* 1082–1094.

Wood, J. V., Saltzberg, J. A., Neale, J. M., Stone, A. A. Rachmiel, T. B. (1990). Self-focused attention, coping responses, and distressed mood in everyday life. *Journal of Personality and Social Psychology, 58,* 1027–1036.

CHAPTER 5

Influence: Getting People to Listen to You

Influence is a concept that bothers people. To have influence means that people will do what you think is best. Influence, then, is a good thing to have. We wish we had more of it. Most of us want as much control over our lives as possible. We also worry that other people, especially groups of people, have more influence over us than they should. Advertisers want me to buy their products, politicians want my vote, and my doctor wants me to exercise more. I am reasonably sure that following my doctor's advice by exercising is in my best interest. If she has enough influence over me to get me to exercise regularly, that would be great. I feel differently about advertisers and politicians. I want to limit their influence over me. In many ways influence is a good thing to have. However, we do not want others to have too much influence over us. If we look at the situation from their point of view, then other people might be just as concerned with how much influence we have over them. If we do manage to acquire a lot of influence, we will want to be careful about how we use it.

The problem for the mental patient in Chapter 4 was to convince hospital staff that a mistake had been made and she should be released. Her predicament is frightening to imagine because—as a mental patient—she had lost her influence. No one would pay attention to what she said. The desire for influence is a major reason why most people prefer the high-status positions in society. For example, people would rather be judges and doctors than clerks and orderlies. Children almost always want to be older rather than younger. High-status positions in society give people influence.

For example, when my son was in trouble at school I had a message at work to call the principal. When I called back, the secretary asked who was calling and I told her, Professor Lovaglia. Usually I would say Michael Lovaglia instead of Professor Lovaglia, but I was worried about my son and did not know what to expect. I used my title hoping people at the school would take me seriously. If school officials were going to make a decision concerning my son, I wanted to have as much influence as possible. Usually I don't use my title because people already take professors too seriously. It hampers conversation. People worry that I will correct their grammar. The point is that people go to school for all those years to get graduate degrees and professional jobs so they will have influence when they need it. For example, if I were still cleaning office buildings, I would not tell the secretary that Janitor Lovaglia was calling. Janitors have little influence in this society—more than mental patients but not enough for people to grow up wanting to be janitors. We want people to take us seriously so that we can get the help we need to solve our problems.

Social psychology can show us how influence works. By examining the research, we can discover how to gain influence, how to use it more effectively, and how to guard against unwanted influence from others. People are social. Almost everything we do is geared toward making an impression on other people. We actively manage the impression we make on other people. From the clothes and jewelry we wear to the cars we drive and the people we become close too, our decisions are shaped by the impression we think others will have of us. We express ourselves in many ways to show other people what we are like. Often we present ourselves to people in ways that we hope will make them feel positively about us. The study of self-presentation and impression management is a major field of research in social psychology.

Sometimes we consciously set out to change other people's opinions. We present arguments as logically as possible to convince people to go along with us. Much of our education focuses on composing convincing arguments. As important as logic is to persuasion, however, people become convinced for many reasons that have little to do with logic. Studying how people become persuaded is another major area of research in social psychology. Have you ever noticed that nobody seems to ever really win an argument? No matter how right you are and how logically you present your case, your opponent in the argument never says, "OK, you have convinced me. You were right." What does it take to change someone's mind?

ARE YOU AS CONVINCING AS YOUR ARGUMENT?

The most logically compelling argument is not very convincing coming from a person we dislike. Think about commission salespeople. People who sell cars or homes go to great lengths to appear friendly and likable. Salespeople are about as different from one another as are people in other occupations. Some salespeople really are friendly and likable. Some are cold and unlikable. But just about all salespeople try to appear as warm and likable as possible because their job is to convince people to buy something. People we like influence us more easily than do people we dislike.

Shelly Chaiken (1980) thought that in some situations people would be more persuaded by arguments while in other situations they would be more persuaded by the person presenting the argument. She set up a situation where people would read persuasive messages on a topic of interest to them. For example, college students participating in the study read a message advocating that the college change from a two-semester system to a trimester system. Students read one of two versions of the persuasive message. The more persuasive version contained six good reasons to change over to the trimester system; the less persuasive version contained only two good reasons to change to trimesters. Then, after students read the persuasive message, they completed a questionnaire that asked for their opinion on whether the college should change to a trimester system. Chaiken predicted that the stronger argument containing six good reasons would be more persuasive than the weaker argument containing only two good reasons. It was. Students who read the strong argument were more convinced that the trimester system was a good idea than were students who read the weak argument.

Chaiken (1980) also wanted to find out whether the same argument would be more persuasive if presented by a likable person than it would be if presented by an unlikable person. Students in her study read the arguments as part of an interview. During the interview, the person making the argument either praised or insulted college students. Not surprisingly, Chaiken found that students liked the person who praised college students and disliked the person who insulted college students. In general, we like people who like us. Would the same argument be more persuasive when the likable person presented it? It was. Students who read the argument given by the likable person were more convinced that the trimester system was a good idea. The overall conclusion of Chaiken's study is that people are persuaded both by the strength of an argument and by the person who presents it.

Chaiken (1980) also made a more subtle prediction. She thought that when people were focused on the content of the message, then the strength of the argument would be more important than the person who presented it. However, when people were not focused on the content, Chaiken thought that the likability of the person presenting the argument would be more important. To find out if she was right, she told half of the people in the study that they would be asked questions about the argument after they had read it and participate in a discussion on the topic. The rest of the people in the study thought they would be asked questions about a different topic. Chaiken predicted that if people expected to discuss the topic of the argument, then the strength of the argument would be more important than the person presenting it. In contrast, she predicted that if people did not expect to discuss the topic of the argument, then the likability of the person presenting the argument would be more important than the strength of the argument. Again she was right. When people were focused on the argument because they thought they would be discussing it, they were more convinced by a strong argument rather than a weak one. However, when people were not focused on the argument, they were more convinced by a person they liked than by a person they did not like.

Chaiken's (1980) study explains why television advertisements can have such a big impact in only a few seconds. Generally, we do not pay close attention to the argument being presented by a TV ad. Because we are not focused on the argument, we are easily convinced by the person who presents the argument, often a likable TV personality. In contrast, when we read an argument, perhaps in a newspaper, then the strength of the argument should be more important than the likability of the author. The idea is that when we read an argument, we can go at our own pace and carefully analyze the argument.

Shelly Chaiken and Alice Eagly (1983) set up a situation to find out whether likability would be more convincing than a good argument for a videotaped message, while a good argument would be more convincing than likability for a written message. The study was similar to that conducted by Chaiken (1980) except that half the people saw a videotaped interview presenting a persuasive argument, while the rest read a transcript of the interview. Chaiken and Eagly predicted that people who saw the videotaped interview would be more convinced by a likable person. In contrast, researchers predicted that people who read a transcript of the interview would be equally convinced by a strong argument whether it was presented by a likable or unlikable person. Chaiken and Eagly were right. On videotape, a likable person was very convincing while an unlikable person was not convincing at all. In contrast, the written argument was equally convincing whether presented by a likable or unlikable person.

Most situations are complicated. Things are happening fast. We seldom have the time to pay close attention to what people are saying. When that happens, our impressions of people have more influence on us than the arguments those people make.

SMILE

We now know why it is important that people like us. They will pay less attention to what we say if they don't. But how do people decide if they like us? What are we supposed to do? Shelley Chaiken's research showed that people like people who like them. Smiling at people is an easy way to let them know that you like them. Even when you do not know people, smiling tells them that you will probably like them. The result is that they will like you more if you smile. And as we have found out, you have more influence over people who like you. So, smile more—especially in situations where you feel threatened.

Smiling got me through one of my most intense social encounters. When I was 21, I worked at a nightclub tending bar and checking IDs at the door. The club featured popular bands and was a rowdy place. It appealed to a wide variety of people from college students to motorcycle gang members. Checking IDs at the door was difficult because teenagers were especially attracted to the scene. Often the club was filled to capacity and people would have to be turned away, sometimes after they had waited in line for hours. Fights broke out frequently. The local police considered the club a nuisance and looked for reasons to shut it down. So it was important that we keep people under the age of 21 out of the bar. I was not very big and usually worked behind the bar rather than at the door. The club was always looking for ID checkers, though, because people did not stay long in that job and we needed a lot of them. Even though it paid better than tending bar, there was too much confrontation at the door.

Working the door appealed to me. It was exciting to a young man who had never been in a fight. I volunteered. One weekday night about midnight, I was checking IDs at the door with a more experienced bouncer. We usually had at least two people working the door—then if something bad happened, one person could call the ambulance. That night, about six members of a national motorcycle gang arrived. The gang had a reputation for violence. They parked their Harley-Davidson motorcycles on the sidewalk in front of the club and clanked up the steps in their chains and leather. Several of the bikers had brought women with them, very young women. This could be trouble. My voice caught in my throat and cracked as I asked for their IDs.

The leader of the bikers was first to the door. He was older than the others, in his forties, but with the youngest woman. She looked about 15. When I asked for her ID, he said, "It's alright, she's with me." He stared hard at me but smiled pleasantly. I wanted to agree with him, to just let it go. I wanted him to like me. Not knowing what to do, I looked for the experienced bouncer, who did know what to do. He was gone.

I decided not to let her in without ID. Maybe I had to prove something. The biker stared at me and smiled. I smiled back. Smiling was about all I could do. I weighed 150 pounds at the time, earring and motorcycle boots included. The tension built as we smiled and talked. He said they did not want trouble, just a quiet drink. He stared harder. I smiled harder. A new recruit to the biker gang had been assigned to watch the bikes. He became impatient with my apparent disrespect for his boss and bounded up the stairs. "Why don't I just kill you," he said. He had something to prove also and was not smiling. With the foolish grin still on my face, I told his boss the first thing that came to mind. I said, "If you kill me the cops will come and you still won't get a drink." Nobody said anything for a long time. We just smiled. Then the leader stopped smiling. He told the women and the new recruit to wait with the bikes and walked into the club. I started to breathe again. My face hurt from smiling so hard. Later, the bikers brought drinks out to the women, which was also illegal, but I did not mind.

Smiling is the most simple and effective tool we have to build relationships with people. For example, babies are famous for their smiles. A human baby is completely defenseless and has no hope of surviving on her own. She cannot talk. How will she persuade people to like her and take care of her? She smiles.

Ann Frodi and Michael Lamb (1980) found an interesting difference between how normal parents and child abusers respond to babies. Everyone got anxious and upset when they saw a baby crying although the child abusers were less sympathetic. The big difference was in the parents' responses to a smiling baby. While normal parents responded positively to the smiling baby, child abusers became

Garfield knows the value of a smile

anxious and upset with the smiling baby just as they had with the crying baby. Smiling does not work on everybody, but most people respond positively to a smile.

Kathi Tidd and Joan Lockard (1978) wanted to find out if smiling had cash value. They wondered what effect smiling would have on a cocktail waitress's tips. Most people would probably agree that a smiling cocktail waitress would get more tips than would a sullen or frowning waitress. Tidd and Lockard had a more interesting idea. They wanted to see if a particular kind of smile would produce more tips. In their study, a cocktail waitress greeted a customer with either a demure, Mona Lisa smile or a broad, toothy grin. Researchers predicted that the broad smile would produce more tips than would the demure smile. Would people tip a waitress more if she approached with a broad smile? The answer is not obvious. The demure smile would undoubtedly appear more sincere. Coming from a stranger, a wide smile exposing as many teeth as possible looks phony, especially on someone who wants something from you. Seeing that many teeth coming at me makes me wonder if they are attached to a barracuda.

How convincing are those big smiles we get from salespeople and cocktail servers? Tidd and Lockard (1978) found that a broad smile made a big difference in a cocktail waitress's tips. When she smiled broadly, the male customers she approached tipped her a total of about $15. When she approached with a demure, sincere smile, an equal number of male customers tipped her a total of about $5. Smiling broadly tripled her tips! It makes sense that men would succumb to a woman's smile. Would women also tip more when their cocktail waitress smiled broadly? They did. When the cocktail waitress smiled broadly, female customers tipped her a total of about $10. When she approached with a demure smile, an equal number of female customers tipped her a total of about $5. Even when a cocktail waitress served women customers, a broad smile had a dramatic effect, doubling her tips. Although a broad smile can seem insincere coming from a cocktail waitress, it has a lot of influence over the amount a customer tips.

Smiling works because it tells people you like them. People like you more if they think you like them. You have more influence over people who like you than over people who don't. A good way, then, to increase your influence over people is to smile at them.

PAYING ATTENTION TO APPEARANCE

Most of us would like to look a little better than we do. We willingly spend a lot of money to improve our appearance. Shoes are a good example. Have you ever noticed how many shoe stores there are in a large shopping mall? How do all those competing shoe stores stay in business? Perfectly normal people may own dozens of pairs of shoes. Why? Certainly not for comfort. One good pair would keep us comfortable. Feet are considered relatively unattractive. We buy all those shoes to make ourselves a little more attractive. By wearing different kinds of shoes, we communicate something about ourselves to other people. Most of us want to be attractive to other people and for good reason. The better we look, the more influence we will have.

How we look has a powerful effect on our lives. Feingold (1992) examined research on physical attractiveness. He concluded that people expect those who are physically attractive to be more sociable, dominant, sexually warm, mentally healthy, intelligent, and socially skilled. Good-looking people, then, are expected to also have a wide variety of socially valuable traits. Physically attractive people are treated better because of the virtues they are expected to have. They are treated better as the research I will describe shows. However, Feingold also concluded that physically attractive people are no different from less attractive people in most ways. Physically attractive people are actually no more intelligent, mentally healthy, or dominant. They are somewhat more socially skilled. Social psychology will explain why.

Despite the importance we attach to how we look, most of us deny how important physical attractiveness is. We think of people who obsess over their appearance as shallow, vain. We like to think that what really counts is character. How good people are and how well they perform determine success. Don't they? Sure, looks make a difference for an actor or a talk show host, but how important can they be for most jobs?

The importance of looks became clear to me while I was selling furniture. At the furniture store where I worked, pay was based about half on an hourly wage and half on commission. The hourly wage was not very high, so it was important to me to sell as much furniture as possible. A small percentage of every sale went to the salesperson who handled the order. Selling on commission generates rivalry among salespeople that can degenerate into hostility. We had rules to manage our competition for customers. For example, when two salespeople were working at the same time, they would alternate as customers entered the store. One salesperson would say hello to the first customer who came in, the other salesperson would say hello to the next customer, and so on. Once a salesperson said hello to a customer, the salesperson expected to work with that customer until a sale was made or the customer left the store. The rule about salespeople alternating with customers worked most of the time unless the store got busy. Then it turned into a free-for-all with salespeople sometimes accusing each other of approaching "their" customer just as she reached the decision to buy a sofa. Also, the customer always had final say in the matter. If a customer approached a salesperson, then that salesperson was supposed to help her regardless of whose turn it was. Appearance, then, could be important. Would customers usually approach the more attractive salesperson?

When I had worked for the store for about a year, a part-time salesperson was hired to work with me during the busier shifts. He was about my age but seemed a little high-powered for a retail sales job. He wore tailored shirts and an elegant gold wristwatch. He always looked like his hair had just been styled. He was over six feet tall and in good shape. He looked like a model in an ad campaign featuring a rising young corporate executive. I hated working with him. I never caught him stealing one of my customers but always suspected him of it. Looking back I realize it may not have been anything he did, but my way of salvaging some self-esteem. It was easier for me to think that he was stealing customers than to admit that they simply preferred him. Whenever we worked together, customers almost always approached him rather than me. I tried to look good at work too, although everything I wear seems to rumple mysteriously after a few minutes. And you probably wouldn't call me fat, maybe lumpy.

One Saturday afternoon, we were both standing at the sales counter when a woman approached with a question. It was my turn, so the poster boy for corporate America graciously stepped behind me and busied himself with paperwork. I turned toward the customer and gave her my most sincere salesperson smile. Not wanting to seem pushy, I caught her eye but let her speak first. She ignored me, then stepped to her left to see around me. She made a noise in her throat to catch the other salesperson's attention. When he looked up, she asked him to help her. All the while I stood chagrined between them. He shrugged a little sheepishly at me, then went off with her to make a sale. Variations of this scene happened so regularly that only one conclusion followed. His appearance made a huge difference in how much furniture he sold. Luckily for me, he did land a better job and was gone in a few months.

Not only do customers prefer good-looking salespeople, but attractive people also get higher ratings for their work. Landy and Sigall (1974) conducted a study to find out whether people would judge a person's work differently depending on how the person looked. To do the study right, researchers wanted to make sure that physical attractiveness was totally unrelated to the work. They asked people to rate the quality of writing in an essay. Physical appearance would not seem to have anything to do with how well a person writes. Would people rate the quality of an essay higher when they thought the author was physically attractive?

Researchers asked male college students to read a short essay by a female college student, then rate the essay's overall quality. In the folder containing the essay, the men also found a yearbook photo of the woman who wrote the essay. Half of the men in the study saw a photo of a very attractive woman. The rest of the men in the study saw a photo of an unattractive woman. Landy and Sigall (1974) predicted that college men would rate the essay higher when they thought it had been written by an attractive woman. They were right. Men rated the quality of the essay higher when they thought it had been written by an attractive woman.

Landy and Sigall (1974) also wanted to find out whether the actual quality of the essay made any difference. Half the men who saw a photo of an attractive woman read a high-quality essay. The rest read an essay that was sloppily written and full of errors. Similarly, half the men who thought an unattractive woman wrote the essay read an essay that was high quality. The rest read an essay that was full of errors. Would the quality of the essay make a difference? Or were men judging writing quality on the basis of the author's appearance alone?

It is a relief to discover that competence does count for something. Landy and Sigall (1974) found that the high-quality essay written by an attractive woman was rated highest. The low-quality essay written by an unattractive woman was rated lowest. Rated in between were low-quality essays written by an attractive woman and high-quality essays written by an unattractive woman. Researchers concluded that both the quality of the writing and the appearance of the author made a difference in how the essay was judged. Beauty counts, but good work counts too.

The impact of beauty goes beyond its effect on other people. How you feel about yourself and how you relate to other people depend on how you look.

Remember that Feingold (1992) had found that attractive people were somewhat more socially skilled than were unattractive people. It is easy to see how attractive people could acquire greater social skills. Because attractive people are considered intelligent, healthy, warm, and sociable, the people around them will treat them in a more friendly and positive way. When we say someone is attractive, we mean people will move toward her, be attracted to her. In contrast, people avoid an unattractive person. Thus attractive people are going to have more opportunity to practice their social skills while having mostly positive social experiences. It sounds logical in theory but will a person really behave in less socially desirable ways because other people think she is unattractive? What if the person does not think of herself as unattractive? Will people who find her unattractive give off clues that cause her to react negatively?

Researchers at the University of Minnesota, Mark Snyder, Elizabeth Decker Tanke, and Ellen Berscheid (1977), wanted to find out whether people's opinions about a person's appearance could affect her behavior even if she was unaware of their reaction to her. Researchers set up a situation where men and women would hold a short get-acquainted conversation by telephone. A man and a woman who had not met before were seated in separate rooms with telephones. The man and the woman were both given a page of standard biographical information about the other person to get the conversation started. For example, the man and woman read about each other's academic major in college and where the person went to high school. The man also received a photo of an attractive or unattractive woman to go along with the biographical information, but the woman received no photo. Half the men in the study thought they would be talking to an attractive woman. The rest of the men in the study thought they would be talking to an unattractive woman. Then the man and woman talked with each other on the phone for 10 minutes.

Snyder, Tanke, and Berscheid (1977) predicted that men who thought they were talking to an unattractive woman would also find her less friendly, likable, and sociable during the phone conversation. To no one's great surprise, the researcher's first prediction was correct. Men who thought they were talking to an attractive woman rated her as more friendly, likable, and sociable than did men who thought they were talking to an unattractive woman. More surprisingly, researchers also predicted that women would respond to the picture that men had of them. When men thought they were talking to an unattractive woman, researchers predicted that the woman would actually become less friendly, likable, and sociable over the phone. Remember that the woman had no idea that the man she was talking to thought she was attractive or unattractive.

The men's impressions of how attractive a woman was had a surprising effect on women's behavior. To find out whether women were actually behaving differently during the phone conversations, researchers brought in 12 people to judge the conversations, which had been tape-recorded. The judges did not know what kind of photo the man in the conversations had seen. They also listened to audiotapes of only the woman's half of the conversations. Judges rated such things as "How animated and enthusiastic is this person?" and "How much is she enjoying herself?" Researchers predicted that independent judges would find that women became more friendly, likable, and sociable as the conversation progressed when the man they talked to thought he was talking to an attractive woman.

That is exactly what happened. When a man thought he was talking to an unattractive woman, the woman became less friendly, likable, and sociable toward him. He treated her differently because of the picture he had of her. She responded in a way that confirmed his impression of her. Attractive people are thought to be more friendly and sociable than are unattractive people. Attractive people respond by being more friendly and sociable, while unattractive people respond by being less friendly and sociable. It is a perfectly self-fulfilling prophecy. (See Merton [1948] for an interesting discussion of self-fulfilling prophecies and the origin of the term.) Now we know why attractive people may become more socially skilled than less attractive people.

Most of us are willing to grant the importance of physical attractiveness in at least one area. Physically attractive women are generally thought to have a great deal of influence over men. And attractive men are known to have influence over women. However, physical attractiveness has powerful effects in many situations where sexual attraction is not an issue.

Leonard Berkowitz and Ann Frodi (1979) at the University of Wisconsin wanted to find out if physically attractive children are treated differently than are unattractive children. Researchers set up a situation in which people decided how harshly they would punish a child. As you might think, there were some ethical problems for researchers to overcome before the study could be done. For example, researchers could not let people actually punish a child. When people came into the laboratory, they saw videotape of either an attractive or unattractive child. People were told that they would supervise the child as she performed a series of tasks. Whenever the child made a mistake, a light would go on. When people saw the light, they were to press one of 10 buttons that produced an annoying noise in the earphones the child was wearing. The button for level 1 produced a mildly annoying noise while the higher buttons produced progressively more annoying noise. The noise became painful at about level 6. People heard the noise produced by each level so they knew how much discomfort they inflicted. However, the child was not actually subjected to the noise that people selected as punishment. Researchers could then see which level of noise each person selected as appropriate punishment for the child. Half of the people in the study worked with an attractive child, and the rest worked with an unattractive child. When the light came on indicating that the child had made a mistake, people pushed one of the noise buttons. Would people select higher levels of annoying noise as punishment for the unattractive child than they would for the attractive child?

They did. People consistently selected a higher level of annoying noise for the unattractive child than they did for the attractive child. That is, people punished an unattractive little girl more harshly than they did an attractive little girl. Berkowitz and Frodi (1979) repeated the study using a boy instead of a girl. The result was the same. People punished an unattractive little boy more harshly than they did an attractive little boy. Now when I send my children off to school in the morning, I pay more attention to how they look than I would have before studying social psychology.

Beauty is important in many situations because we often unconsciously assume that attractive people are more competent than are unattractive people. Even when people think they treat attractive and unattractive people the same, they probably don't. When we expect people to be competent, we treat them better. Remember that painful ritual on the playground where children choose up sides for a game? Two children who want to organize a game become "captains," who select their teams. First one captain picks a child to be on her team from among those who want to play. Then the other captain selects a child. The captains alternate picks until the teams are complete. Children who are more competent at the game get picked first. They are expected to help a team win. Sometimes there is one awkward child who is not picked at all and wanders off by himself. Children usually picked first become leaders. Other children look up to them and follow their advice. Children picked last are ignored, sometimes even ridiculed.

This cruel system for selecting who gets to lead and who has to follow is seen not only on the playground but in the adult workplace as well. People who are expected to be competent and contribute to the group are given better jobs and praised for their work. They are admired and asked for advice. Social psychologists say they have high *status.* As cruel as the system can be, we consider it mostly fair as long as people whom we expect to be most competent really are competent and do contribute more to the group. However, our expectations for who is competent are not always accurate. Sometimes, a characteristic like beauty, which is unrelated to competence, fools us into expecting competence from a person who isn't. A *status characteristic* is something about a person—like beauty—that changes our expectations for how competent that person is.[1]

Webster and Driskell (1983) decided to find out whether more attractive people are also seen as more competent. Researchers showed pairs of photographs to several hundred people. Some people saw a photograph of a highly attractive man and a photograph of an unattractive man. The rest saw a photograph of a highly attractive woman and a photograph of an unattractive woman. Researchers asked people to use the limited information available to them to form impressions about the two people in the photographs. People completed a questionnaire that asked "In terms of things that you think count in this world, how do you compare person A to person B?" The questionnaire also asked how generally competent one person was compared to the other, and how physically attractive one person was compared to the other.

Webster and Driskell (1983) had gone to a lot of trouble to ensure that most people thought the person in one of the photos was highly attractive while the other was unattractive. Thus it is not surprising that the people in their study consistently rated the person in one photo as highly attractive and the other as highly unattractive. More surprising was the fact that gender did not make a difference in the ratings. Men in the study rated the photo of the attractive man just as highly as did women in the study. Women in the study rated the photo of the attractive woman

---

[1]Status characteristics are important in many areas of social psychology. For example, gender and race are also status characteristics. Chapter 7 dealing with social psychology at work and Chapter 8 dealing with prejudice go into more detail on the effects of status characteristics.

just as highly as did men in the study. Both men and women in the study found the photos of unattractive men and women equally unattractive.

The more important question was whether attractiveness would lead people to expect general competence in a person. Would people in the study also rate the highly attractive person as more competent in general? They did. People in the study consistently rated the attractive person as more competent in general and in "things that count" than they did the unattractive person (Webster & Driskell 1983). We expect people to be more competent just because they are physically attractive. Most surprising was that gender was not a factor in the competence ratings. For example, it did not matter whether a man or a woman judged a man's competence. Men expected an attractive man to be more competent than an unattractive man. Women also expected an attractive man to be more competent than an unattractive man. Men expected an attractive woman to be more competent than an unattractive woman. Women too expected attractive women to be more competent. Sexual attraction, then, was not an issue. Attractive people are judged to be more competent than are unattractive people.

Webster and Driskell (1983) showed that beauty is a status characteristic. That is, rightly or wrongly, attractive people are considered more competent in general than are unattractive people. Because beauty is a status characteristic, it makes a difference in how people are treated in the workplace.

Having found that attractive people are expected to be more competent, Webster and Driskell (1983) wanted to discover whether other information could change those expectations. What if an unattractive person had graduated from a prestigious university and become a corporate executive while an attractive person had graduated from a local college and become a store clerk? Would a prestigious education and a high-status occupation raise the expectations that people have for the competence of an unattractive person? Or is beauty the only thing that counts?

Webster and Driskell (1983) also gave people information about the college attended and the job held by the attractive and unattractive people in the comparison photos. When people thought that an attractive woman had attended a local college and worked as a clerk while the unattractive woman had attended a prestigious university and was an executive, would people raise their expectations for the competence of the unattractive woman?

A prestigious education and a high-status job did increase the expectations people had for the competence of the unattractive woman. Webster and Driskell (1983) found the unattractive woman who had a prestigious education and a high-status job was expected to be a little more competent than was the attractive woman from a local college with a low-status job. The results were the same when people judged the competence of attractive and unattractive men. Beauty counts but other things count too. Your education makes a big difference in how competent people expect you to be. Your occupation matters as well. Expectations were highest for attractive people who also had a prestigious education and a high-status job.

Social psychology shows us that physical attractiveness is important. Being concerned with our appearance is not all silly vanity. Because attractive people are expected to be more competent, attractive people have more influence over others than unattractive people do. It is important to look your best in any situation where you want to accomplish something worthwhile with other people. It is also important to remember that physical attractiveness is only one tool you can use to accomplish your goals. It is most effective to back up your attractive appearance with a good education, hard work, and superior performance.

IMPRESSION MANAGEMENT

When we choose clothes to wear or decide whether to smile at someone, we try to manage the impressions that we make on other people. Most of the time we want people to like us. Sometimes we want people to think we are competent. Rather than being a manipulative tactic used only by shallow or insincere people, impression management is a necessary part of social life. People who pay insufficient attention to the impression they make on others can be labeled antisocial, incompetent, or even insane. The theoretical work of Erving Goffman has prompted much research on impression management. Goffman (1959) noticed that an important part of social life resembles a play in a theater, with actors performing in a certain way to make specific impression on the audience. He suggested that normal people in everyday life behave similarly. For example, our homes have backstage and "frontstage" areas just the way a theater does. We entertain guests in the living room that we have tidied up. However, as they arrive, we might shut the door to the bedroom strewn with clothes. The bedroom is backstage. We want to hide the preparations we have made to manage the impressions that people have of us.

Research has shown that people are pretty good at managing the impressions they have on others. Gordon (1996) reviewed 55 of the best studies on the effectiveness of impression management. He concludes that when people try to make themselves more likable to another person, they succeed most of the time. Gordon also concludes that people who try to present themselves as competent sometimes get higher performance evaluations than they otherwise would.

Not only are we pretty good at making people like us, we also can fairly accurately tell how good an impression we have made. DePaulo, Kenny, Hoover, Webb, and Oliver (1987) designed a situation to discover whether people could tell what other people thought of them. In the study, people worked with a number of other people on different projects. For example, a person would take the role of a teacher to give a brief lesson to another person acting as a student. Then people would switch roles so that everyone had a chance to be a teacher and a student at different times. Other projects included a competitive game in which people took turns adding odd-shaped blocks to a pile until it toppled. There was also a cooperative game in which people tried to give their partners clues to the right answer. After each project was completed people would rate how likable and competent they thought their partners were. People also rated how likable and competent they thought their partners would rate them. Researchers could then compare the ratings people made of a person with the ratings that person thought she would get.

Would participants be able to tell how likable and competent other people thought they were? In some ways, yes. People in the study could tell in a general way how likable and competent people thought they were. That is, people who got the highest overall likability and competence ratings also thought that they would get the highest ratings. People were a little more accurate for likability than for competence. People tended to think that others would find them less competent than they actually did. We tend to worry about small mistakes in our own performances that others may not notice.

Researchers also found that people have a surprising lack of ability to judge the impressions they make on particular people. While people knew, overall, how likable and competent their partners thought they were, people could not tell how likable or competent a particular partner thought they were. That is, people thought that everybody they worked with would rate them about the same in terms of likability and competence. However, ratings of a person's competence varied a great deal depending on which partner was doing the rating. For example, the same person might be judged highly competent by one partner and incompetent by another partner. Meanwhile, the person thought that both of her partners had rated her competence about the same.

Attempts at impression management can also backfire. The two common goals of impression management—appearing both likable and competent—sometimes conflict. When people try to make themselves look competent, they may inadvertently give the impression that they are not likable. Just how do people go about trying to make themselves look likable and competent? Which techniques of impression management are effective and which should be avoided?

Godfrey, Jones, and Lord (1986) wanted to find out how people would present themselves to get other people to either like them or think them competent. Researchers brought pairs of people into the laboratory and asked them to get to know each other by talking to each other for 20 minutes about a topic of their choosing. After this get-acquainted conversation was over, people rated how likable and competent they thought their partner had been. Then researchers gave one of the two people from the first conversation specific instructions for a second conversation. Researchers asked one person to "make the other person like you as much as possible." People next got back together with their partner from the first conversation to talk over a topic of their choosing in a second conversation. After the second conversation ended, people again rated how likable and competent they thought their partner had been. Researchers could then compare the ratings people got after the first and second conversations.

When people tried to make a person like them, would that person find them more likable? Godfrey, Jones, and Lord (1986) confirmed that people were successful at making others like them. When people tried to make their partners like them in the second conversation, they got higher ratings for likability after the second conversation than they had after the first. The result was not surprising given that Gordon (1996) came to the same conclusion after examining a number of earlier studies. However, Godfrey, Jones, and Lord also found that when people try to make others like them, their ratings for competence did not change. Not only are people good at getting others to like them, but people need not worry that others will think them less competent because of it.

Trying to get other people to think we are competent is riskier. Godfrey, Jones, and Lord (1986) repeated the study except this time, instead of asking people to make the other person like them, researchers asked people to "get the other person to regard you as extremely competent." Would people who tried to impress another person with their competence actually get higher competence ratings? They did not. When people tried to appear competent in the second conversation, their partners did not rate them as any more competent than they already had in the first conversation. There is also a penalty attached to trying to appear competent. Godfrey, Jones, and Lord found that when people tried to appear competent, their partner rated them as less likable.

How do people go about trying to make another person like them or to think them competent? Godfrey, Jones, and Lord (1986) had videotaped people's attempts to make themselves appear likable or competent. By reviewing the videotape, researchers could identify the techniques used by people in their successful attempts to appear likable and in their unsuccessful attempts to appear competent.

Godfrey, Jones, and Lord (1986) identified a number of techniques used by people who wanted a person to like them. To get a person to like them, people showed more interest in their partner. They were sympathetic. They smiled and nodded more. They maintained eye contact. People listened more and talked less. They pointed out similarities and common acquaintances shared with their partner. Then for good measure, people who wanted to be liked threw in a compliment or two. A little flattery never hurts. These are the effective techniques people use to get others to like them.

People also use a number of techniques to appear competent to others (Godfrey, Jones, & Lord 1986). Keep in mind that in contrast to the techniques used to increase likability, the techniques used to improve the appearance of competence were not effective. When people unsuccessfully attempted to appear competent, they talked a lot about their own accomplishments or achievements. They attempted to control the conversation. They talked more and listened less. They sat up straighter and tried to sound confident. Finally, people who unsuccessfully tried to appear competent avoided talking about areas in which their partner showed competence.

Now we can figure out why trying to appear competent can backfire. Notice that some of the techniques used by people trying to appear competent are opposites of those used by people who want to be liked. People like good listeners, but it is hard to listen sympathetically while trying to dominate a conversation. People like a person who talks about them and their achievements, but trying to appear competent seems to entail avoiding their areas of expertise. People who want to appear competent focus the conversation on themselves and fail. People who want to be liked focus on the other person and succeed.

Forsyth, Berger, and Mitchell (1981) thought that when people try to appear competent, others would find them unattractive. However, when people try to make *someone else* appear competent, people would find them more attractive. In this study, university students participated in a group discussion. Researchers told one group of students that they had done very well during the discussion. Researchers told another group of students that they had done poorly during the discussion. Students then wrote down their thoughts about the reasons for the group's success or failure. When students had finished writing, researchers asked them to judge two examples of what students had written. Students in the group that had done poorly

cathy®   **by Cathy Guisewite**

Cathy learns how to appear as competent as possible

read one example where the person blamed himself or herself for the group's fail-
ure. In the other example, the person blamed the group's failure on other people.
Who would you find more attractive, the person who blamed herself or the person
who blamed others? People in the study felt the same way. A person who blames
herself for her group's failure is more attractive than a person who blames others.
Trying to make ourselves look good backfires when it makes other people look bad.
Results from the discussion group that succeeded support the same conclusion.
Group members read one example where the person took personal credit for the
success of the group and another example where the person gave credit to other
group members. The person who gave credit to other group members was rated as
more attractive. Perhaps the best way to make yourself look good is to help other
people succeed.

Women at work can find the problem of trying to appear competent especially
difficult. Women are still seen as less competent than are men in many work situations. How can women show their coworkers how competent they are without appearing less likable at the same time? Laurie Rudman (1998) investigated the impressions made by women and men who tried to appear more competent. In the
study, people interviewed a person to be their partner in a *Jeopardy* game. Because
success at *Jeopardy* requires quick thinking and a wide range of knowledge, people
in the study wanted to "hire" a competent partner. For the first part of the study,
Rudman wanted to find out if self-promotion would help women who were trying
to be hired. That is, would people prefer a woman partner who presented herself as
competent and assertive? Or would they prefer a woman partner who presented herself more modestly? A research assistant played the role of the partner being interviewed. For half of the people who interviewed the woman partner, she presented
herself as competent and assertive. For the rest of the people who interviewed her,
the woman partner presented herself as modest and self-effacing.

The results of Rudman's (1998) study showed that self-promotion can be an effective tool for women in the workplace. Overall, people were more likely to "hire"
the woman to be their partner when she presented herself as competent and assertive. Both men and women preferred to work with the woman who actively promoted herself. Men and women differed, however, on how likable they found the
self-promoting woman. When the outcome of the decision was important, as it is in

most hiring decisions, men also found the self-promoting woman more socially attractive than they did the modest woman. However, women found the self-promoting woman to be less socially attractive than they did the modest woman. Surprisingly, it seems that men may be more accepting than are women of a woman who tries to assert herself in some work-related situations.

When people could choose between a self-promoting male partner and a self-promoting female partner, both men and women preferred the male partner to the female partner. However, men rated the self-promoting man only slightly higher than they rated the self-promoting woman. In contrast, women had a strong preference for the self-promoting male partner over the self-promoting female partner. Rudman (1998) concludes that the problems faced by women in the workplace may be more complex and difficult than ever. Now that hiring committees are commonly composed of both men and women, a woman applying for a job has the tricky task of promoting herself to appear competent while not alienating people on the committee, especially other women. Chapter 7, "Your Place in the Workplace," looks at the problems women face at work and provides some techniques that can help everyone succeed at work.

WHY APOLOGIZE?

Apologizing is not something that comes easy to people. I know people who simply refuse to do it, ever. It would be interesting to find out what apologies are good for. What effect do apologies have on the person receiving an apology? Can apologizing make you appear more likable or more competent? In other words, is the apology another tool people use to manage the impressions other people have of them?

I have a hard time apologizing too, although I have had a lot of practice in recent years. It seems especially hard to apologize to my children. However, a recent example showed me what a profound effect an apology can have. My youngest daughter, Hannah, is four years old. At her insistence, I removed the training wheels from her first bicycle. Now the driveway is no longer big enough to satisfy her and the street we live on is too dangerous for her to ride on. My solution was to throw her bike in the trunk of the car and take her down to the bike paths that the city has built along the river. She rides her bike and I follow along at a slow walk. She asks me to take her to ride her bike by the river almost every day. Usually I either agree to take her or tell her that we will go tomorrow.

One hot day about a week ago, I came home from work, tired. Hannah ran up to me and asked, "Can we go ride the bike? You said we would go today." I told her that I did not remember saying we would go today, that it was too hot. She did not argue but gave me a puzzled look. I did not realize my nine-year-old son, Kyle, was listening as well, but he was. Then I went to my bedroom to change my clothes. Maybe because putting on shorts and a T-shirt made me feel less hot, I began to think about taking Hannah bike riding. Maybe I had told her we would go today.

Now I was stuck. Although bike riding no longer seemed like a bad idea, I felt that I needed a reason to change my mind. Judging from the look on Hannah's face when I told her we weren't going, that reason ought to be an apology. She had been looking forward to the bike ride all day. It was important to her but I had forgotten all about it, as if it did not matter, as if she did not matter. Rather than apologize to her, however, I decided to forget the whole thing. She was only four years old. By tomorrow she would have forgotten all about it. She could go riding then and everything would be fine.

Why didn't I want to apologize? Maybe I felt that apologizing would make me vulnerable. Admitting I was wrong would open the door for my children to realize I am wrong a lot. An apology tells people that they think too highly of me. Right?

That evening after dinner, the puzzled look my daughter had given me still bothered me. Hannah and her brother were watching TV. I asked Hannah if I had told her that she could go ride her bike today. She looked up at me with a hesitant nod as if she were worried I would contradict her again. My son Kyle had no such worries. He said, "Yes! You did," without looking up from the TV. I told Hannah that I was very sorry I had forgotten my promise and asked if she would like to go ride her bike for a few minutes because it was getting late. She was happy to go, of course, but her reaction went beyond getting to do something that she had given up hope on. Both children looked at me with a combination of joy and wonder.

It does not take much for a father to be a hero to his young children, but I could tell I had given them an enormous gift. By apologizing to them, I had validated their existence, raised them to the level of adults. The look on their faces told me how grateful they were and how high I stood in their esteem. Now that I know the effect that my apologies have, I try not to pass up an opportunity.

Schlenker and Darby (1981) studied how people use apologies. Apologies repair damaged social relationships. When a person offends someone, an apology allows them to go on as before—if the apology is accepted, that is. More serious offenses require more elaborate apologies. For example, bumping into somebody in a crowded hallway requires only a brusque "pardon me." My forgetting my daughter's bike ride required not only an admission of guilt but also a sincere attempt to make up for what I had done. More serious offenses may require all of the following elements of an apology: (1) a statement of intent to apologize, such as "I'm sorry"; (2) an expression of remorse; (3) an offer to repair the damage; (4) self-castigation, saying what a bad person I was to have committed the wrong; and (5) a request for forgiveness, such as "Please forgive me." In a serious situation, an artful apologist will continue elaborating the apology—describing how terrible the offense was, how sorry he is about it, and what a terrible person he must be to have done it—until the wronged person gives up and forgives him. In effect, the wronged person has admitted that the relationship is so valuable that it should continue despite what happened. Everybody feels better and continues as before.

Whether an offense actually occurred is not particularly important. Apologies keep relationships going. Trying to determine if a wrong has been committed before apologizing can further strain a relationship. Remember that reality is socially constructed. It is enough that another person believes he has been wronged. The goal is to repair a relationship rather than to determine guilt. If an appropriate apology will repair the relationship, then it makes sense to do it quickly.

Despite the value of apologies, many of us resist making them. We worry about how apologizing will make us look. What do apologies do to the impressions other people have of us?

Darby and Schlenker (1982) thought that apologies are so important for social relationships that very young children would respond in socially approved ways to apologies. The researchers also thought that as children age, apologies would have a greater effect on their impressions of a person who apologized. Darby and Schlenker read a story to children in the first through the seventh grades. In the story, a child named Pat played on a seesaw with a classmate. Both Pat and the classmate were described as being the same sex as the child listening to the story. After playing on the seesaw for a while, Pat jumped off. The child on the other end slammed into the ground and fell off the seesaw. Children who listened to the story thought that Pat had committed a serious offense "on purpose." The researcher then told children one of several endings to the story. Pat did not apologize, Pat said "I'm sorry," or Pat said "I'm sorry" and offered to help the child who had been knocked off the seesaw. Then researchers asked the children what they thought of Pat. Would children respond more positively to the elaborate apology that included an offer to help than they would to the brusque apology or to no apology at all?

Children who listened to the story thought more highly of Pat when Pat made an elaborate apology. When Pat said "I'm sorry" and offered to help, children thought that Pat was less to blame for knocking the classmate off the seesaw. They also thought that Pat should be punished less when Pat made an elaborate apology (Darby & Schlenker 1982). It is clear that apology can be effective in getting people out of trouble for what they have done.

Surprisingly, children also thought that Pat was a stronger person when Pat made an elaborate apology (Darby and Schlenker 1982). In some ways the effect of the apology was greater for older children than it was for younger children. It seems that apologies can be effective tools to manage the impressions that other people have of us. Not only do people like a person who apologizes appropriately. They may also think her a stronger person. I need not have worried that my children would think less of me for apologizing. Apologizing is often a better idea than I think it is at the time.

I COULD NEVER TELL ANYONE ABOUT THAT

People form impressions of us based on what we tell them about ourselves. Such self-disclosure is especially interesting when what we tell about ourselves is odd or embarrassing. Why would people voluntarily admit to embarrassing behavior? Self-disclosure is similar to apologies in that way. In making an apology, a person admits she did something wrong. We wanted to find reasons that a person would do that. Self-disclosure is more general. Why do people voluntarily confess to their own troublesome or inept behavior? What effect does self-disclosure have on people who hear it?

The value of self-disclosure can be seen in the troubles that politicians have. For example, President Bill Clinton was accused of having sexual relations with a staff member at the White House. When he denied it, he was accused of perjury and obstruction of justice for trying to cover up his affair. Clinton's difficulties may show us something about how confession works. Had Clinton confessed to having sex with someone other than his wife in the White House, it would have been embarrassing for him. However, it would not have seriously marred his presidency. Opinion polls showed that Clinton's popularity increased as the scandal unfolded despite the belief of many people that the affair had occurred. It was Clinton's denial of the affair and the subsequent charge of perjury that caused real problems for the president. The personal indiscretions of politicians rarely cause them serious trouble, especially if they confess their wrongs and seem remorseful. However, trying to cover up those indiscretions brings down many politicians. In terms of politics, President Clinton might have been better off confessing to the affair, rather than denying it, even if it had not occurred.

A wide variety of research in social psychology over the last 30 years has shown that people will like a person more when that person discloses intimate or embarrassing personal details. Nancy Collins and Lynn Miller (1994) conducted an extensive review of research findings on self-disclosure. They conclude that (1) people who disclose intimate information are liked better than those whose disclosures are less intimate, (2) people disclose more to others whom they like than to those they do not like, and (3) people like others more after they have disclosed to them. Self-disclosure, telling people intimate details about ourselves, is one way that we establish and maintain positive relationships with other people. The importance of self-disclosure for personal relationships is discussed in detail in Chapter 9. Here we are more concerned with self-disclosure as a tool that people use to manage the impressions that others have of them. Knowing how and when to disclose intimate and possibly embarrassing details about yourself is one key to successfully living and working with other people. Telling people about yourself is tricky, however. As we saw when people try to make themselves look competent, attempts at impression management sometimes backfire. Knowing when and how to make yourself look bad is an art.

Derlega and Chaiken (1976) wanted to know whether men were expected to keep silent about their problems while women were expected to talk about themselves in certain situations. Researchers set up a situation in which a person might tell her personal problems to a stranger sitting next to her on an airplane. People in the study read about a woman who finds a seat on an airplane. The person sitting next to her asks if she is nervous about flying. In the story read by half the people in the study, the woman responded that she was nervous about flying. The rest of the people in the study read that the woman explained that she was nervous because of the personal problems she was having. Derlega and Chaiken had predicted that people would see the woman as better adjusted mentally if she did disclose her personal problems than if she did not. The researchers were right. People rated the woman's mental health higher when she told another person about her personal problems than they did when she kept it to herself.

But would self-disclosure always be beneficial? Derlega and Chaiken (1976) did not think so. They thought that in this society, women are expected to self-disclose more than are men. When a man was in the same situation the woman was in, researchers predicted that people would rate a man less mentally healthy when he self-disclosed than they would if he kept quiet about his personal difficulties. Researchers repeated the experiment where people read about a person flying on an airplane. This time, the person was a man. When the passenger next to him asked if he was nervous about flying, he either agreed that that he was or explained that he was nervous because of the personal problems he was having. Would people rate the man as *less* mentally healthy when he kept personal information to himself than they would if he told about it? They did. In contrast to the way people rated a woman who told personal information about herself, people rated the man less mentally healthy when he told about his personal problems than they did when the man kept silent about his personal problems. In addition, people had rated the woman considerably more likable when she told about her problems than they did when she kept quiet. In contrast, when a man told about his personal problems, his likability ratings increased only slightly if at all.

In a similar study, Chelune (1976) found dramatic differences in the way people respond to self-disclosure by men and women. In his study, as in the one conducted by Derlega and Chaiken (1976), women were liked more when they disclosed more personal information than they were when they disclosed less about themselves. Results for men were different, however. Chelune found that men were liked *less* when they disclosed more about themselves than they were when they disclosed less. To use self-disclosure effectively, it is important to know what is considered appropriate.

Knowing how and when to tell people about yourself is important. It is not easy to predict how people will respond. Not knowing how people will respond is one reason that we are reluctant to tell other people potentially embarrassing information about ourselves.

Edward E. Jones, whose work on attributions is an important part of the social psychology we can use every day, also laid the groundwork for research on the effects of self-disclosure. Jones and Gordon (1972) wanted to know if the timing of a self-disclosure was important. Would it be better to tell people right away about something that might be embarrassing? Or would it be better to wait until people got to know you before telling them? Researchers thought it might depend on whether a person was responsible for a bad thing that happened. For example, researchers had people listen to an interview between a student and his adviser. In the interview, the student explained why he had dropped out of school for a year. Half the people in the study heard the student explain that he had been expelled for cheating. That is, the student was responsible for the bad thing that happened. He would not have left school if he had not been caught cheating. The rest of the people in the study heard the student explain that he had to leave school for a year because his parents had gotten a divorce. Because it was his parents' divorce that forced him to leave school, the student was not responsible for the bad event. Overall, people in the study found the student a little more attractive when he was not responsible for dropping out of school than they did when he was responsible.

Jones and Gordon (1972) found something much more interesting about the timing of self-disclosure. Researchers set up the interview between the student and his adviser so that the student told his adviser early in the interview about leaving school because he had cheated. When the student was responsible for the bad event because he had cheated and told his adviser about it early in the interview, people in the study found the student quite attractive. Researchers also set up the interview so that the student told his adviser about the cheating late in the interview. When the student waited to disclose his cheating until the end of the interview, it had a dramatic effect on the people who listened to the interview. People in the study found the student much *less* attractive when he was responsible for a bad event *and* waited until the end of the interview to tell about it. In contrast, they still found him attractive when he disclosed the bad event early in the interview. We can conclude from Jones and Gordon's results that if we have to confess our misdeeds, we should do it as quickly as possible. Early confession decreases the likelihood that people will see us as trying to mislead them or cover up.

However, early self-disclosure had the opposite effect when the bad event was a simple misfortune rather than something the student had done wrong (Jones & Gordon 1972). When the student had to leave school because of his parents' divorce, people liked him less when he told his adviser about it early in the interview. They liked the student best when he told his adviser about his parents' divorce late in the interview. In general, this study suggests that people will find us more attractive when we confess a misdeed quickly, but they will find us less attractive if we too quickly disclose a misfortune that was not our responsibility. Early disclosure of misfortune can be seen as a ploy to gain sympathy.

Archer and Burleson (1980) wanted to find out whether people really did give a person credit for confessing a misdeed early. They thought that if people could see a person deciding to answer a question about the misdeed early in an interview rather than late, then people would find the person more attractive. However, researchers also thought that if people knew a person had no control over where in the interview the question about the misdeed occurred, then confessing the misdeed early in the interview would have no effect on how much people liked the person. Only when people thought that a person *chose* to confess a misdeed early in the interview would they give him credit for coming forward.

To test their hypothesis, Archer and Burleson (1980) set up a study in which students at the University of Texas participated in an interview with another student, who was actually a research assistant. The interview was conducted over a closed-circuit television system. People received a list of questions to ask the research assistant. For half the people in the study, the first question on the list was "Has anything bothered you here at the University of Texas?" The research assistant answered by explaining that he had unintentionally gotten his girlfriend pregnant. For the rest of the people in the study, the question "Has anything bothered you. . . ?" was the last question on the list. That way, people in the study knew the research assistant had no choice in when he answered the question. However, he answered it the same way both times by confessing that he had gotten his girlfriend pregnant. Researchers predicted that when the question and the confession came at the end of the interview people would like the person more than they would when the confession came at the beginning of the interview. They were right. People gave the research assistant no credit for confessing his misdeed early in the interview because they knew he had no choice in the timing of the question that prompted the confession. Rather, people liked the research assistant more when he confessed late in the interview. The late confession allowed people more time to form a positive impression of him before they learned about his girlfriend's unwanted pregnancy.

Archer and Burleson (1980) still had to show, however, that people would give the research assistant credit for confessing early if they knew he could *choose* when to answer the question. If people could somehow find out that the research assistant chose to answer the question early in the interview, would they like him more? If people knew he chose to answer the question late in the interview, would they like him less? Because the interview took place over TV, researchers could set up this situation easily. People in the study were seated in a room and watched on TV as the research assistant was seated in another room. As people watched, the research assistant was given the list of questions for the interview and was told to arrange the questions in the order he preferred. People watched as the person put the question "Has anything bothered you here at the University of Texas?" either at the top of the list or at the bottom of the list. Then, people in the study were given the list that the research assistant had arranged so that they could begin the interview. During the interview, when people asked the question "Has anything bothered you . . . ?" the research assistant confessed his responsibility for the unwanted pregnancy. Because people had watched the research assistant choose whether to answer the question first or last, they knew that he had decided where in the interview he would confess. Half the people in the study had watched him choose to confess at the beginning of the interview. The rest of the people in the study watched him choose to wait until the end of the interview to confess.

Now Archer and Burleson (1980) were ready to answer their research question. Would people like the research assistant more when he chose to confess early in the interview than they would when he chose to confess late? Recall that when people knew that the research assistant had no choice in the order of the questions, they gave him no credit for confessing early in the interview. Instead, people liked the research assistant more when he confessed late in the interview. Now researchers were predicting the opposite. They thought that when people knew the research assistant had a choice about when to confess, they would give him credit for confessing early. This would be a surprising reversal of results and a dramatic confirmation of Jones and Gordon's (1972) earlier work.

Indeed, when people saw the research assistant choose to confess early in the interview, they liked him more than they did when they saw him choose to confess later in the interview. That is, they gave him credit for choosing to confess early rather than putting it off until later. Archer and Burleson's (1980) work confirmed Jones and Gordon's (1972) conclusions. Confessing a misdeed early shows strength; people will like you more if you do it early rather than wait until you have made a good impression. In most other cases, however, it is better to wait before telling people about bad things that have happened to you. For example, a misfortune you experienced that was beyond your control should not come up too early in a conversation or a relationship. Otherwise, it might be seen as a ploy to gain sympathy.

Why does self-disclosure increase how much people like us? If we knew this, then we might gain insight into the most appropriate ways to tell people about ourselves. Which details of our lives should we disclose? If we blurt out extremely intimate details to strangers, they may think we have little self-control. In contrast, if we never talk about ourselves, people will think us secretive and untrustworthy.

Jones and Archer (1976) explained that our need to predict whether a person we meet is trustworthy is important.[2] If people think that a person who tells intimate personal details is more trustworthy, then people will feel more comfortable in turn telling about their own difficulties. The resulting exchange of information leads to a relationship based on trust. When two people confide in each other, each has given the other potentially valuable information. It is flattering to receive a valuable gift from someone. Therefore, we like her more. We can use this explanation to predict that people will like a person who self-discloses personal information when that information seems valuable to them.

Taylor, Gould, and Brounstein (1981) wanted to find out whether people would like a person who self-disclosed more because they thought that person found them special in some way. In other words, do people like a person who self-discloses more because they find it flattering to be singled out to share that person's secrets? When a person tells us something really personal about herself, we might think that person finds us special, perhaps trustworthy. If we think another person thinks highly of us, then we are likely to find that person more attractive.

People who participated in Taylor, Gould, and Brounstein's (1981) study conducted a get-acquainted interview with a partner who was actually a research assistant. For half the people in the study, the partner disclosed personal information during the interview. For the rest of the people in the study, the partner did not disclose personal information. As we would now expect from the studies on self-disclosure that we already examined, people liked the partner more when she disclosed intimate details about herself than when she did not. During the study, researchers also gave people information about why their partner had disclosed more personal information. Some of the people in the study found out that their partner had disclosed intimate details about herself because of "something about my partner." That is, people thought that something special about themselves prompted their partner to be especially revealing about herself. Would people find that flattering and like their partner more because of it?

They did. Taylor, Gould, and Brounstein (1981) found that people like their partner best when she disclosed intimate details about herself because of something special she felt for her partner. When people thought their partner self-disclosed for other reasons, they did not like her as much. However, no matter what the reason for the partner's self-disclosure, people always liked the partner more when she disclosed intimate details about herself than they did when she talked about less personal things. Here we see two different impression-management techniques at work. People like us more when they think we find them special. People also like us more when we share intimate details of our lives with them.

It would still help to have an explanation for why people like us more when we tell them intimate details about ourselves. Jones and Archer (1976) thought it was because by telling people about ourselves, we give them valuable information. If that explanation is correct, then people will like us more only when they see the information we give them as valuable. If they place no value on the personal details we disclose, then they will not like us any more than they already did.

---

[2]Similar ideas can be found in Wortman, Adesman, Herman, and Greenberg (1976).

Archer and Cook (1986) set up a situation to test the idea that self-disclosure increases liking because the disclosed information is considered valuable. In Archer and Cook's study, people were to hold a get-acquainted interview similar to earlier research settings that studied self-disclosure. People in the study used a microphone to speak about themselves to a partner in another room. They were told to select topics from a list to talk about and to check off each topic as they mentioned it. After they had finished speaking about themselves, people in the study listened to their partner—a research assistant—talk about herself. Half the people heard the partner disclose intimate details about herself, in particular, her anxiety about having premarital sex with her boyfriend. The rest of the people in the study heard the partner talk about less personal details of her life. She mentioned her boyfriend but did not talk about sex. As in earlier studies, people liked their partner more when she disclosed more intimate details about her relationship with her boyfriend than they did when she talked only about less intimate matters.

This study differed from earlier ones, however, because half the people in the study were given a questionnaire that the partner had filled out for an earlier study. In the questionnaire, people learned that the partner had disclosed the same personal information about her boyfriend to people in the earlier study. The rest of the people in Archer and Cook's (1986) study did not find out that the partner had already revealed the personal information to others before she revealed it to them. Researchers predicted that people would find the partner's information more valuable if it was scarce. That is, when people thought that the partner casually revealed the information to others, people in the study would find the information less valuable than they would if they thought the partner revealed it only to them.

Archer and Cook (1986) then predicted that people would find the partner more attractive when she told only them intimate details of her relationship with her boyfriend. Researchers predicted that people would find the partner less attractive when they found out the partner had also revealed the same intimate information to others. Results of the study supported researchers' predictions. People in the study liked the partner more when she disclosed the personal information only to them. Assuming that scarce information is more valuable, Archer and Cook conclude that part of the reason people find others who self-disclose attractive is because they value the information they have been given. To use self-disclosure for impression management, it is important to tell people intimate details about ourselves that others will appreciate and find useful themselves.

Again we have found that considering another person's point of view is crucial to getting along with people. Recall from Chapter 2 how considering another person's point of view as well as your own is the key to successful social relationships. Blurting out the embarrassing and intimate details of our lives to everyone we meet won't make them like us. That does not mean we should talk only about trivial things. People appreciate someone confiding embarrassing or intimate details when the information might help them solve their own problems. When the personal information you confide can help people solve their own problems, you have given them a valuable gift. They will appreciate how hard it is for you to open up to them about sensitive topics. They will trust you more because of it. They will think you are a stronger person. And if you have the courage to open up to people about yourself, they will like you.

WHAT'S IN IT FOR ME?

OK, people will like us more if we tell them embarrassing things about ourselves. That is not enough reason for most of us to do it. For one thing, we have found that it is important to tell only appropriately embarrassing things at the right time. Self-disclosure is tricky business. Maybe there are more compelling reasons to tell other people the intimate details of our lives. Maybe confession and self-disclosure in general are good for us. One benefit that has already been mentioned is that self-disclosure builds solid and lasting relationships between people. Chapter 9 on intimate relationships will explain the role of self-disclosure in building and maintaining relationships. A more surprising benefit of self-disclosure in general and confession in particular is that people who confide in others are healthier than are people who keep things to themselves. Self-disclosure has physical as well as social benefits.

James Pennebaker at Southern Methodist University has conducted a research program to find out how self-disclosure affects our physical health. Recall from Chapter 4 that Pennebaker's research showed that when people wrote about their most profound emotional experiences, they encountered fewer health problems for several months afterward (Pennebaker, Colder, & Sharp 1990).[3] It turns out that writing about yourself is another form of self-disclosure. By writing about yourself, you are confiding your problems to someone. That someone is you. Self-disclosure can have more profound effects when you confide in someone else.

Pennebaker and O'Heeron (1984) wanted to find out if talking to someone about a tragic event would improve people's physical health. To find people who had recently suffered a tragedy, researchers sought out the spouses of suicide and accidental death victims. This was not an easy study to undertake. It was important that people not be hurt by the study in addition to the loss they had already suffered. Researchers, however, had reason to believe that people would benefit from talking about their lost loved one. That was their reason for conducting the study.

People who had recently suffered the death of a spouse were asked to fill out a questionnaire (Pennebaker & O'Heeron 1984). The questionnaire asked how much people were troubled by obsessive thoughts about their spouse's death. Other questions asked about how much people confided in others as they grieved. The questionnaire included two sets of health questions. One set of health questions asked about diseases and symptoms that people might have experienced *before* their spouse died. A second set asked about diseases and symptoms that people might have experienced *after* their spouse died.

After researchers collected people's answers to the questionnaire, they could compare how much people talked about their tragedy with how much it continued to bother them. That is, Pennebaker and O'Heeron (1984) could find out whether people who talked about their problems were coping with them better. Researchers could also find out whether people who confided in others about their problems were healthier than were people who did not confide in others. Researchers' suspicions about the benefits of confiding in others were supported by the results. The

---

[3] Also see Smyth, Stone, Hurewitz, and Kaell (1999) for a recent study that shows asthma patients improved after writing about their stressful experiences.

more people confided in others about their grief, the less they were troubled by obsessive thoughts. Perhaps more important, the more people confided in others, the healthier they were. That is, people who did not confide in others reported an increase in illness after the death of their spouse. However, people who did confide in others reported much less increase in illness. Telling people about your troubles helps keep you healthy.

While the results of Pennebaker and O'Heeron's (1984) study were exciting, they were not conclusive. Because people in the study were located after the tragedy had occurred, other explanations for the results were possible. For example, maybe naturally healthy people find it easier to confide in others, or have more opportunities to decide than do sick people. Or maybe some people did not remember the health problems they had before the tragedy as well as others did. It is hard to be sure that confiding in others actually makes people healthier. A laboratory study that could gather more complete information would help.

Pennebaker, Hughes, and O'Heeron (1987) brought people into the laboratory to study the physical changes that confession produces. Researchers attached people's hands to a machine that measures small changes in electricity conducted through their skin. When stress is high, as when people are trying to hide something, skin conductance goes up. It makes sense. Sweaty palms conduct electricity better than dry ones do. When people feel less inhibition, when they are not trying to hide something, skin conductance is low. People's hands are dry. After hooking people up to the skin conductance monitor, researchers asked them to talk about the most traumatic or stressful events in their lives. As in all research with people, responses covered a wide range of topics. Some people went into great depth about their troubles. Other people tried to distance themselves from their troubles. They tried to keep it light and talk about trivial things. Researchers recorded changes in the electrical conductance levels as people confessed their troubles.

Pennebaker, Hughes, and O'Heeron (1987) found that when people spoke in depth about the personal effects of stressful events, their skin conductance levels went down. This means they were feeling less stress. In contrast, when people tried to distance themselves from their troubles, for example, when they stuck to trivial topics, their skin conductance levels went up. This means they were feeling more stress. Researchers concluded that confession does have real physiological effects on people. Confiding in others can reduce stress; trying to avoid confiding in others can increase stress. Not only will people like you more and think you are a stronger person if you confide in them, but confiding in people can improve your health.

MORE WAYS TO MANAGE IMPRESSIONS

People use many techniques to change the impressions that others have of them. This chapter has covered smiling, improving our appearance, apologies, and confiding in people as ways to improve the impressions we make on other people. The wide variety of impression management techniques is one reason to think that managing other people's impressions is an important human activity. Some techniques are not only subtle but also surprising.

One reason people help others is to make themselves look better. It is not surprising that people sometimes have less than pure motives for the good things they do. In most cases, what people do is more important than why they do it. Not always. Gilbert and Silvera (1996) thought that in some situations people would help others to make themselves look good but also to make the other person look *bad*. When you see a person rushing to help somebody, you will think more highly of the person who helps. Now think about your impression of the person being helped. Sure, you may be sympathetic. We all need help sometimes. Still, the person being helped appears weaker, less competent, than she did before the help arrived.

When people are competing with each other in some way, as happens in many work situations, making you look incompetent can be a way to make another person look better by comparison. In competitive situations, then, a person might help someone who does not need it to make the person being helped appear less competent. Gilbert and Silvera (1996) thought that human beings are devious enough to try to manage the impressions other people make. One way to make a rival look weak is to help her when she does not need it. A helping strategy also has the advantage of making the helper look strong while making a rival look weak. In a competitive situation, would normal human beings really help someone just to make her look bad?

Gilbert and Silvera (1996) set up a situation that gave people the opportunity to make someone look weak by helping her. People in the study were assigned to help someone solve anagrams, rearranging jumbled letters into a word. To help the person solve the anagram, people could supply the first several letters as a hint. For example, if someone was given the anagram U N I M A O T N, the person helping might provide the hint, M O U _ _ _ _ _. People in the study were allowed to choose how many letters the hint would contain. If people provided only the M, then they would be providing less help than if they provided MOU or MOUNT. By counting up the number of letters that people provided in their hints, researchers could tell how much help they were giving.

Here is the tricky part. Researchers predicted that if people want to make someone look bad, they will help her more when she *does not* need it. The idea is that helping people when they do not need it robs them of the credit they deserve. Observers would think the person succeeded not because she was competent, but because she had help. In contrast, if people want to make someone look good, they will help her more when she *does* need it. Observers would give her some credit for success on a task that she might have failed without help. Would people try to make a person look bad by helping her more when she did not need it?

To find out, Gilbert and Silvera (1996) first gave people an anagram task to find out who was really good at anagrams and who was not. Researchers picked a few of the best anagram solvers to get help as well as a few people with normal anagram ability. The rest of the people in the study would be helpers. Then the people who were to get help, the anagram whizzes and the anagram plodders, were given new sets of anagrams to solve. The rest of the people in the study, who were going to help, got the answers to the anagrams in advance. The helpers also knew which people being helped were quite good at anagrams (whizzes) and which people being helped were not so good at anagrams (plodders). Now the situation was set up so that people had the opportunity to help a person succeed. A whiz would not need much help to succeed but a plodder would need more help.

Researchers told helpers that the anagram test was being used to determine whether the person being helped received a job in a later study. The helpers' hints and the person's answers to the anagrams would be reviewed later by a person who would decide whether the person who solved the anagrams was suitable for the job. Thus helpers knew that how much help they gave could make a difference in how competent the anagram solver looked. Researchers predicted that when people were trying to *help* someone get a job, they would help more if the person was a plodder who needed more help. In contrast, researchers predicted that when people were trying to hinder someone from getting a job, they would help more if the person was a whiz who needed less help. People would actually provide more help to a person to try to make her look bad. Surprising but true—people did just that.

Gilbert and Silvera (1996) asked half of the helpers to do their best to *help* the anagram solver get the job. As researchers predicted, helpers gave more help to plodders who needed it than people gave to whizzes who did not need it. That is, people realized that helping someone who might fail made her appear more competent. The person would succeed where she otherwise might have failed. However, helping someone who would succeed on her own made her appear less competent. The person succeeded anyway, but an outside observer might think she succeeded because she got help, not because she was competent. Exactly the opposite occurred when researchers asked the rest of the helpers to do their best to *prevent* the anagram solver from getting the job. As we would expect, helpers provided few letters as clues to the anagrams to plodders who needed the help to succeed. A good way to make someone look bad is not to help. However, an indicator of how devious human beings can be is that helpers gave more letters as clues to whizzes who did not need the help. When people wanted to make the anagram solver look bad, they helped *more* when she did not need it.

Helping someone who does not need it is one way people try to make a person look bad. You can now look at the behavior of your coworkers in a new light. Why are they helping you? By helping, are they trying to make you look good or bad? More important, does it work? Gilbert and Silvera (1996) also found that observers who rated the ability of whizzes found them to be less competent when they received more help. Not only is helping a person who does not need it a strategy that people use to make a person look bad, but it also works.

While people regularly attempt to manage the impression they make on the people around them, they usually do not try to make other people look bad. Human beings are devious but rarely malicious. One way to excuse a poor performance is to make another person look exceptionally competent. That is, people sometimes help others win at their own expense. By helping somebody else win, a person can justify losing without having to admit he is incompetent. This strategy is similar to self-handicapping (Berglas & Jones 1978). Recall from Chapter 2 that people, especially men, sometimes do things that increase the chance of their own failure. Such self-handicapping explains a poor performance without a person having to question his own ability. For example, I inadvertently drank too much brandy the night before taking the Scholastic Aptitude Test (SAT) when I was applying to college. My drinking would explain a poor score, leaving intact my belief in my academic ability. One way to excuse losing is to help your competitor win. By helping your competitor beat you, you appear to be a good sport and you look less incompetent when you lose. Should you win despite helping your opponent, you will appear even more competent.

Shepperd and Arkin (1991) set up a situation to find out if people really would help another person win, even if it meant they would lose. The earlier self-handicapping study had found that men self-handicapped more than women did. That is, men were more likely than were women to create a reason to do poorly. Shepperd and Arkin also wanted to find out if men, more than women, would try to help other people outscore them. For the study, researchers brought people into the laboratory to see how well they would do on a new test of mental ability. People in the study were told that their performance on the test would be compared with the performance of another person who would be taking the test at the same time. Because test scores of two people were being compared, people were in competition with each other. Most people would want to outscore the other person taking the test with them. Then researchers let people choose the kind of music their *partner* would listen to while taking the test. People were given the choice of five kinds of music. One of the musical selections was said to help people a great deal when taking tests. Another was said to help people only a little. One musical selection was said to have no effect on test taking. Another was said to interfere somewhat with test taking. The last selection was said to interfere a great deal with test taking. If you were in competition with someone taking a test, which kind of music would you select for your rival to listen to during the test? Would you select music that would make the other person do better or worse?

Researchers gave people little time to think about which kind of music to pick for their partners to listen to during the test. Thus, people did not have time to consider what was fair or proper before making a choice. They had to go by what felt right to them at the moment. Shepperd and Arkin (1991) predicted that people, especially men, would pick music that they thought would increase the test score of their rival. That is, men would give their opponent an advantage that would increase their own chances of losing. For men, the prediction was correct. When men were in competition with another person, they more often picked music that would increase their rival's performance than they did when they were not in competition with the person. Women, however, did not try to give their rival an advantage. Women more often picked music for the other person that would decrease performance. It seems that men will actually help a rival outscore them in order to look less incompetent when they lose. Why men but not women behave in such a peculiar way is still a mystery.

This chapter has described a variety of ways in which people try to influence the way other people think about them. Some are basic to all people. Babies smile so that people will find them attractive and help them survive. Adults do the same thing. By making ourselves attractive to other people, we get them to listen to us, to consider our needs. Impression management is a major human activity. Human beings are social animals. Whenever people have to get along with the people around them, they try to manage the impressions that others have of them. How can I make myself more attractive? How can I make people like me? How can I make people think I am competent? These are questions that concern all people who are not isolated or mentally disturbed. It is not a simple matter of vanity or self-promotion.

Further Reading

Of General Interest

Hatfield, E., & Sprecher, S. (1986). *Mirror, mirror . . . : The importance of looks in everyday life.* Albany: State University of New York Press.

Leary, M. (1995). *Self-presentation: Impression management and interpersonal behavior.* Boulder, CO: Westview.

Pennebaker, J. W. (1990). *Opening up: The healing power of confiding in others.* New York: Morrow.

Recent and Technical Issues

Baumeister, R. F., & Cairns, K. J. (1992). Repression and self-presentation: When audiences interfere with self-deceptive strategies. *Journal of Personality and Social Psychology, 62,* 851–862.

Chaiken, S., & Maheswaran, D. (1994). Heuristic processing can bias systematic processing: Effects of source credibility, argument ambiguity, and task importance on attitude judgment. *Journal of Personality and Social Psychology, 66,* 460–473.

Cialdini, R. B., & De Nicholas, M. E. (1989). Self-presentation by association. *Journal of Personality and Social Psychology, 57,* 626–631.

Gilbert, D. T., & Jones, E. E. (1986). Exemplification: The self-presentation of moral character. *Journal of Personality, 54,* 593–615.

Gonzales, M. H., Pederson, J. H., Manning, D. J., Wetter, D. W. (1990). Pardon my gaffe: Effects of sex, status, and consequence severity on accounts. *Journal of Personality and Social Psychology, 58,* 610–621.

Graziano, W. G., Jensen-Campbell, L. A., Shebilske, L. J., & Lundgren, S. R. (1993). Social influence, sex differences, and judgments of beauty: Putting the *interpersonal* back in interpersonal attraction. *Journal of Personality and Social Psychology, 65,* 522–531.

Hodgins, H. S., Liebeskind, E., & Schwartz, W. (1996). Getting out of hot water: Facework in social predicaments. *Journal of Personality and Social Psychology, 71,* 300–314.

Mikulincer, M., & Nachshon, O. (1991). Attachment styles and patterns of self-disclosure. *Journal of Personality and Social Psychology, 61,* 321–334.

Mori, D. A., Chaiken, S., & Pliner, P. (1987). "Eating lightly" and the self-presentation of femininity. *Journal of Personality and Social Psychology, 53,* 693–702.

Pegalis, L. J., Shaffer, D. R., Bazzini, D. G., & Greenier, K. (1994). On the ability to elicit self-disclosure: Are there gender-based and contextual limitations on the opener effect? *Personality and Social Psychology Bulletin, 20,* 412–420.

Rhodewalt, F., & Agustsdottir, S. (1986). Effects of self-presentation on the phenomenal self. *Journal of Personality and Social Psychology, 50,* 47–55.

Shaffer, D. R., & Ogden, J. K. (1986). On sex differences in self-disclosure during the acquaintance process: The role of anticipated future interaction. *Journal of Personality and Social Psychology, 51,* 92–101.

CHAPTER 6

Persuasion: What Will It Take to Convince You?

This chapter, like Chapter 5, is about influence. How do you convince people to do what you think is right? We have seen that convincing people is easier if they like us and think us competent. However, after we have made the best possible impression on a person, we still have to present an argument. We have to persuade them. Social psychology can show us how to be more persuasive.

In school you have already learned how to argue logically. Most people think highly of logic. Yet logic and persuasion are distinct skills. The most logical argument you can make will need help to be persuasive.

No matter how highly we value logic, we are seldom as logical as we would like to be. Recent studies of how our brains work show that human logic is effective only when coupled with an emotional response. When we make a decision, the best we can do is to use logic to carefully weigh the alternatives, then decide on the course of action that feels best to us. Without that emotional tiebreaker, the feeling that one course of action is better, there is rarely strong enough evidence on one side or the other to allow us to make a confident decision (Damasio 1994).

Curiously, the more important and difficult the task, the more we rely on the opinions of others rather than on logic. Persuasion becomes more important when the stakes are high. That is why salespeople who deal with major transactions involving large amounts of money earn high commissions and salaries, whereas retail sales clerks often earn little more than the minimum wage. I can be reasonably logical in deciding which brand of vitamins to buy. I read the labels and choose the brand that gives me the vitamins I need at a reasonable cost. Buying a house or a car or a business is different. It has to feel right. Salespeople who make customers feel comfortable are much more likely to successfully close an important sale.

Baron, Vandello, and Brunsman (1996) studied how easily people are persuaded to make a wrong choice. Researchers set up a situation in which people tried to find the correct answer to a problem while other people suggested the wrong answer. When would people be able to ignore the bad advice and give the correct answer? Sometimes the problem was easy to solve and people could be confident that their choice was probably correct. Other times, the problem was difficult and people were uncertain about their choice. Researchers also made getting the correct answer more or less important to people. For example, some people in the study were offered a substantial amount of money for getting the right answers while others were simply asked to see how well they could do. When the outcome was important to people, would they be able to ignore bad advice, or would they be persuaded to make the wrong decision?

As we might expect, people more often were persuaded to make the wrong decision when the choice was difficult. The less certain we are that an answer is correct, the more likely we are to rely on the advice of others, even if they are wrong. Baron, Vandello, and Brunsman (1996), however, had made more interesting predictions about the effect of important decisions on people's ability to ignore bad advice. They predicted that when a decision was easy but important, people would make the right decision, ignoring the bad advice they were given. In contrast, they would more frequently make the wrong decision when it was easy but less important. This makes sense. When a decision is unimportant, people may let themselves be persuaded because going along is easier than resisting, and a wrong decision costs them little. But researchers thought that the opposite would occur when the decision was difficult, when people were less certain that they were correct. Researchers predicted that for difficult decisions, people would be persuaded more easily to make the wrong choice when the outcome was important to them.

Baron, Vandello, and Brunsman (1996) showed people a photograph of a man then later asked them if they could pick him out of a photo lineup composed of several men. Half the people in the study were shown a photo lineup in which the men looked very different from each other, making it easy to pick out the man they had seen earlier. The rest of the people in the study were shown a photo lineup of men who looked nearly identical, making a correct identification difficult. Before people made their decision about the photo lineup, they watched as two research assistants made the wrong choice. Would people be able to resist the influence of two others who were suggesting the wrong answer?

They could when the task was easy but also important. People made the most accurate identifications when they could easily identify the man they had seen earlier and when they had a large incentive to get the correct answer. But, just as Barron, Vandello, and Brunsman (1996) had predicted, people made the least accurate identifications when identifying the man was difficult and they had a large incentive to get the correct answer. That is, people were more easily persuaded by the research assistants to make the wrong decision when the decision was both difficult and important.

Persuasion counts. When the decision to be made is both difficult and important, persuasion counts more than logic. How do we protect ourselves from people who try to persuade us to make a wrong decision? Only with difficulty. Gilbert, Tafarodi, and Malone (1993) found that we initially accept what others tell us even when we should realize it is false. Then, if we have the time and inclination to be skeptical, we can sometimes succeed in overcoming our initial acceptance and reject the false information.

One way that we protect ourselves against the bad advice is by considering the person trying to persuade us. We like to know why people are trying to persuade us to do something before we make our decision. In particular, we look for evidence of bias, for some reason that a person might be trying to persuade us to do something that is in her interest rather than our own.

When a person gives us advice, the position she is in makes a difference in how persuasive she will be. For example, when a used-car salesperson suggests we buy a car because the previous owners were an elderly couple who only drove it to the grocery store once a week, we are skeptical. We hesitate to go along with the suggestions of the used-car salesperson because we know that her interests conflict with our own in important ways. Certainly, the salesperson would not mind if she sold us the best possible car. However, more important to her is selling us a car at the highest possible price. The more she charges for a car, the higher her commission from the sale. Her position as a car salesperson, not her personal character, makes persuading a customer a difficult challenge. That is why good automobile salespeople are well paid. They manage to convince a large proportion of skeptical shoppers to buy cars from them.

A doctor is in a different position when we go to her for advice. Suppose you have been feeling a little discomfort after eating a heavy meal, so you go to the doctor. After examining you, she suggests surgery to remove your gall bladder. On the surface, the doctor's job seems more difficult than the car salesperson. You consulted the doctor for an upset stomach and she suggests major surgery involving weeks of recovery and considerable pain, something you usually try to avoid. In contrast, the car salesperson suggests that you buy a car you may actually want. Yet most people would accept the doctor's diagnosis and go ahead with the surgery. Few patients take it upon themselves to ask for a second opinion before surgery. Most car shoppers would do at least a little checking before accepting the advice of a car salesperson.

A doctor more readily persuades us than does a salesperson because we do not expect the doctor's interests to conflict with our own. Usually, the doctor who diagnoses our troubled gall bladder is not the surgeon who will charge thousands of dollars to remove it. We do not expect doctors to be motivated by the money our illness may bring in. Sometimes doctors and other professionals betray our trust in their motives. What if you found out that the doctor who recommended gall bladder surgery was trying to patent a new gall bladder removal procedure that would make her millions of dollars? You would be more skeptical of her advice because you see that the doctor's interests do conflict with your own in an important way. She wants to see the new procedure proven effective as quickly as possible. To do that, she needs a lot of gall bladder patients. Maybe your gall bladder is really OK. Generally, however, we expect doctors to have our interests in mind when they suggest a medical procedure. Thus doctors easily persuade patients to undergo unpleasant treatment while car salespeople have difficulty persuading people to buy a car they really want.

THE UNEXPECTED IS CONVINCING

When we are trying to persuade people to do something that helps us, we are in the same position as the car salesperson. Because we are pushing a course of action that benefits us, the person we are trying to persuade expects us to exaggerate the benefits and minimize the costs of our proposal. Sudden evidence that those expectations are wrong can be highly persuasive. The more skeptical a person is, the more surprising and effective the result. When a person you are trying to persuade expects you to be biased in favor of the proposal, show her that you are not.

For example, suppose you are due for a promotion at your company from middle management to the executive level. However, there has been a recent downturn in business. Cutbacks are necessary. You realize that everybody will have to give up something. Factory workers will be laid off. There will be a hiring freeze. Maybe some managers will be let go as well. Your boss asks you for recommendations. Most people would take the opportunity to argue strongly against cuts in their own department. They would try to show how vital their contributions are to continued company success and so their own department should be spared. That is, most people would argue for their own interests, as expected. They would not be very persuasive. Instead, you could do the unexpected. You might advocate canceling bonuses for middle managers, your own included. Your credibility would increase because you had taken an unexpected position. Your ability to persuade your boss will have increased as well. True, you might not get a bonus because of it, but your chance of getting that promotion goes way up.

Have you noticed that a good car salesperson will tell you which car *not* to buy? I went shopping for a used car recently. The salesperson at the lot where I eventually bought a car was showing me around. I told him that I wanted a car that was big enough for the kids but did not cost very much because it would mostly be used to drive to work. He showed me several cars that were too expensive. So far, he had confirmed my expectations. His interests conflicted with mine. I wanted inexpensive transportation, he wanted a big commission on an expensive car with a high profit margin. We continued to stroll around the lot looking at cars. I noticed one that was marked with a special sale price on the windshield. When I asked him about it, he told me that he would not sell me that car. It had engine problems. Despite the low price, it was not a good deal. Suddenly, his advice seemed more credible. He had violated my expectations. I expected him to try to sell me the car I was interested in. He need not have told me about the engine, but he did. He had dramatically disconfirmed my expectations that he was only out to make a sale. It seemed to me that maybe he did care that I found a good car at a reasonable price. By apparently arguing against his own self-interest, he had increased his ability to persuade me.

Wendy Wood and Alice Eagly (1981) demonstrated the persuasiveness of someone unexpectedly arguing against the position he had been expected to take. Researchers proposed that when a person assumed to be biased toward a position argues against that position, he demonstrates that the assumption of bias is false. Therefore, he becomes more persuasive because he appears to be an unbiased source of advice.

Wood and Eagly (1981) set up a situation in which a person conveying a persuasive message either confirmed or disconfirmed the assumptions that people held about his views on restricting access to pornography. Half the participants in the study learned that a man had previously advocated unlimited free speech. The rest of the participants learned that the man had previously advocated restrictions on free speech for the public good. Participants were also divided into two groups based on whether they favored restricting pornography. Those who favored restricting pornography then listened to the man try to persuade them that unrestricted access to pornography was best. Those who opposed restricting pornography listened to the man try to persuade them that restricted access to pornography for the public good was best. Thus all participants listened to a man argue for a position that they opposed. Half of them had expected him to oppose their position. The rest were surprised because they thought the man would agree with them but he instead opposed their position. Researchers predicted that the man would be more persuasive when his opposition was unexpected and that he would appear less biased.

When the man's opposition was unexpected, would the information he provided be more convincing? It was. After the man argued against people's position on pornography, Wood and Eagly (1981) measured their opinions on the issue again. Participants changed their opinions more to agree with the man when his opposition to them was unexpected than when they assumed from the beginning that he would hold views opposite their own. Also as researchers had predicted, when the man's opposition to them was unexpected, participants rated him as less biased. By disconfirming people's preconceived ideas about his position, the man demonstrated that he was unbiased. Thus people were more willing to accept as true the information that he provided.

We expect people to push for whatever will do them the most good. Sometimes, however, people put aside their own needs to help others or to promote group goals. Still, the expectation is strong that people will put their own needs first. Thus it is surprising when a person argues against her own self-interest and in favor of the group's interest. As Wood and Eagly's (1981) research showed, one way to make yourself more persuasive is to advocate the unexpected. People will expect you to be biased toward what helps you. Surprise them by putting aside your own needs. Not only will you be more persuasive, but your status in the group will rise as well. Chapter 4 showed how our status in a group is based on how much others expect us to contribute to group goals. That is, we become personally successful by helping other people succeed rather than by focusing on personal success. As paradoxical as it sounds, my problems are none of my business. Chapter 7, "Your Place in the Workplace," shows how to effectively promote your personal goals by focusing on group success rather than personal success.

FEELING GOOD HELPS

Children usually realize that it is easier to persuade a person who is in a good mood. When you were young, would you try to gauge your parents' mood before asking for money? You had probably figured out that when your parents were happy, they were easier for you to persuade. Salespeople often tell jokes to try to get customers in a good mood. Taking clients out for a good meal has a similar effect. Baron (1990) found that people were easier to persuade when he put them in a good mood using a pleasant scent. Apparently, money spent on perfume is not wasted.

Forgas (1998) took that idea one step farther. He predicted that negotiators would be more effective bargainers and produce better outcomes when they, as well as the person they were trying to convince, were in a good mood. Forgas proposed that when negotiators were in a good mood, they would be more cooperative and avoid conflict. The result would be outcomes beneficial to both sides. People were brought into the laboratory and placed in either a positive or negative mood. They were either criticized or praised for their performance on a short test. Then they negotiated in groups over which new courses to add to a psychology department's schedule. Those who were criticized for their test performance reported being less happy and more sad than did those praised for their test performance. Also, happy people used more cooperative and less competitive negotiating strategies than did sad people, just as Forgas had predicted. Happy people were also more successful at getting their ideas accepted by the group.

Recall from Chapter 4 how effective optimism is for producing positive outcomes in many social situations. Maintaining a positive mood is important for success in many work and social situations.

FAST TALKING

The fast-talking salesperson is a cliché. But is fast talk more persuasive than slow talk? Why talking fast should be more persuasive than talking at a normal rate is not entirely clear. It might be more difficult to understand what is being said if a person is talking too fast. Also, fast talk is commonly associated with people like car salespeople who are considered untrustworthy. In contrast, the ability to speak rapidly and fluently is highly valued. Those who speak rapidly and fluently are demonstrating high ability. Also, rapid speech can give the impression that the speaker is knowledgeable, that pauses and hesitation are unnecessary. Thus there are good arguments that fast talk should increase persuasiveness and equally good arguments that it should not.

Miller, Maruyama, Beaber, and Valone (1976) decided to find out whether fast speech is more persuasive than slower speech. They proposed that fast speech increased persuasiveness by increasing both the credibility and perceived knowledge of the speaker. Thus despite that fact that fast talkers have a reputation for low credibility, researchers predicted that fast talk would nonetheless increase credibility and persuasiveness.

Research assistants asked people in shopping malls to listen to a short audiotape and give their opinions on the topic for a local college radio station. In the first study, people listened to an audiotape that warned of the dangers of coffee drinking. The research assistants randomly assigned each person to listen to either a fast version of the talk on the dangers of coffee drinking or a slower version. Then people were asked for their own opinions about coffee drinking. Because the research assistants had selected people to listen to the fast-speech or slow-speech tape completely by chance, individual differences in preference for coffee drinking would be similar in the fast-speech and slow-speech groups. Just as researchers had predicted, people who listened to the fast-speech version of the tape agreed about the dangers of coffee drinking more than did those who listened to the slow-speech version (Miller et al. 1976). Not only was the fast-speech version of the tape more persuasive in convincing people of the dangers of coffee drinking, but people who listened to the fast-speech version rated the speaker as more knowledgeable.

Miller and colleagues (1976) conducted a second study to directly test whether fast speech increased persuasiveness by increasing the speaker's credibility. An alternative explanation would be that fast speech is persuasive because it interferes with a listener's ability to argue against the position. Information is simply coming in too fast to be adequately countered. For the second study, the speech on the audiotape was either fast or slow, as it had been before. It could also be more or less complicated. In one version, the speech used a more complicated argument and sentence structure. In another version, the speech was simpler. Researchers predicted that the complicated argument would make it difficult for a listener to argue against the message whether it was delivered fast or slow. In contrast, a simple argument would be easier to understand and argue against when delivered slow, but difficult to argue against when delivered fast. Thus the simple argument would be more persuasive when spoken quickly. However, the complicated argument would be equally persuasive when spoken fast or slow.

Again, results supported researchers' predictions that fast talk increased the speaker's persuasiveness by making him appear more credible. For both the complicated and simple versions of the tape, listeners were more persuaded when the argument was delivered quickly. In addition, listeners rated the fast talker as more intelligent, more knowledgeable, and more objective than they rated the slow talker. Thus any difficulty in understanding rapid speech is more than offset by the positive impression it gives of the speaker. People associate rapid speech with a wide variety of positive personal characteristics. If you want people to think you are intelligent, knowledgeable, and objective, speak rapidly and fluently.

CAN QUESTIONS LEAD?

In courtroom dramas on TV, attorneys often object if the opposing counsel asks a leading question. Why? What exactly is a leading question? Does it really have so much persuasive power that asking a leading question in a courtroom is taking unfair advantage?

When you ask a leading question, you want the question to imply the answer you desire. That is, the question itself is used as a form of persuasion. It is a subtle way to argue your position, so subtle that people can change their minds before they realize that they have done so. Then, once people have answered the leading question, they have committed themselves to a particular position. Once committed, people are reluctant to appear inconsistent by changing their minds. The leading question gains people's agreement without their ever having to make a conscious decision.

Salespeople make good use of leading questions. Buying a roomful of furniture is a major purchase, a big decision. Many shoppers are understandably reluctant to make the final decision to spend several thousand dollars on furniture they will have

live with for at least a few years. They ask themselves if they can afford it, will it
t, do the colors clash, what will their mother think? The salesperson, waiting im-
patiently, wants to hurry the process along. What can she do? She probably wants to
say "So buy it already. It's just a sofa." But that would not help. Instead she asks a
leading question: "How soon would you need your furniture delivered?" The customer might answer "Right away" or "Not for a few months, until we move into our
new house." Either answer serves the salesperson's purpose. The question assumes
that the customer will need the store's delivery service. That is true only after the
customer buys the furniture. By answering the question, the customer implies that
she will go ahead with the purchase. The question helps push her into a decision
that she had been uncertain about until she answered it.

If the salesperson were really good, she would have already found out that the
customer was in a hurry to get the furniture, before the salesperson asked the question about delivery. Then she would have checked to make sure there was an open
slot in the delivery schedule that afternoon and that the customer's furniture was in
stock. Armed with that information, the salesperson casually asks her leading question: "Oh, by the way, how soon would you need your furniture delivered?" When
the customer answers "Right away," the salesperson immediately replies: "I think
there is one opening left on today's schedule. Would you like your furniture this afternoon?" At that point, pressure on the customer is all but overwhelming. However, in most cases, the customer will not be aware of any sales pressure at all. The
salesperson has only asked a casual question about delivery and tried to be helpful.
But the salesperson's leading question triggered the internal pressure felt by the
customer. She is aware of how much she wants furniture for her bare apartment.
She can see how beautiful her home would look with the new furniture. She needs
it right away. And the salesperson has just made it all possible today. Few customers
could say *no* in such a situation.

Not only can leading questions be used to persuade the person who answers
them, but leading questions also persuade people who watch someone else answer
them. Members of a jury, for example, might be persuaded by a lawyer's leading
question instead of the evidence. That is why leading questions are forbidden in
courtrooms. A person accused of burglary might take the stand in his own defense.
On cross-examination, the prosecuting attorney might try to ask the leading question, "How many houses have you robbed?" Or the classic, "When did you last rob
a house?" A good defense attorney would immediately object to the prosecutor
"leading the witness." Those are leading questions because they assume that the defendant has robbed houses. Even if the defendant denies robbing any house, the
jury is left with the impression that the prosecutor knows that the defendant has
robbed at least one or two. The prosecutor, then, has used a question to testify
against the defendant, something that a lawyer is not allowed to do. Only witnesses
can testify in court.

To investigate the power of leading questions to persuade, Swann, Giuliano,
and Wegner (1982) proposed two ways in which leading questions can persuade
people who watch another person answering the questions. First, the question itself
suggests the answer desired by the person who asks it. People watching might use
the question itself as evidence. Second, the person who answers the question with-

out thinking it through may give the desired answer, providing further evidence to people watching. That is, leading questions might be persuasive in themselves. Or leading questions might persuade because of the answers that are given to them.

Swann, Giuliano, and Wegner (1982) set up a situation to determine whether leading questions were persuasive in themselves or required the answers in order for them to be persuasive. Researchers brought people into the laboratory and asked them to watch an interview between two research assistants. One research assistant asked the other a series of questions about how introverted or extroverted she was. Half the people in the study watched while the research assistant asked the other only about her introversion. For example, "In what situations do you wish you were more outgoing?" and "Tell me about some time when you were left out of some social group. How did you handle these feelings?" The rest of the people in the study saw the research assistant asking only about extroversion. For example, "What would you do if you wanted to liven things up at a party?" and "In what situations are you most talkative?"

The questions were leading because they asked only about either introversion or extroversion. People watching the conversation might think that the person asking the questions knew something about the other's personality and so asked questions to confirm that knowledge. That is, people watching might assume that the person being asked questions about introversion was actually more introverted, and that the person being asked about extroversion was actually more extroverted. Notice, too, that examples of either introverted or extroverted behavior are easy for most people to recall. So most people's answers to the questions would probably make them appear to be more introverted or extroverted than they really were. Had the same person been asked a balanced set of questions about both introversion and extroversion, then a more accurate picture of that person's personality would emerge. Researchers wanted to know whether both the leading questions and their answers were necessary to persuade or whether the leading questions alone could convince people.

Swann, Giuliano, and Wegner (1982) then set up the situation so that some of the people heard only the leading questions that were asked but not the answers given to them. Others heard both the leading questions and the answers. Then people rated the personality of the person who answered the questions. For example, people judged whether the person was more talkative or quiet and more shy or outgoing. How would people judge the research assistant when she was asked only about extroversion? Would they judge her as more extroverted? Would they judge her as more introverted when she had been asked only about introversion? Would it matter whether people heard both the questions and the answers, or would the leading questions alone be enough to persuade?

Leading questions were found to be powerfully persuasive. People who watched the research assistant being asked only about introversion judged her to be a basically shy, introverted person. People who watched the research assistant being asked only about extroversion judged her to be a basically outgoing, extroverted person (Swann, Giuliano, & Wegner 1982). Researchers also found that it was the leading questions themselves that persuaded people. It made little difference whether people heard only the questions or both the questions and the answers.

ey judged her personality based only on the questions she was asked, whether or
ot they heard her answers. Because people apparently use leading questions themselves as evidence, the rule against using leading questions in court has a solid basis in social psychological research.

PERSUASION BY INCHES

Have you noticed that big building projects always seem to cost much more than
was originally estimated? No matter how high the original estimate, the project almost always ends up costing millions, sometimes billions of dollars more. It is not
that accurate estimates are too difficult to make. If accuracy were the problem, then
the original estimate would be too high only about half the time and too low the
rest. The error here is too one-sided to be accidental. Taxpayers, certainly, do not
like having to pay additional billions of dollars for a new highway. Yet contractors
continue to give low estimates then ask for increases along the way. No matter how
annoyed people get, the practice continues. Social psychology explains why.

An initially low estimate is a powerful persuasive tool, whether you are buying
a car or the government is buying a highway. When people are shopping for a car,
they are often strongly attracted to one more expensive than they can easily afford.
The salesperson's job is to persuade them to buy a car that will strain but not break
their financial resources. Suppose you are shopping for a car. You have made a firm
resolution to spend no more than $12,000. At one dealership, however, you are at-
tracted to one that costs $16,000. You realize this is out of your price range and start
to move on. At that point, salespeople are taught to ask, "Would you be interested if
I could get the price of this car down to $10,900?"

There are two reasons for the salesperson's question. First, notice that it is a
leading question. He did not say that he could get the price reduced by $5,000. He
only asked if you would be interested. However, by asking the leading question, he
implied that a price of $10,900 was at least possible. Second, you would probably
answer yes to the question. (A good salesperson would already have found out that
it was in your price range.) Once you agree that you are interested in that car at that
price, you have made a commitment. We are all taught to keep our commitments. It
is difficult for people to stop and reverse themselves once they have started something. By agreeing that you would be interested, you committed yourself in a small
way to buying that car. If the salesperson is good at his job, then you will buy that
car and be happy with it, but the price you pay will be closer to $16,000 than it will
be to $10,900. Had the salesperson accurately estimated that you might be able to
buy the car for $14,900, you would not have been interested. To the salesperson's
credit, you probably like your new car more than any you could have found for less
than $12,000. On the other hand, your financial situation may be shaky for a while
because of it.

Cialdini, Cacioppo, Bassett, and Miller (1978) investigated why giving a very
low initial cost estimate is such a persuasive technique. Researchers called people
on the phone to ask them to participate in a psychology study. Half of the people
were told immediately that the study would take place at 7 A.M. The early hour

made it unlikely that many people would agree to participate. The rest of the people were told about the study and that it would take place at a variety of times during the day. Then all of the people in the study were asked if they would like to participate first. Only after people said that they were interested in participating were they told that they would be needed at the 7 A.M. session of the study. Researchers wanted to know if getting people to agree that they were interested in the study first, before they knew how early they would have to arrive, would increase the number who eventually showed up for a 7 A.M. study.

Cialdini and colleagues (1978) showed that giving a low initial cost estimate effectively persuaded people to participate in their study. When researchers told subjects up front that the study would take place at 7 A.M., less than a third (31 percent) agreed to participate. However, when researchers got people to agree that they were interested in participating before telling them what time the study would take place, more than half (56 percent) agreed to participate. But would more people really show up for the study after having had a chance to consider their decision? Saying yes on the phone is one thing. But if people actually get out of bed in the morning to come to a study, then they really must have been persuaded. Cialdini and colleagues found that giving a low initial cost estimate was even more effective when it came to changing people's actual behavior. When researchers forthrightly told people about the 7 A.M. study time, less than a quarter (only 24 percent) actually showed up for the study. However, when researchers got people to agree that they were interested before telling them about the early starting time, more than half (53 percent) showed up on time. Almost all of those who agreed to participate actually appeared. Once we commit in even a small way to participating in a project, we are unlikely to drop out, even if the cost of continuing increases dramatically along the way.

MENTIONING A LITTLE TO GET A LOT

Charitable organizations that solicit contributions face an interesting dilemma. If they ask for large amounts of money from people, then more people will say no. However, if solicitors ask for small amounts, more people will say yes, but rarely will large amounts be given. How can solicitors convince as many people as possible to contribute without decreasing the average amount that each person gives?

Cialdini and Schroeder (1976) found a solution to the problem faced by charitable organizations that required adding only five words to the end of a request for a contribution: "Even a penny will help." In their study, research assistants solicited funds for the American Cancer Society. All used a standard request for funds: "Would you be willing to help by giving a donation?" However, half the research assistants added the sentence "Even a penny will help." Almost twice as many people contributed when they were told that even a penny would help. More surprisingly, their contributions were no smaller than the contributions given by those who were not told that a penny would help. Researchers concluded that mentioning the penny legitimized a small donation, making it more difficult for people to say no.

However, because the amount suggested—a penny—was so small, people did not use it to estimate the size of a reasonable donation.

WHO WILL HELP YOU?

Most people realize that if you want people to help you, it is good to help them. The practice of giving and receiving gifts is universal in human culture. From a very young age, we learn to give things to people in the hope that we will get something else in return. We have no guarantee that the people we give gifts to will give us gifts in return, or give us gifts of equal value. However, we are all taught that giving gifts is a good thing and that we should not keep too close an account of who gives us what in return. The idea is that by giving gifts we start to form lasting relationships with people. For example, in my large extended family, it would not be practical for everyone to give everyone else a Christmas present. We would all be broke and spend the whole year shopping. Instead, we draw names and everyone gives one other person a gift. I give my aunt a scarf. My nephew gives me a sweater. Almost no one gets a gift from the person to whom she or he gave one. Nonetheless, gift giving works to maintain good relationships among people. Although I do not see my relatives often, I feel comfortable asking for help from my aunt or nephew when I need it. A good way to persuade people to help you is to start by giving them a gift, doing them a favor, providing some small service.

Salespeople and charitable organizations know something more surprising about giving gifts and doing favors. Another good way to persuade people to help you in the future is to get them to do you a small favor first. This is the opposite of how we are taught the social world works. We grow up thinking that we can expect about as much help from other people as we are willing to give in return. If someone does us a favor, then that person should be less likely to do us another favor right away. It is as if we have withdrawn some of our credit in the goodwill bank account. We will not be eligible for another favor until we make a deposit by helping someone else. But there are good social psychological reasons to continue helping someone we have already helped.

Recall from a previous section that once people commit to a project, they are likely to continue with it although the cost involved inches steadily upward. We feel the same way about people, but to a greater degree. It is important to us to keep and maintain our personal relationships. So once we have committed to helping a person, we are likely to agree to help the next time we are asked. We will continue to help even though the second favor requested of us is bigger than the first. Have you noticed that if you send a small donation to a charitable organization, they will send you requests for more money every couple of months? The more money that you give, the bigger and more frequent are the requests that follow. Aren't charities worried that they will wear out donors with repeated, escalating requests for money? Apparently not.

Freedman and Fraser (1966) showed that by getting a person to do you a small favor first, you increase the chance that she will do you a bigger favor later. To test this surprising idea, researchers contacted people by telephone. Researchers wanted to find out how many people would agree to a big favor that researchers would ask of them. Researchers requested that they be allowed to enter people's homes and for several hours catalog their personal belongings. Most people would be hesitant to grant such a request over the phone. Half the people contacted were first asked for a small favor. Researchers asked people merely to answer a few questions for a consumer survey. Then, three days later, researchers called back with the big request. The rest of the people in the survey were only asked if they would agree to the big favor, allowing researchers to come to their homes and make a list of their possessions. Would more people agree to let researchers come into their houses after they had first agreed to the small favor of answering a few survey questions?

Getting people to agree to doing a small favor first had a major effect (Freedman and Fraser 1966). When people were first asked to answer a few survey questions, more than half (53 percent) later agreed to let researchers come into their homes. (Imagine how successful you would be if you called strangers and asked if you could come over and go through their stuff for a couple of hours!) In contrast, when only the large request was made, just 28 percent, a little more than a quarter, agreed to let researchers come into their homes. By asking for a small favor first, researchers nearly doubled the percentage of people who would agree to grant their major request.

The lesson is clear. If you will need someone's help in the future, get that person to help you in small ways now, thus increasing the likelihood of agreement to an important request later. Note that as with the low initial bid technique of the previous section, getting people to do you a small favor requires no pressure. Persuasion starts to occur before a request is ever made. The more people help you, the more people will want to continue helping you. They become committed to your success.

The technique of gaining people's commitment by getting them to do you a favor can work for customers as well as salespeople. The one time in my life where it seemed that I got an especially good deal on a used car is an example. I had moved back to California from Idaho. I was working, selling furniture, but I no longer needed the truck that I had used to deliver waterbeds and hot tubs. I had decided to go back to school and needed a reliable car. A few blocks from the furniture store where I worked was a car lot where a national car rental company sold the rental cars to the public after they were a couple of years old. One day, as I drove by the lot, a Mustang convertible caught my eye. What better car to drive to college in California? After driving by that car several days in a row, I wanted it badly. I stopped by the lot after work to find out more about the car. With tax and license, the total price would be a little over $9,000. The salesperson told me that I would have to get my own financing. Also, the company had a strict "one-price" policy. Car prices were not negotiable. The best price for each car was plainly marked on it. No haggling. While this seems a fair way to sell cars, it leaves the dealer firmly in control of the ultimate price that customers pay. I decided to try a little social psychology to get the price down.

I returned to the car lot prepared to buy the car. Nonetheless, I let the salesperson go through his entire sales routine. I drove the car a second time. I let him tell me at length about the company's one-price policy that was such a benefit for customers because it relieved them of the anxiety of negotiating. We practiced putting the convertible top up and down. I asked him to show me how to operate everything on the car. I asked him to help me make sure that everything worked. In social psychological terms, I was gaining his commitment to sell me that car. Every time I asked him to help me with something, to show me something, he became a little more committed to completing the sale. The only thing salespeople have to work with is their time. While he was spending time with me, he could not work with anyone else. The more time he spent with me, the more important it was to him that our meeting result in a successful sale.

Eventually he suggested that we go to his desk to "get some information" from me. He was getting impatient. At his desk, we talked about price again. He repeated the company's no-exceptions one-price policy. No negotiating. I told him that I had already arranged a loan and that the price seemed reasonable. However, $9,000 was more than I was prepared to pay. Instead, I gave him a cashier's check for $8,000 and asked him to sell me the car for that amount. He laughed a little nervously at that point. He knew I was serious—$8,000 is a lot of money and a cashier's check has more impact than a personal check. He told me that he could not do it. It was against company policy to lower the price. I paused for what seemed like a long time, then said, "OK, let's go look at the car again." More time commitment from the salesperson.

I had already noticed a small tear in the outer shell of the convertible top, perhaps half an inch long. It seemed minor but might get worse. I pointed it out to the salesperson and asked how much a new convertible top would cost. He said that he did not know. I smiled and said, "Why don't we find out?" Back at his desk, I went through the yellow pages and asked him to call convertible top repair shops. More commitment; he was doing me a favor. We eventually agreed that a new convertible top would cost about $1,200 dollars. I suggested that we subtract the price of a new top from the price of the car and complete the sale. He said that he couldn't do that. I asked him what he could do. He said he would have to find out. Would he do that for me, please? More commitment. I told him that I was taking my new girlfriend to lunch and would be back in an hour or two.

The salesperson had spent a substantial amount of his working day with me. He had nothing to show for it yet. He was committed. When my girlfriend and I got back from lunch, the salesperson agreed to drop the "nonnegotiable" price by $500. After a little more bargaining, I wrote him a personal check for about $150 to add to the cashiers check of $8,000 that I had already given him. I had saved about $1,000. By getting him to help me repeatedly in small ways, I gained his commitment to help me in a bigger way. When I asked him to help me get the price I wanted, he found it difficult to refuse. As for the tear in the convertible top, a tube of vinyl repair goo fixed it nicely. Many good things got started that day. I drove to college with the top down and made it to graduation. Then I married my girlfriend.

TO PERSUADE THEM, LET THEM PERSUADE YOU

Cialdini, Green, and Rusch (1992) put an interesting twist on the idea that people want to help people who have helped them. Because people feel the need to recip-

Dilbert discovers the value of giving in

rocate, researchers proposed that if someone has persuaded you to do something in the past, then that person will be easier for you to persuade to do something in the future. Salespeople experience the situation often. When I sold furniture to a person in business, I felt obligated to use their services as well. When a family that owned a dry cleaners bought both dining room and living room furniture from me, I started taking my clothes to their cleaners, although it required driving across town.

Cialdini and colleagues (1992) proposed that a person would be persuaded more easily by someone who had yielded to her arguments on some unrelated topic. That is, once a person has persuaded you of something, that person will feel the need to reciprocate, return the favor, by letting you persuade her on some other issue. Researchers first asked people to give their opinions about the minimum drinking age. For half the people in the study, a research assistant at first disagreed but then admitted to being convinced by their arguments. For the rest of the people in the study, the research assistant remained unconvinced by their arguments. Then in the second part of the study, the research assistant's opinions about whether to require comprehensive exams in college were given to people. Researchers wanted to find out if people would agree more with the researcher after the researcher had agreed with them about the drinking age issue.

After the research assistant was persuaded by their arguments, people were more likely to be persuaded by the research assistant on a different topic. Cialdini et al. (1992) were correct. Researchers asked people to estimate how much their attitude had changed after listening to the research assistant's arguments. When the research assistant had agreed with people's opinions on the earlier topic, people reported that on average their attitudes had been changed 27 percent by the research assistant. That is, the research assistant's brief statement of her or his opinions had been highly persuasive. However, when the research assistant had been unconvinced by people's opinions on an earlier topic, people reported that on average their attitudes had been changed only 6 percent by the research assistant.

To get people to agree with you, first agree with them. The implications go well beyond any individual negotiations. These research results suggest a personal style that will increase your success in social life. Most arguments people get into are silly because the outcome doesn't matter very much. But those minor disagreements set the stage for major conflict when an important issue does arise. When I was in high school I loved to argue. I practiced and studied ways to construct a sound argument. I believed that logic would prevail. It was important for me to be right and for people to acknowledge that I was right. An implication that I had not considered was that by acknowledging I was right, people would be admitting that they were wrong. People do not like to admit that they are wrong.

For several years I argued every chance I got. It puzzled me, however, that no matter how brilliant my argument, the people I argued with never seemed to be convinced. After a particularly heated argument, I would review it in my mind for days to make sure I had been right. Yet later I would find that the person I had argued with remained unconvinced. My logic was sound enough but my social psychology was weak. I had ignored the importance of reciprocity in human relationships. To convince somebody of something, it helps to let that person convince you of something else first. And because the outcome of most arguments doesn't matter very much, it pays to agree with other people most of the time. Save your arguments for situations where the outcome is truly important to you. Agree with people unless you have good reason not to. Let them convince you. That was exactly the opposite of the way I had approached my relationships with people. I wanted to show people that I was right. So I argued about everything. But people were not convinced. A better way to approach the people in your life is to agree with them as much as possible. Show them how right they are. Then, when an issue comes up that is very important to you, you will be more likely to convince them that on this rare but important occasion, you might be right.

STATUS AS THE MOST SUBTLE WAY TO PERSUADE

Most of this chapter has described effective, subtle, and sometimes devious techniques that salespeople and organizations use to persuade people. You have seen how you can benefit from using similar techniques when you need to persuade someone to help you. But recall the example at the beginning of this chapter. Some people do not seem to need such techniques to persuade others. The doctor merely tells you that an operation is necessary and you agree to let her remove part of your body. Why doesn't your doctor need the subtle techniques of persuasion commonly used by salespeople?

The answer is *status*. Your status is your standing within a group based on your prestige, the respect that other group members give you. Doctors have high status in our society. They are respected, honored. The magic of high status is that people will try to find out what it is you want them to do, and do it for you, without your ever having to make a request. I noticed myself doing this just last week. By watching my diet and starting to exercise, I recently lost most of the excess weight I had carried around for years. I have more energy and feel healthier. Then last week it occurred to me that I should go to my doctor for the first time in years to get a physical examination. Why should I want to go to the doctor now that I feel great? I usually avoid going when I am sick. What I really wanted was my doctor's approval. I wanted the doctor to tell me what a good job I had done getting rid of that extra body fat. Her approval is important to me because of her high status. My doctor never told me I should lose weight, although she did hint last time that a little exercise would help. However, I thought my doctor would approve if I lost weight. Thus the opinion I expected her to have influenced my behavior without her having to express that opinion directly. When people have high status, their opinions count.

Techniques of persuasion can be highly effective in specific situations, but to wield real influence, a person needs high status. Chapter 7 shows how status operates in the workplace to smooth the careers of some people and place barriers in front of others. It also shows how to increase your status and influence at work.

Further Reading

Of General Interest

Bacharach, S. B., Lawler, E. J. (1984). *Bargaining.* San Francisco: Jossey-Bass.

Cialdini, R. B. (1993). *Influence: Science and practice.* New York: HarperCollins.

Damasio, A. R. (1994). *Descarte's error: Emotion, reason, and the human brain.* New York: Grosset/Putnam.

Pfeffer, J. (1992). *Managing with power: Politics and influence in organizations.* Boston: Harvard Business School Press.

Recent and Technical Issues

Axsom, D., Yates, S., & Chaiken, S. (1987). Audience response as a heuristic cue in persuasion. *Journal of Personality and Social Psychology, 53,* 30–40.

Fleming, J. H., Darley, J. M., Hilton, J. L., & Kojetin, B. A. (1990.) Multiple audience problem: A strategic communication perspective on social perception. *Journal of Personality and Social Psychology, 58,* 593–609.

Frey, K. P., & Eagly, A. H. (1993). Vividness can undermine the persuasiveness of messages. *Journal of Personality and Social Psychology, 65,* 32–44.

Gorassini, D. R., Olson, J. M. (1995). Does self-perception change explain the foot-in-the-door effect? *Journal of Personality and Social Psychology, 69,* 91–105.

Kruglanski, A., Webster, D. M., & Klem, A. (1993). Motivated resistance and openness to persuasion in the presence or absence of prior information. *Journal of Personality and Social Psychology, 65,* 861–876.

Petty, R. E., Schumann, D. W., Richman, S. A., & Strathman, A. J. (1993). Positive mood and persuasion: Different roles for affect under high- and low-elaboration conditions. *Journal of Personality and Social Psychology, 64,* 5–20.

Vorauer, J. D., & Miller, D. T. (1997). Failure to recognize the effect of implicit social influence on the presentation of self. *Journal of Personality and Social Psychology, 73,* 281–295.

Zarnoth, P., & Sniezek, J. A. (1997). The social influence of confidence in group decision making. *Journal of Experimental Social Psychology, 33,* 345–366.

CHAPTER 7

Your Place in the Workplace

Most of us spend most of our adult lives working, so work is important to us. We want to get the best job that we can and do it well. Some people are highly successful in their occupations. They are promoted and their coworkers look up to them. Others struggle. Social psychology can explain why some people glide smoothly toward success while others who work just as hard struggle uphill. Research can also identify techniques to help those who are struggling to succeed.

The following story tells about common problems faced by people engaged in promising business careers. The story is about a woman named Lauren and some of her problems are unique to women. Not all women have the same career problems at the same times in their careers. However, most women will see many of Lauren's problems soon after they enter the work force. Some of Lauren's problems will also be familiar to men, especially young men and members of minority groups. The goal is to use social psychology to explain why Lauren faces the problems she does, then describe research that supports those explanations. Happily, the research also identifies useful techniques to help you overcome similar problems in your working life.

LAUREN'S STORY

A young woman named Lauren graduated from high school near the top of her class. She left home and went away to a good college where her academic success continued. She graduated with honors and started a career in business. Her academic record and her major in communications landed her a job on the fast track in a large corporation. Lauren was aware, of course, that women face hurdles in a business career that men do not face. However, she assumed that she would overcome whatever obstacles she encountered through hard work, perseverance, and her personal ability. After all, she had proven in school that she could outwork and outthink most men.

Lauren put her personal life on hold while she concentrated on her career. She found that in addition to the skills she had learned in school, paying attention to details, and the ability to plan, she also had a knack for dealing with people. She truly liked the people she worked with and took an interest in their lives. She was soon promoted to a management position. A little more than half the new college graduates hired with Lauren were women. She noticed that women made up somewhat less than half of those promoted with her. She was not particularly surprised.

Lauren felt that many of the women she worked with did not take their careers seriously. They were as likely to talk about the career of the man in their life as about their own. They talked about the children their friends were having or about the children they would someday have. One or two had already taken maternity leave. Occasionally, Lauren would pass a group of the women she had worked with before her promotion. They would be gathered around someone's desk in the open staff room—Lauren now had a private office—passing around pictures of the newest addition to someone's family. Somewhat wistfully, Lauren would continue without pausing. She missed the comfortable friendship of women who cared about the same things that she did. She remembered the way they had little celebrations for each other's birthdays, the way they truly cared about each other. Lauren also knew that few of them would ever be promoted.

Lauren did take her career seriously and she avoided the common traps that snare so many women in business. She enjoyed the company of men and dated casually but avoided serious romantic entanglements. She made certain her romantic behavior was above reproach to head off the gossip that dogged the careers of women who like to party. She pushed the thought of children to the back of her mind. Success, she thought, would take about 10 years. By then she would be firmly established in the corporation and could think about a personal life.

At home, Lauren tried to make up for her lack of close relationships at work. She spent some of her rapidly growing income on remodeling and decorating her condominium. What had once been rooms as sterile as her office at work became a warm and inviting home. She kept in touch with her friends from college. They visited as often as they could but they had careers of their own, careers that took them to different parts of the country or even overseas. Lauren also made friends with her neighbors; some were single career women like herself, but others were raising families. One of them would usually drop by for coffee whenever Lauren was home. She had made sure when she bought the condo that it was in a neighborhood with families and young children. In the evenings and on Sunday mornings—she worked most Saturdays—she walked her dog in a beautiful park a block away and watched the children play.

At work, her success continued. She received another promotion. At that level relatively few promotions went to women. She felt that her work and ability were being recognized. She believed that hard work and talent really were the keys to success, woman or not. In her new position, though, she began to feel the strain and notice its effects on her. She felt brittle, unable to relax. Her relations with her subordinates remained cordial, but not as friendly as before. As she rose up the management ladder, the employees under her, both women and men, challenged her suggestions more frequently. She often had to push her ideas forward by sheer force of will. And when she did, she could feel the whispering behind her back, the conversations that died out when she entered the room—conversations among people she had thought of as friends who now excluded her. So be it, she thought. If she had to choose between friendship and respect, she would settle for respect. Her relations with her superiors were becoming more difficult as well. It was nothing she could really pinpoint. The higher she rose in the corporation, the more trouble she had getting her ideas across. It was not as if upper management opposed her. Rather, they just did not seem to consider her ideas. Although most of top management was male, Lauren's sex did not seem to be a factor. She reminded herself that it was lonely at the top. Success always has a price, and she was willing to pay it.

She could not help noticing that the men at her level seemed to handle the job more easily. They certainly worked hard. However, they also spent huge amounts of time talking about things that had nothing to do with work. Lauren had learned that if she wanted to maintain her contacts, then she would have keep up on a number of subjects. She kept up with professional basketball and football and knew a little about baseball (too many players and too many games). She drew the line at hockey. She knew the cars that counted and why. Men especially talked about themselves. They talked about where their careers were headed, their most recent triumph, what the company could do for them, and whether they should move to a bigger company with more opportunity. Here Lauren found herself slipping into the female role, a cheerleader for them. She knew that if she talked that way about herself, no one would be leading cheers for her. She found herself resenting the men's ability to relax, their easy confidence that career success was automatic. When men made mistakes they seemed to recover easily. Lauren could not help feeling that even her small mistakes would be held against her forever.

In her late twenties, Lauren fell in love. She met him at a management training seminar. He was a little older, being groomed for a vice presidency. They married. Lauren took her first maternity leave. By the time Lauren's second child arrived, her husband's steadily growing salary allowed her to take a year off work. Lauren hoped that when she returned it would be as a part-time consultant. Perhaps she could work out of her home.

Lauren's career had hit the glass ceiling, a nearly invisible barrier that curtails the rise of women into the ranks of upper management. Men's careers also usually reach a plateau. Large corporations are job pyramids, with many opportunities at the bottom but only a few at the top. The difference for Lauren and most women is the short time it takes for a career to peak. Many women in their thirties are already considering some form of semiretirement, sometimes accepting a less prestigious job with a lighter schedule. Many others continue to pursue full-time careers, not for the satisfaction they will gain, but because their alternatives are limited. They need a job to support themselves and their families and no better jobs are available. In contrast, college-educated men do not usually feel the inevitable leveling out of their advancement opportunities until well into their forties.

Lauren's story is an example. It is not the experience of all women. Some top business executives are women, more than ever before. Many have the respect of the people they work with. Lauren might well see her career as a success, her shift in career path a preferred choice. Then why does Lauren's story seem so discouraging? Women do succeed, and when they do, they succeed for the same reasons that men do: a good education, ability, and hard work. Yet all women in the work force face Lauren's problems to some extent.

Women's Second Shift

Our society puts the responsibility for maintaining a home and raising children directly on women. Granted, men are expected to lend their support, especially financial support, but the responsibility for home and children still falls mainly on women. Where children are involved, this is a full-time job. Nevertheless, women also work outside the home. Most women come home from the office to a "second shift" managing a home and children. Arlie Russell Hochshild's 1989 book, *The Second Shift,* showed that we have made less progress in this area than many people think. Many husbands now believe they share the work at home but their wives still do much more than half the total workload.[1]

Lauren's story shows how women are torn between the different roles they play. We all play more than one role in society. A person is not just a worker but also a woman, perhaps a wife as well, and a mother. Men also play several roles. However, men's roles do not conflict with each other as consistently as do women's various roles (Thoits 1986). A man who works hard and devotes a lot of time to building a successful career is not necessarily a bad husband and father. Rather, within appropriate limits, a man's success at work complements his role at home. By being successful at work, he can provide his family with comfort and security. His wife's prestige in the community depends in part on his success. Except in cases where work is so demanding that a husband is rarely home, success at work increases the likelihood of a successful home life for a man. Women's roles operate differently.

Women's roles conflict with each other more than men's roles do, which adds to the burden of the second shift. Professor Robin Simon at the University of Iowa conducted in-depth interviews with married men and women. She found that conflict among the roles of worker, spouse, and parent caused more guilt and lower self-evaluations for women than for men (Simon 1995). A woman's success at work does not raise her husband's prestige in the community the way a man's success does for his wife. Moreover, husbands can feel threatened if their wives are too successful. Women also do not get much credit for providing financial support for their children. Women can feel that they are stealing the hours spent at work from their families. Women get less satisfaction at work than do men. Success at work is less enjoyable when women see it as coming at the expense of their families. As one woman told Simon, "Guilt is probably the number one emotion because if I didn't work, that time could be devoted to my kids or my home life or my wifely duties or whatever" (1995, p. 186).

Can Social Psychology Help Lauren?

Remember that social psychology usually makes us uncomfortable. Lauren's story makes many people uncomfortable. She has less control over her life than we like to think we have over our own. She did everything right. She was smart and worked hard at her job. She exceeded the expectations that her superiors held for her. Yet

---

[1]Hochshild's *The Second Shift* makes fascinating reading and contains stories of working women in their own words.

she did not get what she had hoped from her career. People start to feel uncomfortable when they wonder why.

Social psychology explains why trying to understand Lauren's career makes us uncomfortable. Recall the fundamental attribution error from Chapter 1. We tend to blame individuals for what happens to them when outside forces often play a large role. There is the nagging doubt about Lauren: Was she somehow inadequate? It is easy to think that if the men she worked with aren't having a problem, then it must be her problem. Are we about to blame the victim again for an unjust situation? Fortunately, research will help us find a more valid explanation. However, knowing that social psychology can help people understand Lauren's career may not be comforting.

People also feel uncomfortable because they do not want to believe that Lauren's story could become their own. It feels better to believe that people make their own opportunities, that ability and hard work are more important to success than who a person is. When I was in grade school, my teachers liked to repeat that anyone in the United States could grow up to be president. It was not true. They did not mean that a woman could grow up to be president of the United States, nor did they mean that an African American could be president. It is still not true today. Maybe we are closer now to a day when it will be true.

The belief that ability, education, and hard work are all that matters for success may not be accurate. But it was a good thing for me to believe. I set higher goals for myself because of it. I persisted in working toward those goals longer than I otherwise would. The illusion that we have control over our lives keeps us working. Recall from Chapter 4 that some illusions are positive. Social psychology makes us uncomfortable when it threatens our illusion of control over our lives.

Nonetheless, social psychology can help. Chapter 4 also explained how positive illusions can be nurtured and maintained even as we learn more about the social world. The research described in this chapter shows you techniques to improve your influence at work. Research provides us with reliable tools. You will decide whether they apply to the situations you find yourself in and whether you use them.

Some people have an easier time getting to the top

SOCIAL PSYCHOLOGY AT WORK

William James pointed out that we become what we do. Recall from Chapter 2 that one way we figure out our identities, who we are, is by observing how we behave. The more time we spend at some activity, the more it defines who we are. A successful career often requires more than 50 hours a week. The more time we spend working, the more our identity is tied up with our work. Other social theorists emphasized the importance of work in determining what we believe. Kanter (1977) pointed out that Karl Marx, who promoted communism, and Adam Smith, who provided the philosophical basis for free market capitalism, both agreed that much of what people think and believe is shaped by their work. For example, the impact that a job has on my self-image was made clear to me when I worked for my brother as a janitor. I showed up for work at a large office building. My brother issued me the standard janitorial equipment: a vacuum cleaner, feather duster, rag to wipe out ashtrays, plastic bags for the wastebaskets, a bottle of spray cleaner. Cleaning office buildings is still fairly low-tech. He also gave me some advice. He warned me that people working in the offices did not think much of janitors and would ignore me. He said this could be hard to take and not to let it bother me. We cleaned the building after 5 P.M. so we would not meet many of them. The warning sounded strange to me at the time. Why would I care about the opinion of an office worker I did not know? But I did care and it was hard to take.

I became invisible, a nonperson. In the halls, people would try so hard not to notice me that they would bump into me unless I scrambled out of their way. The building was only a few stories tall but very long. Hallways stretched the length of a city block with elevators on each end. How far would people go to avoid having to acknowledge me? I was waiting for the elevator in my T-shirt and jeans with my low-tech janitor equipment when a man and a woman, both dressed in business suits, approached. They had been talking as they walked toward the elevator, but they stopped while they waited for it. An uncomfortable silence developed. I turned to them, smiled, and said, "Hi." They looked away from me, then at each other. Neither said anything. Then they both turned at the same time and walked the entire length of the hallway to the other elevator. It was easy to see that being a janitor could be hard on a person's self-image. As Kanter put it, "The job makes the person" (1977, p. 3).

Lauren and many successful women are caught in a trap. Even though they may feel ambivalent about a successful career, their self-image depends on it. They may happily choose to emphasize their important family responsibilities over a single-minded pursuit of success at work. Yet the nagging doubt remains. Could she have pulled off the magic trick of a successful career and a successful family life if she had worked a little harder?

Is the career path typified by Lauren inevitable for women? Must women accept being eased to the sidelines of corporate life before achieving their goals? It is interesting to note that for many women, the turn away from a career and toward family comes after career disappointments rather than before (Kanter 1977). Women's greater involvement with their children is not sufficient to explain their lack of career success. Disengagement from work is not something women choose but something that happens to them. Even while equal opportunity laws and women's impressive academic success generate entry-level opportunities for women, many are pushed out of their careers just short of success. To find ways for women to overcome the obstacles to a successful career, we first have to understand the problem.

STATUS AT WORK

Human beings have always worked together in groups. Individuals working together can accomplish a lot more than individuals working alone. But working in groups requires organization. People have to know what to do and the timing has to be right. For example, when neighbors in early America got together for a barn raising, everyone had to pull at once or the barn wall would not go up. One way to coordinate work so that everyone knows what to do is with a social hierarchy. Hierarchy means that society is arranged in layers. Each of us has a position in society, a status. Status positions are not just different from each other; they are ranked. Some are higher than others are. Most people can tell what their social rank is relative to the people around them. The army is a classic example. Army personnel wear their social rank on their uniforms. In other cases, the cues that indicate rank are more subtle. All human societies have status hierarchies. Some people are in charge and give the orders. Others obey the orders and do the work. No matter how informal the work group, when people got ready to raise the barn wall, somebody had to yell "pull" and the others had to obey. Status hierarchies promote efficient group work.

A set of related theories in social psychology called *status characteristics and expectation states theories* explains how status hierarchies develop at work. They explain why some people have an easy time succeeding at work while others struggle. The theories have been supported by hundreds of research studies starting in the 1950s. Later in the chapter, I describe some of the relevant research in detail, especially where it applies to techniques that can help you succeed at work. First, however, it will help to describe how the theory explains the problems that Lauren faced. Overviews of research supporting the theory that follows can be found in Berger, Fisek, Norman, and Zelditch (1977), Berger and Zelditch (1985), Berger and Zelditch (1993), Berger, Zelditch, and Anderson (1989), Foschi and Lawler (1994), Szmatka, Skvoretz, and Berger (1997), and Webster and Foschi (1988).

In an efficient work group, an individual's social status results from how much she can contribute to group goals. The more a person can contribute, the more honor and prestige she is given in the group. Everyone shares in the rewards of a successfully completed group project. Status hierarchies encourage group members to contribute as much as they can. The result is a successful group. At least, that is the way it might be if people really knew how much each person could contribute. In work groups, people are not sure how much to expect from group members. They have to guess. Status hierarchies are not based on how much each individual contributes. Rather, status hierarchies are based on how much each individual is *expected* to contribute. People honor those who are expected to contribute most to the success of the group. Being human, people are sometimes wrong. Some people contribute more than expected. They do not receive the honor and prestige—the status—they deserve. For example, the contributions of women in corporations are often overlooked or devalued. In contrast, white men in corporations often receive credit for contributions made by others and escape blame for their mistakes.

Work is important. People depend on it to survive. Because work is important, a person's status in society depends on how much she is expected to contribute at work. Status is important as well. Because people do not know exactly how much a person will contribute, they form expectations for a person's ability. That is, they use shortcuts, rules of thumb. People guess based on various bits of personal information. Social psychologists call those bits of information *status cues*. Some status cues are personal characteristics that are clearly relevant to group work. For example, a person with a lot of education is probably someone who can work effectively. People expect that a person with a college degree will contribute more to a work group than will a person who dropped out of high school. Other cues can also be relevant. People expect a person who speaks clearly and fluently to contribute more to the group than one who mumbles haltingly.

In contrast, people also use irrelevant information to decide how much a person will contribute. As people look around in society, they notice that certain kinds of people have most of the high-status positions. The big contributors share some common characteristics. It is easy to assume that those characteristics are related somehow to their contributions. For example, high-status workers in society are mostly men. Most business executives are men. Most doctors, lawyers, judges, scientists, college professors, astronauts, war heroes, movie stars are men, in fact, white men. Because most high-status positions are filled by men, people assume that men are more capable than women of contributing to group goals. It is a short and reasonable leap to an often wrong conclusion. Worse, expectations often become reality.

Thomas and Thomas (1928) wrote that what men believe to be real is real in its consequences. Ironically, in framing that remarkable insight, "men" was used to mean all people.[2] At work, men do contribute more than women, don't they? Men have made most of the medical breakthroughs and scientific discoveries, built the biggest buildings, supplied us with water and electricity. Most of the great chefs of the world have been men. A reasonable person could easily come to expect a man to make greater contributions than a woman will. It would also be wrong. There is a self-fulfilling prophecy at work here.

When people expect men to make bigger contributions, men are given high-status positions that allow them to make bigger contributions. Not only that, the contributions of men and women are evaluated differently in comparable situations. Because men are expected to be more competent, people look for the benefits of what men have done. Because people expect women to be less competent, they look for the flaws in what women have done. Even when a man and woman have made exactly the same contribution to group success, people often rate the man's contribution higher.[3] They see it in a better light, filtered through their expectations. One

---

[2]Perhaps more ironic, the idea is often referred to as the "Thomas Theorem." W. I. Thomas is usually given sole credit for the idea although it appeared in a book co-authored with his wife, Dorothy S. Thomas.
[3]Foschi and Foddy (1988), Foschi, Lai and Sigerson (1994), and Biernat and Kobrynowicz (1997) also show how men and women are evaluated according to different standards.

reason that expectations are so troublesome is because they are often not conscious beliefs. People can *believe* completely in the equal abilities of men and women yet still *expect* that men will outperform women.

Our expectations for the way men and women will perform are based on gender as a *diffuse* status characteristic in society. The effects of gender are diffuse because they spread out to include competence in many areas. That is, men are assumed to be more competent than women in a wide variety of situations. According to common gender stereotypes, men are better at sports, math, decision making, driving, working with tools, logic, chess, computers, business, science, surgery, and war. In few of these activities do men possess a relevant ability that gives them an advantage over women. For example, male upper body strength gives men an advantage over women in most sports. For most occupations, however, the superior performance of men results from a self-fulfilling prophecy. Men are put in high-status positions because they are expected to outperform women. Then, because they are in high-status positions, men are able to outperform women. Expectations are confirmed. People expect men to succeed as managers in the workplace. They expect women to fail.

Kay Deaux (1984), a professor at Purdue University, explained how attributions give men an advantage over women at work. Recall that certain kinds of attributions allow us to predict how people will behave in the future. If we decide that a person's behavior results from some underlying stable personality trait, then we can feel confident that the person will behave the same way in similar future situations. For example, if we think a person got an A on a test because he is very intelligent and a hard worker, then we will confidently predict that he will do well on the next test also. However, if we think he happened to sit next to the smartest person in class and copied her answers, then we would not be able to predict how well he would do on the next test. Maybe the seats next to ace students will not be available during the next test. His previous success depended on a temporary aspect of the situation. Attributions to temporary conditions that are internal to a person also prevent us from making predictions about future performance. For example, a person may have failed a test because he had the flu that day. The next time he takes a test, he may do well or poorly. We just do not know. Attributions to stable character traits of a person allow us to predict his or her future performance. Attributions to external factors in the situation or to temporary internal conditions do not allow us to predict future performance.

Deaux (1984) suggests that people make different attributions for the performances of men and women based on their different expectations for male and female success. When coworkers' performances meet expectations, people make stable internal attributions. Because expectations are met, people need not think much about the causes of the performance. The tendency toward correspondence bias takes over. That is, people commit the fundamental attribution error. For example, people expect men to succeed and assume it is because of men's underlying competence. People expect women to fail and assume it is because of women's underlying incompetence. People have to think harder when performances contradict their expectations. Deaux suggests that people are less likely to succumb to correspondence bias when their expectations are not met. People will make more attributions to factors in the situation or to a temporary condition of the person. For example, when a man fails, people might attribute it to bad luck or to factors in the situation over which he had no control. His failure violated expectations, so people had to look around for unusual reasons for it. A woman succeeding also violates expectations, so people look for unusual explanations in the situation. They might think that she was lucky. Expectations for how people will perform determine the kinds of attributions people make for their performances.

Because people expect men to succeed and women to fail at high-level jobs, they tend to make different attributions for their success or failure (Deaux 1984). When men succeed, people attribute their success to ability and assume they will perform well in the future. When men fail, people attribute their failure to some external or temporary factor and reach no conclusion about their future performance. In contrast, when women succeed, people attribute their success to luck or some other external factor and cannot predict their future performance. When women fail, however, people attribute their failure to lack of ability and assume they will continue to perform poorly in the future.

It is easy to see how, over the course of a career, such differences in attribution could give men a real advantage when it comes to promotions. Blatant discrimination against women need not occur for men to gain nearly all upper management positions. Usually, hiring and promotion committees will say that they really wanted to find a woman for the position, but a male candidate was clearly superior. Over the course of a career, the subtle difference in coworkers' attributions for the performances of men and women will have built up into a clear advantage. When superiors evaluate a man's performance, his failures will be excused. His successes will be credited to his competence. Superior future performance will be predicted. In contrast, women will not be credited with their successes. They will be dismissed as lucky. Her failures, however, will be seen as due to lack of aptitude. Poor future performance will be predicted. With a number of such assessments on the record in a personnel file, a man and woman who had performed identically over the years will have dramatically different records. The man's will be a record of achievement, his failures excused. The woman's record will show her failures, with her successes dismissed. This attribution process works without anyone intending to discriminate against women. Thus it is not enough that people come to believe that discrimination in the workplace is wrong. Expectations are not conscious beliefs. To make effective social changes, we have to change the situation.

USING STATUS CHARACTERISTICS TO YOUR ADVANTAGE

To change the way you are evaluated at work, it is first necessary to understand how status characteristics put some people at a disadvantage. Status characteristics are distinctive parts of a person's identity such as gender, race, age, occupation, and education. People use status characteristics to form expectations of a person's competence. Sometimes expectations are correct. A person with a college education may well be more competent than one who did not finish high school. However, people also estimate people's competence from status characteristics that are often irrelevant to the kind of work they do. A man, for example, is no more likely than a woman to be a competent juror. Yet when it comes time to elect a jury foreman, men are usually picked. *Status characteristics theory* explains how status characteristics are used in groups of people to create a status hierarchy. In human groups, people are ranked in terms of their expected value to the group. Some are given great honor and prestige and have a lot of influence. Others are ranked lower and not valued as highly. Sometimes a person's status ranking reflects her competence and ability to contribute. Too often it does not.

Status characteristics theory has developed as a scientific research program.[4] Researchers started with a basic theory then added to it. Each new addition to the theory was tested with solid research. As a result, we now understand how status hierarchies form in work groups. That understanding has led to techniques for overcoming the obstacles faced by low-status workers.

Status characteristics theory explains how status characteristics determine a person's social rank and ultimately how much influence that person will have. The theory starts with the status characteristics that people use to make guesses about a person's competence. A person can always be either high or low on a status characteristic. For the status characteristic gender, men are high and women are low. It is unfair but true. That may be changing slowly. Still, in this society men are expected to be more competent than women in many ways.

People try to determine each other's status characteristics when they meet. Have you noticed how uncomfortable people are when they cannot determine whether a person is a man or a woman? We are not comfortable with other people until we form expectations for how they will behave. When describing another person, people usually start with three status characteristics, gender, race, and age. Think of the descriptions given of wanted criminals—white male about 25 years old, for example.

Status characteristics are important. An introduction usually includes a status characteristic, occupation. "Here, meet Rhonda. She's an advertising executive." And if occupation was not included in the introduction, it comes up early in the conversation. "What is it you do?" People also find ways to slip their education credentials into conversations. "We met in college." People quickly gather enough information about each other's status characteristics to rank themselves and others. In fact, the process can be entirely unconscious.

People rank each other according to their status automatically, without conscious thought. That makes the process of status formation in groups highly resistant to conscious attempts to change it. For example, men usually dominate important group discussions. Contributions from high-status people are expected to be more valuable, and so high-status people contribute more to discussions. On university campuses now, students are careful to consider women and minority groups. Still, men usually dominate classroom discussions. It is not that they try to exclude women and minorities. In fact, when men are asked why they dominated the discussion, they often reply that they did not. They say that they were careful to let

---

[4]Good overviews of status characteristics research can be found in Berger, Cohen, and Zelditch (1972), Berger, Fisek, Norman, and Zelditch (1977), Berger and Zelditch (1985), and Webster and Foschi (1988).

women and minority students speak. The men are amazed when shown videotape of the discussion in which they clearly dominate, often interrupting women and minority students. Change is slow. Women may participate more in class discussion than they used to, but when a discussion is important, notice that men will still take over.

People use the status information available to make guesses about people's competence. If two people are different on a particular status characteristic, then people will use it to rank each other. Relevant or not, people use gender when they rank a man and a woman. Pugh and Wahrman (1983) set up a situation to show the effects of gender when men and women work together. Gender was not at all relevant to the task involved. A black and white image was projected on a screen. Work teams had to decide whether black or white covered more of the surface area of the image. Women worked with either a male or female partner. Researchers recorded how often the partner was able to influence a woman to change her mind. Women changed their minds to agree with a male partner more often than women changed their minds to agree with a female partner. Male and female partners acted identically. The partner's gender alone made the difference in influence. Pugh and Wahrman repeated the study. This time, they showed people that women were just as competent as men were at the task. Even though people were well aware that women were just as competent as men, men still had more influence than women. Pugh and Wahrman repeated the study a third time. This time, they showed women that they were clearly more competent than were men at the task. Only when women were clearly shown to be *more* competent than men did women gain influence *equal* to men. Women who have succeeded in business often remark that they have to be more competent than men to receive equal treatment.

Status characteristics theory also shows how people combine information about various status characteristics when they form expectations about someone's competence. People use all the status information available. For example, people expect a woman with a college degree to be more competent than a woman with only a high school diploma. If the college-educated woman is also a doctor, then people raise their estimate of her competence. If she is a cook, they will lower their estimate. The effects of status characteristics combine. That is important for people struggling for equality at work.

When a person is struggling with the disadvantages of low status, it can seem as if the disadvantage is the only characteristic that matters. "My college degree doesn't matter, people only see a black man" is a commonly heard sentiment. The disadvantage of being a woman in a corporation can also seem insurmountable. "I am a vice president of the company and the CEO asked me to get him a cup of coffee in a board meeting." The effects of race and gender sometimes seem to minimize or eliminate the effects of other characteristics. That is, when race and gender are involved, the effects of other status characteristics might not count.

Pugh and Wahrman (1983) demonstrated that status characteristics do combine. Even though gender is an important status characteristic, other status characteristics can counter its effects. In their study, Pugh and Wahrman showed that women could achieve influence equal to men at work. But first women had to show that they were *more* competent than men. It was not enough for women to show that they were equally competent. Webster and Driskell (1978) have shown that other status characteristics combine with race in the same way.[5]

The effects of status characteristics have also been shown to combine in a precise way. Berger, Norman, Balkwell, and Smith (1992) set up a situation where they could test the influence produced by different combinations of status characteristics. People worked with partners who were different from them on as many as seven status characteristics. The study made it possible to tell how much influence was gained by adding a single positive status characteristic to several negative ones. That is, how big an effect does a single, inconsistent status characteristic have when a person is disadvantaged in several ways? For example, a person might be a poor black woman but have a Ph.D. Results showed clearly that a single inconsistent status characteristic has a big effect on a person's influence, much bigger than if there was only one status characteristic. In contrast, each additional consistent status characteristic has a smaller effect. Adding one more positive characteristic to several other positive characteristics has little effect. Therefore, adding a positive status characteristic will help a disadvantaged person more than it would an already advantaged person. For example, a college education will have a much bigger positive effect on the status of a poor black woman than it will on the status of a rich white man.

We can see how status characteristics operate in the lives of people around us. Suppose your status is low on several characteristics. Perhaps you are a woman, relatively poor, with a low-status job as a food server or receptionist. People around you treat you in a particularly disconcerting way. They ignore you. Even the people who care about you do not seem to take you seriously. One of the major early insights of social psychology is that our self-image depends on how others see us. We see ourselves reflected in the faces of the people around us. Charles Horton Cooley (1902) called this the *looking-glass self* because people around us act as mirrors for our self-image. If the people around you think you are not worth much, it is easy for you to agree with them. You may feel depressed. Then you start to wonder if you exist at all. But suppose you are working your way through college. The struggle and expense and time eventually pay off. Your social position changes dramatically on the day you graduate. Your high-status education has a big impact because it combines with several inconsistent status characteristics. Those around you immediately start listening to you. People ask your advice. You have become an important person in their eyes, all the more so because your accomplishment was unexpected. Soon you will start to see your own value as well. Once you have discarded your old self-image, you gain the confidence to get a better job. Your new life transforms you into a different person.

Understanding how status characteristics combine offers hope for a better society. We often have reason to be pessimistic. Those with many advantages just seem to get more. The rich get richer and the poor get poorer is a common lament. We now see that it does not have to be this way. Education is going to have a bigger effect on the lives of disadvantaged people than it does on the already privileged. For example, a white man grows up in a wealthy family and pays little attention to

---

[5]See Chapter 8 for a detailed account of the Webster and Driskell (1978) study.

school. He knows that he will have a good job in the family business. Nonetheless, the family pushes him through college. Certainly getting an education was easier for him than for the woman who struggled to work her way through. However, education has less effect on the social position of the privileged man. In contrast, we saw how getting a college degree transformed the life of a poor woman with a low-status occupation.

The results are not guaranteed. People with college degrees sometimes remain food servers or cab drivers. Education provides the opportunity but the opportunity has to be used. A college degree will help you find a high-status occupation. However, if you remain in a low-status job, pretty soon people will forget about your college degree because it will not apply to the situation you are in. Also, high-status jobs are not easy to get. A lot of people want them. University professor is a good example. Most people who get Ph.D.s would like to be university professors, but there are few openings. The problem is not new. After Albert Einstein got his Ph.D., he worked for years in the Swiss patent office before finally finding a job in a university. High-status jobs may be hard to get but that is no reason for people with a college degree to continue working as food servers. The degree qualifies people for a wide variety of high-status jobs. If they have difficulty getting their dream job, they can explore a variety of good alternatives.

Results of status characteristics research suggest strategies to improve all our lives. The effects of status characteristics combine to determine our social position. True, race and gender have important effects that are beyond our control. However, because the effects of status characteristics combine, we can counter the effects of race and gender by changing our status on other characteristics. Education, for example, is a powerful status characteristic and one that you can control. Get as much education as you can. After you get a bachelor's degree and have worked for a few years, consider going back to get a master's. That is the unmistakable conclusion of status characteristics research. Education is the best investment you can make because you are investing in yourself, in who you are.

There are mental traps to avoid along the way to a better life. A surprising number of people of all ages think they are too old to go back to school. How can people get past the idea that school is just for children? It was not easy for me. I dropped out of college after my freshman year. It felt too much like high school. I tried to enroll a couple of times during the next 14 years but gave up each time. Thinking of myself as a student made me so uncomfortable. Finally, I just gave up. My life had been going nowhere. The future looked bleak. At least going to school would be something to do. One spring, I took two classes at a community college and finished them both. That was my goal, to finish. It did not bother me that I did not get A's. My outlook had changed. I took the summer off. By the time fall quarter started I was more than ready to go back. School, no matter how much trouble it was, at least gave me a sense of motion, the possibility of progress. I took more classes. My grades improved. Thinking of myself as a student no longer made me uncomfortable. For one thing, many of the other students were old too. In some colleges, the typical student is in her thirties or even forties. Quite a few are older than that. When I transferred from the community college to the local branch of a state university, I had a wonderful professor. She tried to teach me to write poetry. She had gotten her Ph.D. from Stanford University at the age of 59. It is never too late to go back to school.

Perhaps the best advice ever given by an advice columnist came in the form of a question. A person had written complaining about the advice she had been given. She had worked in the same routine job for years and was sick of it. She was not qualified for a better one and had asked for advice. The columnist had told her to go back to school. In exasperation, she wrote back asking if the columnist realized that it would take her six years to get a degree because she would have to go to school part time while she worked. Did the columnist realize how old she would be in six years? The columnist replied by asking how old she would be in six years if she did not go back to school.

The United States has more opportunities for education than any other country. One thing we do well is school. In the United States there is always another chance to get an education, even for people who drop out of high school. A friend of mine had a troubled childhood. His parents were drunks. His mother died when he was in junior high school. He got in trouble at school. During his freshman year in high school he just stopped going. He had been spending more time with the dean of students than he had with his teachers. He remained enrolled in school until he was 16 but finished almost none of his high school courses. Then he dropped out completely. He used drugs heavily. At one point he became so depressed that he attempted suicide. He injected insecticide into a vein. When I met him, he was in his twenties, just finishing a drug rehabilitation program. There he had decided to get a general education diploma. He thought he would feel better about himself if he had at least the equivalent of a high school diploma. The local community college offered classes to prepare people for the GED exam. Never a person to do things the easy way, he enrolled in a college-level history course instead. No one told him that he could not take a college course without finishing high school first. He completed his history course and passed his exam. More important, he had discovered that he could succeed in college. He took more courses. He transferred to a university and graduated. Then he got a master's degree in education. He can now be the dean of students in the high school that threw him out. The community college is a wonderful American idea. There is always another chance to go to school.

ATTRIBUTIONS, EXPECTATIONS, AND STATUS CHARACTERISTICS AT WORK

We saw how attributions give men an advantage over women at work. Deaux (1984) suggests that people make different attributions for the performances of men and women based on their expectations for whether or not people will succeed. More than for women, people expect men to succeed and attribute men's successes to their character. Men get credit for their success. In contrast, people expect women to fail, so people attribute women's successes to luck or some other external factor.

People's different expectations for men and women are self-fulfilling. Men are given more opportunities to grow and succeed because they are expected to contribute more. Then men contribute more because of the opportunities they have been given. Expectations are confirmed. To change the way women are treated in the workplace, we need to understand how expectations affect people's behavior.

Status characteristics research has already shown us one way to change expectations. We can add positive characteristics to counteract the ones that keep us at a disadvantage. Elizabeth Cohen (1993) has used status characteristics research to develop a remarkable program for schoolchildren. Status hierarchies that develop in school settings are just as rigid as those found in the workplace. The disadvantages of status hierarchies are similar as well. Student participation in most school activities is determined by such status characteristics as race and reading ability. High-status students participate more and learn more. Low-status students participate less, learn less, and are likely to lose interest in school. Cohen's program teaches students to value a wider range of abilities, for example, reasoning, being precise, and using visual thinking. That is, she creates many more status characteristics. With a wide variety of characteristics, almost all students will be high on some and low on others. When the effects of the characteristics combine, equality results. The program is in operation in grade schools around California and in Israel. It is especially effective where teachers have to cope with students who speak different languages. Low-status students in Cohen's program participate more equally with high-status students. There is also an unexpected added benefit. Academic performance improves for all students.

In work settings, it may not be possible to create new status characteristics that people will use. Adults are more set in their ways than children. They may not adapt to new ways of evaluating people as easily as do children. For women and minority group members to achieve equal status at work, we need to discover techniques that an individual worker can use to counteract her status disadvantage. Professor Cecilia Ridgeway, chair of the Sociology Department at Stanford University from 1994 to 1997, conducted a remarkable program of research that does just that.

Ridgeway (1982) pushed status characteristics theory a step further. The theory says that we use status characteristics to rank people because we need to predict how much people will contribute to our group. We want to know who will help us be successful. We give high status to people who we expect are competent because competent people can contribute more to our success. Ridgeway pointed out that competence alone was not enough to ensure that a person would contribute to group goals. A competent but very selfish person might contribute less to the group than would a less competent person who was motivated to contribute to the group. High status in a group, then, should result not just from expectations of competence but also from expectations that a person will be group-motivated.

According to Ridgeway (1982), we assume that high-status people are group-motivated, another example of a self-fulfilling prophecy. We give people high status because we expect them to be group-motivated, and we assume that if a person has high status, then he must be group-motivated. Just as with expectations of competence, we often have little direct evidence to decide whether a person is motivated to contribute to our group. We use shortcuts, the same shortcuts we use to form expectations for a person's competence; we use status characteristics. We assume that people with valued status characteristics are group-motivated even when they talk and act selfishly. In other words, we give white men the benefit of the doubt when it comes to group motivation. We assume that white men will contribute to the group no matter how selfish they seem. In contrast, we assume women and minorities to be selfishly motivated. Status characteristics do them a double disservice. Not only are their contributions devalued and ignored, but they also are assumed to have been motivated by selfish concerns. Although discouraging, this insight produced knowledge that women and minority group members can use to increase their influence and status in the workplace.

Ridgeway (1982) set up a situation to investigate whether group motivation would make a difference in the influence that women have in a work group. Groups with four members worked together to solve word problems. One member of each group was a confederate of the researcher. Social psychologists call a person trained to act in a certain way during an experiment a *confederate*. In half of the groups, the confederate was a man. In the other half, the confederate was a woman. If group members changed their minds to support the answer proposed by the confederate, then the confederate had influence over them. If they chose some other answer, then the confederate did not demonstrate any influence. As expected, men had more influence over group decisions than did women, even though all confederates, both men and women, acted exactly the same way. Gender alone produced the difference in influence.

Group motivation was then added to the setting (Ridgeway 1982). Confederates (both men and women) presented themselves as group-motivated to half the groups. Confederates presented themselves as selfish to the other half. A group-motivated confederate was friendly and cooperative. For example, he or she would say "I think it is important that we cooperate here." Selfishly oriented confederates acted in a self-confident and somewhat critical manner. They said they were primarily interested in earning points for themselves. Would acting in a group-motivated manner increase the influence of women in the work group? It did. When a woman who presented herself as group-motivated worked in a group with three men, her influence doubled. That is an important finding. Women can increase their influence in work groups by presenting themselves as group-motivated.

The theory makes another interesting prediction. The contributions of men are expected to benefit the group even when men act selfishly. Thus men have a lot of influence regardless of how they present themselves. The theory predicts that when men present themselves as group-motivated, it will have little effect on their influence over the group. That is exactly what happened. The influence of men increased only slightly when they presented themselves as group-motivated. In fact, women who presented themselves as group-motivated had influence equal to selfishly motivated men, and group-motivated women had almost as much influence as group-motivated men. Acting in a group-motivated way increased the influence of women much more than it increased the influence of men. Ridgeway (1982) demonstrated that by acting in a group-motivated way, women can attain influence virtually equal to that of men. Surprisingly, the influence of men and women remained almost equal *even when men acted in a group-motivated way as well.* Ridgeway tested the theory using gender as the status characteristic. However, because the theory has been well tested, there is reason to believe the group-motivation technique will also work for minority group members.

Recall the problems Lauren had with her career in the story that opened this chapter. We can now better understand why Lauren's strategy could not completely overcome her status disadvantage as a woman. She achieved initial success and promotion by copying the style of the successful men around her. She worked hard, taking every opportunity to demonstrate her competence. She acted in an assertive manner so that she would be noticed and taken seriously. Nonetheless, as she was being promoted, she felt herself being marginalized, forced to the sidelines. Her coworkers regarded her as selfishly motivated. Her success did not produce expectations that the group as a whole would succeed. The harder she worked, the more assertive her style, the less she appeared to be a team player. Her relationships at work became less satisfying. She felt she had to fight to get even small things done. She received little cooperation.

Shackelford, Wood, and Worchel (1996) showed that the strategies women use to cope with their status disadvantage at work do help increase expectations of competence. However, these strategies may also make it more difficult for women to get along with coworkers. Shackelford, Wood, and Worchel set up a situation in which women worked with men to solve problems. They investigated three factors that might increase women's influence in work groups: (1) a clear demonstration of competence, (2) assertive, even aggressive behavior as opposed to quiet conforming behavior, and (3) a group-motivated as opposed to selfishly motivated behavioral style. To demonstrate the woman's competence, team members were given an aptitude test related to the ability required. In half the groups, the woman received a high score, suggesting she would do well at the task. In the other half the woman received a low score. To demonstrate assertive behavior, a woman interrupted others with her suggestions and challenged others' estimates. To demonstrate group motivation, a woman made cooperative statements similar to the ones that Ridgeway (1982) used. "This research is important, so let's all confer so we can come up with a group answer." A woman presented herself as selfishly motivated by making statements such as "I think it is important that you cooperate with me. I know what I am doing." By observing how many times the group members changed their minds to agree with the woman's assessment of the correct solution, Shackelford, Wood, and Worchel could then tell whether competence, assertive behavior, or group-oriented behavior increased the woman's influence.

The results of Shackelford, Wood, and Worchel's (1996) experiment supported the validity of the strategies women commonly use to succeed in the workplace. Women's influence at work increases when they demonstrate competence and when they act aggressively. The results also showed why women encounter resistance. As predicted by status characteristics theory, when the woman in the study clearly demonstrated her ability by scoring high on the test, she had high influence in the group. Women who acted aggressively also had high influence. Even with no clear demonstration of competence, a confident, assertive manner convinced group members of the woman's competence. However, even in this brief task, Shackelford and colleagues found problems for the aggressive woman's relationships with other group members. Group members did not like the aggressive woman much. In contrast, a woman who presented herself as group-motivated had high influence without triggering dislike from coworkers. This is an important result. If a woman can be successful at work without triggering an emotional backlash from coworkers, she will be more likely to enjoy her success.

EMOTION AT WORK

Jeffrey Houser and I conducted a study that showed how damaging negative emotional reactions of coworkers can be (Lovaglia & Houser 1996). People worked together with partners who either made them angry or made them happy. Workers exchanged gifts before beginning the group project. To make a person happy, the partner would give a beautiful flower, a carnation in an attractive vase. To make a person angry, instead of giving a gift, the partner would send a card that read, "NO GIFT. I came here to make money not friends." People in the study had spent their own money to send the partner a nice gift. They definitely had a negative emotional reaction when they received the dismissive response from their partner. How much influence would the partner have? When people had received a nice gift and felt positively toward their partner, their partner had quite a bit of influence over them. In contrast, after sending no gift, the partner had very little influence. You can have little influence over people who are angry with you. Managing your own emotions and the emotions of others are important skills necessary for your success in the workplace.

We also investigated the more general effects of emotions. What if a person were angry at someone else? Would a person's emotional reaction to someone else alter the partner's influence? We introduced people to a stuffy administrative assistant who put them in a bad mood (Lovaglia & Houser 1996). They had completed a questionnaire by filling in the bubbles on a computer-ready answer sheet, the kind where you fill in the bubbles with a number 2 pencil. However, the researcher had given them a pen instead. When people mentioned that they needed a pencil, the researcher told them to just go ahead and fill it out. The administrative assistant came by a while later to collect the answer sheets. She complained that a pen had been used instead of a pencil and said that the person who filled it out should know better. When people began to protest that they had been told to use a pen, the administrative assistant cut them off by quickly leaving the room and slamming the door. Being criticized for following directions produced a definite negative emotional reaction in people. Then people were introduced to their partner and worked on the group project. Would the partner still have little influence when people were angry at someone else? Yes. Partners had very little influence over people who were upset at the administrative assistant. The moods people are in, their emotional reactions, make a difference in how much influence you will have over them, even if you were not the cause of their emotion.

Children know about their parents' moods. When you were a child, would you try to wait until your mother was in a good mood to ask for something special? The effect of emotion on influence became clear to me when I was looking for a job in the middle of a recession. The economy was in terrible shape. I had moved back to

California from Idaho to look for a job. But unemployment in California was almost as bad. Still, I had sent out application letters. One day I got a phone call from the headquarters of a chain of Scandinavian furniture stores. They wanted me to come for an interview. A torrential rainstorm boiled over San Francisco Bay as I drove the 50 miles to the head office. I found the building without trouble, but I desperately drove up and down streets looking for a parking place, convinced I would be late and miss my chance at a job. I finally parked several blocks from the building and ran to it through the rain. I arrived anxious and drenched, having neither raincoat nor umbrella. The receptionist told me to take a seat and wait. The vice president who would interview me had been detained on another matter. I waited and worried. After about half an hour, the receptionist told me that the vice president had called. He would be back soon. I waited. The storm continued outside. After an hour or so, I thought about going home. How interested could they be in me if they made me wait an hour? I stayed because it was raining so hard. After two hours and fifteen minutes, the vice president arrived.

He was in an exceptionally good mood. He bubbled over with enthusiasm and good cheer. My resentment at being kept waiting disappeared. He told me that he had been out buying a new truck for the warehouse. He talked about his early career. He had started in the business delivering furniture, then moved up to warehouse manager. He still loved trucks. He went into great detail about the wonderful truck he had bought and the good deal he made. He finally got around to asking me questions about my background in furniture sales. My answers could not have helped me much because I knew little about the furniture business. But whenever I had trouble answering a question, he said "never mind," then answered it for me. After a few questions, he jumped up and literally grabbed the company's chief furniture buyer in the hallway. The joyous vice president introduced me to him as "the perfect person for our South Bay store." Unemployment was high. Hundreds of people had applied for that job. Certainly many of them were more qualified than I was. Despite my meager qualifications, I got the job because the vice president's good mood made me look particularly attractive to him. He was so happy about acquiring a new truck that he decided to get a new employee too.

Baron (1987) conducted a study that demonstrated the effect of mood on evaluations in the workplace. He gave people the job of interviewing a candidate for an entry-level management position. First, the researcher placed them in a bad mood by criticizing their performance on a test. Or the researcher placed them in a good mood by praising their performance. Then people interviewed the job candidate. People in a good mood rated the candidate's character and qualifications higher than when they were in a bad mood. They also decided to hire the candidate more often when they were in a good mood. The job candidate always had exactly the same qualifications and acted the same way. People's mood alone changed their evaluations and hiring decisions. Social psychology tells us to pay attention to the moods of our coworkers.

Jeff Houser and I also discovered that the effects of emotional reactions and status characteristics combine to determine the influence a person will have (Lovaglia & Houser 1996). You might not be able to control your status characteristics. Race and gender, for example, are not easy to change. However, we can learn to manage our emotions and pay attention to the emotional reactions we create in other people. Because the effects of emotional reactions and status characteristics combine to determine influence, emotions can be used to increase the influence of low-status people. In the study, we made half the people angry. We made the other half happy. They then worked with a partner who was either a high school student about to drop out with a D+ average or a graduate student with a straight A average doing biomedical research. We asked people to rate the intelligence of their partner. Would people in a bad mood give low estimates of the graduate student's intelligence? Would people in a good mood give high estimates of the high school dropout's intelligence? Yes, they did. People in a bad mood evaluating the graduate student and people in a good mood evaluating the high school dropout rated their partner's intelligence the same. That is, people's emotional reactions can cancel the effect of status characteristics. A high-status partner had much less influence when a person was in a bad mood. A low-status partner had much more influence when a person was in a good mood.

You can use the knowledge that effects of emotion and status characteristics combine. For example, if you are a woman and want to increase your influence at work, then you want to avoid creating negative emotional reactions in your coworkers. Rather, by creating positive emotional reactions in them, you can increase your influence. Alice Eagly and her colleagues (Eagly, Karau, & Makhijani 1995; Eagly, Makhijani, & Klonsky 1992) have found that women develop distinctive leadership styles that are effective. The goal is to display a high level of competence and assertiveness without triggering negative emotional reactions. To be effective, women leaders have had to be attuned to the emotional reactions of their people and encourage positive emotions.

Women leaders have developed effective ways to overcome the Pollyanna image of the dutiful and meek secretary. Creating positive emotions in others is only part of increasing your influence. You must also control your own emotions to prevent others from gaining undue influence over you. Resist flattery and the courteous dismissal of your ideas. Keep focused on your goal of contributing and making your contributions count. Use your coworkers' emotions to help you succeed.

First Lady Hillary Rodham Clinton's performance during the health care debates on Capitol Hill is a good example of the strategies used by successful women. Kathleen Hall Jamieson (1995) describes how Clinton's active role in shaping public policy galvanized public sentiment against her. She was ridiculed for everything from her hairstyle to using her birth name, Rodham. For the health care hearings, Clinton responded to the extremely negative emotional reactions with thorough preparation. She demonstrated a commanding grasp of the subject and the subtle problems involved. Her clear demonstration of competence changed the way even her adversaries saw her. When asked about his new attitude toward Hillary Clinton, Republican Robert Dole said that he was used to smart women, and he was grateful that Clinton did not ask for blood. And while health care reform was not successfully implemented that year, Hillary Rodham Clinton's performance was successful in establishing her reputation as a political presence. A clear demonstration of competence is the first step in a successful work strategy.

It is also necessary to act assertively, to be noticed. Jamieson (1995, p. 200) tells how Supreme Court Justice Ruth Bader Ginsburg's nickname in law school was "Bitch." Ginsburg commented, "Better bitch than mouse." However, care is necessary when using an aggressive style. A woman who is too threatening, who creates too much fear and anger, can easily be swept aside no matter how competent. Hillary Clinton walked a fine line during the health care hearings. According to a *New York Times* article, "But no previous First Lady has occupied center stage so aggressively or disarmed her critics more effectively" (reported in Jamieson 1995, p. 47). When acting aggressively it is important to disarm the negative emotional reactions that follow. For best results, make it clear that you are not selfishly motivated, that you intend your contributions to help the group. For Clinton's work on the health care plan, it was clear that she was trying to contribute to the national good. It was hard to argue that the outcome would help her personally. Certainly, her position as First Lady would be easier if she stayed away from public policy. She was not pushing a personal agenda. She talked of the impact health care reform would have on the country, not the impact her performance would have on her. Aggressive behavior for selfish ends creates negative emotional reactions. You can disarm that negative emotion by presenting yourself as group-motivated.

Social psychology provides ways for low-status workers to increase their influence. Implications for the strategy women use on the job are clear. To maximize influence, you can demonstrate your competence without arousing negative emotional reactions. Clear demonstrations of competence are crucial for women who wish to attain influence in the workplace. However, your position in the status hierarchy depends not just on your competence, but on expectations that other people have for your competence. Your contributions will be more effective if people notice them. You can act assertively to avoid being ignored or overlooked, but couple assertiveness with discretion. To change people's expectations, not only must your contributions be noticed, but the benefits of your contributions must be noticed as well.

You can overcome the assumption that your efforts are selfishly motivated. Assertive behavior by people seen as selfish creates negative emotional reactions among coworkers. You can defuse negative emotional reactions that hamper competent and assertive women by carefully presenting yourself as group-motivated. You can emphasize group goals and group success rather than your personal success. Kay and Hagan (1998) found that women who successfully became partners in law firms did so by presenting themselves as focused on their legal careers rather than their home lives, by bringing in corporate clients, and by endorsing the goals of the law firm.

The techniques described in this chapter can help you obtain the influence and respect you deserve. They are available if you need them. Should you choose to use them, positive job evaluations, promotions, and better relations with coworkers are likely to result.

Further Reading

Of General Interest

Conley, F. K. (1998). *Walking out on the boys.* New York: Farrar, Straus and Giroux.
Hochshild, A. R. (1989). *The second shift.* New York: Avon Books.

Jamieson, K. H. (1995). *Beyond the double bind: Women and leadership.* New York: Oxford University Press.

Kanter, R. M. (1977). *Men and women of the corporation.* New York: Basic Books.

Recent and Technical Issues

Biernat, M., & Kobrynowicz, D. (1997). Gender- and race-based standards of competence: Lower minimum standards but higher ability standards for devalued groups. *Journal of Personality and Social Psychology, 72,* 544–557.

Butler, D., & Geis, F. L. (1990). Nonverbal affect responses to male and female leaders: Implications for leadership evaluations. *Journal of Personality and Social Psychology, 58,* 48–59.

Halberstadt, J. B., & Niedenthal, P. M. (1997). Emotional state and the use of stimulus dimensions in judgment. *Journal of Personality and Social Psychology, 72,* 1017–1033.

Rudman, L. A. (1998). Self-promotion as a risk factor for women: The costs and benefits of counterstereotypical impression management. *Journal of Personality and Social Psychology, 74,* 629–645.

Ruggiero, K. M., & Taylor, D. M. (1994). The personal/group discrimination discrepancy: Women talk about their experiences. *Journal of Applied Social Psychology, 24,*1806–1826.

Stangor, C., Lynch, L., Duan, C., & Glass, B. (1992). Categorization of individuals on the basis of multiple social features, *Journal of Personality and Social Psychology, 62,* 207–218.

Troyer, L., & Younts, C. W. (1997). Whose expectations matter? The relative power of first- and second-order expectations in determining social influence. *American Journal of Sociology, 103,* 692–732.

CHAPTER 8

Why I'm Prejudiced

It took me a long time to discover that I was prejudiced. It took even longer to admit it. The evidence built up slowly and painfully until I could no longer deny it. There was the time I felt a tingle of fear in the back of my neck when a well-dressed African-American college student walked behind me as I got cash from an ATM. Another time I hesitated momentarily before shaking the hand of a black coworker. Evidence of prejudice is measured in tenths of a second. But looking into his eyes I knew that he noticed. My prejudice and inability to admit it would just add to a long list of my character flaws had not some good research come of it, research that might actually help people. Social psychologists, it turns out, have made major contributions to the study of prejudice because of the peculiar way that we look at the world. A social psychologist would say that maybe my prejudice is not evidence of a personal character flaw but of a more general social process. Maybe that means we can find a way to help.

Having admitted my prejudice, my previous understanding of it no longer made sense. I had understood prejudice the way many people do. I thought that only mindlessly hostile people were prejudiced. Certainly enlightened people like me were not. That view of prejudice made admitting my own prejudice difficult. Unless I wanted to see myself as a mindlessly hostile person, my understanding of prejudice would have to change.

It turns out that everybody is prejudiced, some less than others perhaps, but prejudice is part of normal human thoughts and feelings. We humans discriminate between *us* and *them* with surprising ease. The flimsiest justification lets us think of ourselves as good and them as bad. I live in farm country where there are no large cities and many small towns. It is not uncommon for young people in one small town to dislike those from a neighboring small town. Hostility rises out of competition between high school athletic teams and romantic rivalries. *We* consider ourselves better in major ways than *they* are. But how much difference between us and them is there, really? Outside observers visiting those small towns have difficulty finding any difference between the two other than the town name painted on the water tower.

Doonesbury

BY GARRY TRUDEAU

Prejudice is communicated in subtle ways

An example of serious prejudice toward a minority group in Japan shows how arbitrary the distinction between us and them seems to outside observers. The village people—Burakumin—are a minority of about a million people who live in small segregated communities throughout Japan.[1] The disadvantaged position of the village people is striking because there are no noticeable racial, language, or cultural differences between the village people and the majority Japanese. Nonetheless, oppression of the village people dates back hundreds of years. They traditionally have been confined to low-status occupations such as itinerant entertainment, gardening, waste disposal, and animal slaughter. Japan had a civil rights movement during the 1960s, as did the United States. Civil rights legislation mandating equal opportunity for the village people passed with the support of a broad majority of Japanese voters. Despite some improvement in the lives of the village people, discrimination remains a problem. Village people are still more likely to work as unskilled laborers than are other Japanese and they are more likely to be on welfare.

Attempts to improve educational opportunity for the village people shows how persistent the problem can be. Up to the 1960s, the children of village people were known as terrible students who were often delinquent and frequently dropped out of school. While civil rights legislation lessened overt discrimination, problems with education persisted. Twenty years later, the dropout rate for the children of village people was still about twice that of majority Japanese. Grades of village people students remained lower than those of majority students (Shimahara 1984). Why can't village people in Japan take advantage of the educational opportunities provided since the 1960s? The same question is asked in the United States about African Americans. Before we try to answer that question, let's look at research that shows just how arbitrary prejudice can be.

MINIMUM REQUIREMENTS FOR PREJUDICE

Will people become prejudiced against others just like them who happen to belong to a different group? What if people were divided into two groups, the only distinction between the groups being that one was called group X while the other was

---

[1]Information on the Burakumin comes from Shimahara (1984).

called group Y? Researchers wanted to find out if even minimal distinctions between groups were enough to produce prejudice. Henri Tajfel and his colleagues (1971) divided people into groups based on arbitrary and trivial distinctions. They found that people separated into such groups gave more money to members of their own group, thus discriminating against members of the other group. Other researchers have repeated the experiment using different ways to separate people into groups with only minimal distinctions between them. Results of these experiments consistently show that people discriminate against members of another group when only trivial distinctions exist.[2]

In an extreme example, Louise Lemyre and Philip Smith (1985) divided people into two groups based on a slip of paper that people blindly drew from a bag. Those who drew a slip with the word "Red" on it were assigned to the Red group. Those who drew a slip with the word "Blue" on it were assigned to the Blue group. People then had the opportunity to reward members of their own group and the other group. Even though the only distinction between the two groups was whether the word Red or Blue was written on a slip of paper, people rewarded members of their own group more highly than members of the other group. Human beings are so prone to prejudice that it arises whenever people are divided into groups of *us* and *them.*

Researchers have found that categorizing people into groups of *us* and *them* also affects the way we think about people. Howard and Rothbart (1980) divided people into two groups based on a trivial distinction. Then people read a list of favorable and unfavorable statements from members of the other group and from members of their own group. "I took two disadvantaged kids on a one-week vacation" is an example of a favorable statement. "I had two brief affairs with other people while I was married" is an example of an unfavorable statement. Later people were asked to remember the statements they had read from each group. People found it easier to remember negative statements made by members of the other group than negative statements made by members of their own group. We overlook the faults of people close to us but we easily recall the shortcomings of members of other groups.

Once people are categorized as different, they are assumed to have many of the characteristics of their group. The characteristics are often negative. We call a generalization about all members of a group a *stereotype.* For example, African Americans are stereotyped as poor, lazy, athletic, musical, and hostile. The perception that African Americans are hostile creates real problems for racial relations. Because whites see blacks as hostile, whites fear blacks and retaliate with hostility of their own, sometimes with little or no provocation. Blacks, fearful of the unpredictable and sometimes violent response of whites, are less friendly than they otherwise would be. It is a perfect self-fulfilling prophecy. Whites see blacks as hostile. Whites' responses to blacks then increase black hostility. Recall from Chapter 7 that what people believe to be real is real in its consequences (Thomas & Thomas 1928).

---

[2] Other studies of the "minimal group" effect include Allen and Wilder (1975), Billig and Tajfel (1973), Brewer and Silver (1978), Locksley, Ortiz, and Hepburn (1980), Tajfel (1970), and Turner (1978).

The human tendency to categorize and stereotype makes racial relations more difficult because we tend to see what we expect to see. When white people see a black person do something that might or might not be aggressive, white people see it as aggressive because they expect hostility and aggression from a black person. In the same situation, a white person's behavior might not be seen as aggressive at all. The white perception of black hostility means that African Americans have to behave much more carefully than do European Americans.

Just how careful African-American men have to be became clear to me when a student asked me for help with her boyfriend, who had been arrested. He was being held in jail on a high bail. His bail was high because of a previous arrest. Both my student and her boyfriend are black. In the first incident, her boyfriend had gotten out of a late movie. He and some friends, who were white, decided to go to a local fast-food restaurant. The restaurant closes at midnight. The assistant manager was locking the doors just before midnight as a large number of people arrived from the movie. The crowd of young people brushed past the frustrated assistant manager, who called the police. The boyfriend of my student went in with the others but did not touch the assistant manager. When the police arrived, the assistant manager accused the boyfriend of pushing him out of the way. The boyfriend is tall and stands out in a crowd of white students. The assistant manager is white. The police made one arrest out of all the people who had pushed into the restaurant. My student's boyfriend, the only black person in the restaurant, was charged with assault. Stereotypes lead us to see the behavior we expect, sometimes when it has not occurred.

A couple of months later, my student was riding with her boyfriend as he drove his pickup truck. They got in an argument. She became angry and demanded to get out of the truck. He pulled over as she jumped out. He stopped the truck and followed her. When he caught up with her, he grabbed her and asked her to get back in the truck. She agreed. The police arrived a few minutes later. A witness in a passing car had seen the couple arguing and called the police. The police arrested the boyfriend. Based on what the witness said, police charged him with first-degree kidnapping. The witness said that she had seen the boyfriend force my student into the pickup truck. The witness is white. My student told the police that she had gotten into the truck willingly. When she came to me, her boyfriend had been in jail for almost a week on the kidnapping charge. Bail was set at $50,000. The witness saw a man arguing with a woman. But it became a kidnapping because the man was black. Because stereotypes change the way we see a situation, the lives of European Americans are very different from the lives of African Americans. Few white men consider the possibility that they could be charged with kidnapping for arguing with their girlfriends. Black men find it a necessary precaution.

Duncan (1976) set up a situation to determine whether white people really do see the behavior of a black person as more violent than the same behavior of a white person. He brought white people into the lab and showed them one of two videotapes. The videotapes showed two young men having a discussion. The discussion gradually becomes more heated until one of the young men shoves the other. The shove is not particularly violent. The man who was shoved does not lose his balance. The shove could have been meant to make a point in the argument, to dramatize. Or it could have been done in jest, a playful act. It might also have been a violent act, a prelude to further attack. Which was it? White people who saw the video-tapes were asked to decide for themselves. Was the shove intended to be playful or to dramatize a point in the argument? Or was it a violent attack?

Some people saw a tape of a black man shoving another man. Other people saw a tape of a white man shoving another man. Duncan (1976) predicted that white people would see the black man's shove as a violent act. However, the same shove by a white man would be seen as playful or to dramatize a point in the argument. The study supported Duncan's predictions. When white people saw a black man shoving another man, nearly all of them described it as violent or aggressive behavior. In contrast, when a white man did the shoving, most white people described it as playing around or dramatizing a point in the argument. The same behavior that is excused as clowning around when done by white men is seen as a violent attack when done by black men. One reason the arrest rate for African Americans is so high is because witnesses see the behavior of black men as violent or criminal when the same behavior of white men would be seen as innocent.

The self-fulfilling nature of stereotypes is complete when a witness who sees hostile behavior by a black person becomes convinced that it is typical of African Americans in general. The stereotype leads me to see hostile behavior where it may not exist. Then, having seen what I believe to be hostile behavior, I become more convinced that hostile behavior is typical of African Americans.

A negative experience with just one member of a different group affects the way we feel about that group as a whole. When we look at members of our own group, we see individuals with a wide variety of individual differences. We treat negative behavior by one of our own as a symptom of that person's individual problems. For example, we might read a newspaper story about a local athlete who has been arrested for drugs. If we are white, we see a white athlete's arrest as an example of that individual's drug problem. We do not see it as a symptom of more severe drug problems among whites than blacks. If we are black, our reaction to a black athlete's arrest is the same. We do not see it as a symptom of more severe drug problems among blacks than whites. But when we look at members of a different group, instead of individuals with a lot of variety, we see similar examples of the typical group member. We do not make the fine distinctions among individuals that we do with people close to us. When we encounter negative behavior by a member of a different group, we generalize. We think that negative behavior is typical of all members of the group. Whites see the arrest of a black athlete for drugs as an example of problems in the black community, not just the problem of an individual person.

Henderson-King and Nisbett (1996) set up a situation to see how white people react to the hostile behavior of either a black person or another white person. Would a white person who witnessed one brief incident of hostile behavior by a black person then associate hostility more strongly with blacks in general? Researchers also predicted that whites who witnessed the same hostile behavior by a white person would *not* then associate hostility any more strongly with whites in general. In the study, white people waited in a waiting room for the study to begin. Then either a white or a black person entered and spoke rudely to a research assistant. The hostile person said in a rude voice, "I've waited long enough. I'm outta here." Then he walked out of the room. Would exposing people to this mild example of rude behavior be enough to trigger the stereotype that blacks are hostile? For comparison, researchers also exposed people to positive behavior by a black or a white person. People waiting for the study to begin witnessed either a black or a white person politely agree to wait an extra 25 minutes to help a researcher finish an experiment.

White people exposed to rude behavior by a black person rated all black people as more hostile (Henderson-King and Nisbett 1996). However, the positive behavior of the black person did not improve the general impression that white people had of blacks. Not only do we remember better the negative behavior of a member of a different group, but we also will generalize that negative impression to the group as a whole. More surprising, researchers found that when whites were exposed to hostile behavior by a white person, whites rated white people in general as *less* hostile than did whites exposed to *positive* behavior by a white person. Negative behavior by a person of our own group has the opposite effect of negative behavior by a person from a different group. We see negative behavior by a member of our own group as the exception that proves the rule: *We* are generally good (with a few exceptions) and *they* are generally bad.

Another student of mine told me about his experience with how easily negative stereotypes become activated. He and a few friends were drinking beer and playing pool at a bar near the university. One friend had put his wallet on the bar. He picked up his wallet and looked inside. "I had a hundred-dollar bill in here when I laid it on the bar and now it is gone," he said. Visibly upset, he looked around the room. When he spotted a black student, the only African American in the bar, he said for no apparent reason, "It's him. He must have stolen my hundred-dollar bill." The other friends knew that the black student had not come near the wallet. They managed to talk their friend out of confronting the black student. Nothing more came of the incident, although the potential for violence was clear to everyone. My student told me that up until then he had no reason to think his friend was prejudiced. He also no longer thought African Americans oversensitive or paranoid for worrying about prejudiced reactions. One of his friends found the money on the floor under a barstool.

IS PREJUDICE AUTOMATIC?

My emerging understanding of prejudice created some disturbing problems. If I was prejudiced when my education and upbringing had taught against it, then prejudice must be somehow automatic. Did that also mean there was nothing we could do about it? Is real progress possible?

Normal people are prejudiced because a big part of the process is automatic. Prejudiced responses continue after people learn that prejudice is wrong and decide to behave differently. When humans belonged only to relatively small groups—the extended family or the tribe, for example—prejudice against outsiders served a purpose. Preference for our own group helped ensure that our family would survive. In modern society, individuals are members of very large groups—a nation, for example—composed of diverse people and many smaller groups. Automatic prejudiced reactions against other subgroups in society now interfere with social success. One of the first steps to overcoming prejudice is to realize that prejudiced reactions are a normal part of being human and will require constant work to overcome. Realizing I was prejudiced was at least a start toward something better.

Patricia Devine investigated automatic prejudiced reactions while she was still a graduate student at Ohio State University. She wondered why problems with prejudice continue even among people who seemed relatively unprejudiced. Why isn't it enough to realize that prejudice is wrong?

Devine (1989) first gave a test for prejudice to almost 500 people. The test she used is designed to detect prejudice even when people try to hide it. Using the results of the prejudice test, Devine then selected the most prejudiced people and the least prejudiced people for the second part of her study. She wanted to find out if both the most prejudiced people and the least prejudiced people had similar automatic prejudiced reactions.

If prejudiced reactions are automatic, then the least prejudiced people should have the same automatic prejudiced reactions as the most prejudiced people. Detecting an automatic prejudiced reaction is tricky. Devine thought that low-prejudiced people would try to block their automatic prejudiced reactions whenever they were aware of them. That meant she had to design a situation where people would not be aware that their reactions were prejudiced. The study of automatic reactions in other contexts had been pioneered by Bargh and Pietromonaco (1982). Devine adapted their method to detect automatic prejudiced reactions.

In Devine's (1989) study, a word was projected on a screen for a fraction of a second. People watching would notice that something flashed on the screen, but it would go by so quickly that they would not know what the word was, or even that it was a word. To be sure that the word was not recognized, jumbled letters were projected on the screen immediately after the word was flashed. Most people would not notice the brief flash that preceded the jumbled letters on the screen. All they would notice was a group of jumbled letters. Devine thought that by flashing words associated with the common stereotype of African Americans, she might activate people's automatic prejudiced reactions. Because people were unaware of those racially charged words, she also thought that low-prejudiced people would not be able to block their prejudiced reactions. If prejudiced reactions were automatic, then low-prejudiced and high-prejudiced people would react the same to the racially charged words. She showed people either a series of racially charged words (for example, blacks, Negroes, poor, lazy, athletic) or a series of neutral words (for example, water, then, would, thought, something).

Devine (1989) predicted that she had activated the prejudices of one group of people by showing them racially charged words. She could then compare the reactions of people who had been shown the racially charged words with the reactions of people who had seen the neutral words. If she had succeeded in activating prejudice, then people who saw the racially charged words would react in a more prejudiced way than would people who saw the neutral words.

To find out whether prejudice had been activated by the flashed words, Devine (1989) asked people to judge the behavior of a man named "Donald." Donald's race was *not* identified. People read a paragraph in which Donald demands his money back from a store clerk and refuses to pay his rent until his landlord paints his apartment. Donald's behavior might be seen as reasonable or aggressive and hostile, depending on the way that people saw the situation. If people's prejudice had really been triggered by the racially charged words flashed on a screen, then they would read more hostility into Donald's behavior than would people who had seen neutral words. Remember that hostility is part of the stereotype of African Americans, but none of the flashed words referred to hostility in any way.

In this situation, people could not block any automatic prejudiced reactions they might have. They had no way to tell that the study was about prejudice. All they saw was a series of jumbled letters flashed on a screen, and then they judged the behavior of a person whose race was not mentioned.

Devine (1989) predicted that people who had seen the racially charged words would find Donald's behavior more hostile than would people who had seen neurtral words. Along with being stereotyped as poor, lazy, and athletic, African Americans are stereotyped as hostile and aggressive. Devine wanted to know if people who had seen the racially charged words would find Donald's behavior more hostile. None of the racially charged words flashed on the screen had anything to do with hostility. If people who had seen the racially charged words found Donald's behavior more hostile, it would be due to their automatic prejudiced reactions to African Americans.

Flashing racially charged words on a screen for less than a tenth of a second was enough to activate automatic prejudiced reactions. People who saw racially charged words rated Donald's behavior as more hostile than did people who saw neutral words. Devine (1989) showed that automatic prejudiced reactions could be detected and measured.

Devine's (1989) most important prediction was that people who scored low on the prejudice test would have the same automatic prejudiced reactions as people who score high on the prejudice test. Recall that her theory says that all people are prejudiced, but those who score low on prejudice tests are able to consciously block some of their automatic prejudiced reactions, when they are aware of them. Of course in her experiment, people are not aware of their prejudiced reactions because all they see are jumbled words on a screen and a paragraph about Donald, whose race is not mentioned. Would low-prejudiced people have the same automatic prejudiced reactions as high-prejudiced people?

They did. It did not matter whether people were outright bigots or firm believers in racial equality; people had the same automatic prejudiced reactions. In Devine's (1989) study, when people were shown the racially charged words, they found Donald's behavior more hostile. It did not matter whether they had scored very high or very low on a prejudice test. They had the same automatic prejudiced reactions.

Do those automatic prejudiced reactions that we all have really affect our behavior? It would not be so bad if, as a result of our prejudice, we merely think that some people are more hostile than are others. In contrast, if our prejudice causes us to be more hostile as well, then prejudice remains a major problem for society. No matter how tolerant and well educated we are, no matter how strongly we believe in racial equality, we cannot always be aware of our automatic reactions and correct for them. In some situations we will not be aware of them. In other situations events will be happening too fast for us to consciously react. My hesitation before shaking a black colleague's hand took little more time than one of those racially charged words that Patricia Devine flashed on the screen. But it was enough time to do damage.

If people's prejudice were automatically triggered, would they then react in a more hostile way to an annoying situation than they would if their prejudice were not triggered? Bargh, Chen, and Burrows (1996) set up a situation where they could measure people's hostile reactions. Researchers presented people with a series of tedious problems, judging the number of different colored circles that appeared for a few seconds on a computer screen. People judged the number of circles on more than 100 screens. Just before each screen of circles appeared, the computer flashed a man's picture for less than a tenth of a second. The man's picture went by so fast that people were not aware that anything had happened. All they saw was the picture of the colored circles on the computer screen. For half the people in the study, researchers flashed a picture of an African-American man. The rest of the people in the study saw a picture of a European-American man.

After people had been repeatedly exposed to a picture of either a black man or a white man, researchers provoked a hostile reaction from them. After judging 130 pictures of small, different-colored circles, a research assistant came in and explained that the computer had failed to save the data and it had all been lost. The person would have to repeat the study, all 130 times. A hidden video camera recorded people's facial expressions when they heard the news. Bargh, Chen, and Burrows (1996) predicted that people who had been exposed to the subliminal picture of a black man would react with more hostile facial expressions than would people who had been exposed to a picture of a white man. Researchers thought that seeing a picture of a black man would activate automatic prejudice. Because the question of race did not come up during the experiment, people would not be able to consciously block their prejudiced reactions. They would react in a more hostile way because of their prejudice.

Would white people react in a more hostile way just because they had seen a picture of a black man? They did. Bargh, Chen, and Burrows (1996) had observers watch the videotapes and judge the hostility of people's reaction to hearing they would have to repeat the tedious experiment. Observers did not know which picture people had seen subliminally, the picture of the black man or the picture of the white man. After the hostility ratings were complete, however, it turned out that observers agreed most of the time on how hostile each person's reaction was. More important, observers had rated the expressions of people exposed to a picture of a black man as more hostile than the expressions of people exposed to the picture of a white man.

Now we can see why prejudice continues to be a problem. We are all prejudiced and prejudiced reactions can be automatically triggered. (Social psychology does make us uncomfortable.) When prejudice has been triggered we react in a hostile manner. Our hostile reaction invites a hostile response, and the problem continues. In some situations, when we are aware of ourselves and we have enough time, we can block those prejudiced reactions, replacing them with more socially acceptable behavior. But many times we cannot. Overcoming prejudice is a constant battle we fight within ourselves.

WHY ARE PEOPLE SO UPSET?

As my understanding of my own prejudice grew, I also had to abandon the idea that prejudice and racial discrimination were major problems in the past that had, to a large extent, been solved. When I thought that prejudiced people were mindlessly hostile, it was easy also to think that the civil rights legislation of the 1960s gave people a roughly equal chance of success in this country. I thought that as soon as people got used to the idea, they would realize that treating each other equally was the right way to live. But if I was prejudiced when my upbringing and education had taught the opposite, then African Americans must face a constant barrage of minor insults mixed with some major ones. Further, prejudice would be virtually invisible to European Americans. Because it was not happening to them, there would be no reason for whites to notice. As a result, racial tension and mistrust stay at a high level. Many whites wonder what all the fuss is about while many blacks wonder whether whites are evil or just blind (Shipler 1997).

Sometimes the extent and power of prejudice becomes clear to everyone. In late 1996 and early 1997, a tragedy occurred in the lives of several young people in Indiana (Terry 1997). Leif O'Connell was in love with Annie Fulford, his 17-year-old girlfriend. They met at a high school basketball game. Annie soon became the center of Leif's life. They planned to announce their engagement when Annie turned 18. Leif had shown Annie's mother the ring. Their marriage promised to fulfill his lifelong dream, a stable and loving home life. Then the young couple went to visit Annie's brother in a poor part of town. Annie and Leif accidentally walked into the middle of a drug deal gone bad. She was caught in the crossfire and killed. After Annie's funeral, Leif spent many hours at her parents' house, staring at the box containing her cremated ashes, crying. Leif is white, as was Annie. The drug dealers accused of killing her were arrested and held in jail without bail. All of the men accused in Annie's death are black.

About a month later, Robert Wardlow Jr. was shot to death as he walked along a street in a largely black section of South Bend, the Indiana town where Leif lives. Police at first thought Robert was the accidental victim of a gang-related shooting. Drug-related violence was common in the area. Robert was 20 years old and had avoided trouble. He stayed away from gangs. He worked with his mother doing odd jobs at a convention center. He loved video games and food. He wanted to go to art school. Police soon discovered that Robert's death was not drug-related. They arrested Leif O'Connell, Annie's boyfriend, for Robert's murder. Robert had nothing to do with Annie's death. Robert, however, was black.

Police say that Leif and a white friend also shot five other black men over a two-week period. The shooters selected black men at random. None of the black victims were involved in any way in Annie's death. Yet police say that Leif and his friend shot black men to avenge Annie's death. Robert died and the other men were shot only because they were black.

Leif does not seem to fit our image of a racist murderer. He is not active in hate groups. There is no evidence of prejudice in his past. Leif took ballet lessons for eight years but quit to keep his friends from teasing him about it. He has a 4-H club trophy and an award for being the best-behaved boy in church. Yet Annie's death triggered Leif's underlying prejudice. When he lost Annie, Leif's emotional reaction against all black men was apparently so severe that he murdered an innocent African American and wounded five others.

The story of Leif and Annie and Robert is so disturbing because we all can understand Leif's behavior at a basic emotional level. Sure, we know it is not logical to kill innocent people because someone killed a loved one. If white drug dealers had killed Annie, Leif would not have shot random white men. Would he? It does not feel like something a person would do. But if you are not black, imagine how you would feel if a black criminal killed someone you love. It would certainly trigger some fear of blacks in general and maybe some anger. While most people would not act on their prejudice, it would be there. If you are black, imagine how you would feel if a white criminal killed someone you love. Robert's father was angry that a white man killed his son for no reason. He said he wants to stay angry. I would too. We all are prejudiced.

Perhaps the most curious aspect of prejudice is the strong emotion that accompanies it. It makes some sense that people would give more money to people of their own group than to people of another group, as they do in those "minimal group" experiments described earlier. After all, we have a better chance of benefiting if others in our own group have money than we do if some other group gets it. But prejudice provokes extreme fear and hatred. Why? We respond with fear and hatred when we have been threatened. Any threat to ourselves or our social positions triggers prejudice. Without threat, prejudice might remain a manageable preference for members of our own group. We are prejudiced to the extent we feel threatened or fearful.

Rogers and Prentice-Dunn (1981) studied the effect that threat has on prejudice and aggressive behavior. Since the 1960s, most white Americans have come to believe that people should be treated equally regardless of their race. In fact, because race is such a touchy issue, white Americans will often go out of their way to avoid the appearance of prejudice. For example, when asked to judge the essays of fellow college students, white students gave more positive feedback about the essay when they thought a black student wrote it than when they thought a white student wrote it (Harber 1998). It is understandable, then, that many whites feel that blacks are now treated more than fairly in society. However, Rogers and Prentice-Dunn thought that any positive bias toward African Americans would be limited to situations where emotions did not trigger prejudice. The researchers predicted that when white people are threatened, they would react more aggressively toward a black person than they would toward a white person.

Rogers and Prentice-Dunn (1981) brought people into the lab to act as assistants in a behavior modification clinic. In the behavior modification procedure, a patient would be wired to a heart rate monitor and to an electrical shock generator. The people acting as research assistants would watch the heart rate monitor. Their job was to administer mild electrical shocks to the patient whenever the patient's heart rate dropped below a certain level. By pressing one of ten switches, people could choose what level of shock to administer from very mild (switch 1) to most severe (switch 10). They could also change the duration of the shock by holding down the shock switch. In the study, a researcher acted as the "patient." No real shock was ever delivered, but people acting as clinical assistants thought they were administering electrical shocks to a patient. They were told that only mild (switch 1) shocks were needed. Stronger shocks would only cause the patient greater pain without greater benefit. Half the people gave shocks to a black man. The other half gave shocks to a white man.

When white people in the study were not threatened or emotionally upset, they gave milder shocks to the black man than they did to the white man. Thus when prejudice has not been triggered by emotion, people may overcompensate to avoid the appearance of prejudice. Rogers and Prentice-Dunn (1981) thought people would behave quite differently after they had been threatened. They tried the study again, but this time the patient insulted the people acting as clinical assistants. For example, people overheard the patient say that the clinical assistants looked too dumb to follow instructions properly. Having been insulted, would the white clinical assistants retaliate more harshly against the black patient than the white patient?

They did. Rogers and Prentice-Dunn (1981) found that the white people acting as clinical assistants were angered by the insults from the patient. In their anger, white people shocked the black patient more severely and for longer periods of time than they shocked the white patient. When threatened and angry, people act on their prejudices, despite otherwise good intentions.

More evidence that threat triggers prejudice comes from studies of lynchings and legal executions of African Americans in the south. Between the emancipation of slaves in the 1860s and the great economic depression of the 1930s, about 3,000 African Americans were lynched by white mobs in the south (Beck & Tolnay 1990). Researchers thought that these lynchings might be more frequent during tough economic times. The idea is that people feel threatened during a sagging economy. Jobs are harder to get and easier to lose when the economy is bad. Farmers may fear losing their farms and their homes. If prejudice is triggered when people feel threatened, then whites in the south would be more likely to lynch blacks when whites felt threatened by tough economic times. Lynchings would increase even if blacks had nothing to do with white financial difficulties. Threat and fear in general trigger prejudice.

A number of studies confirm that lynchings and executions of African Americans were more frequent in the south during tough economic times. Beck and Tolnay (1990) found that lynchings increased when the price of cotton was falling, cotton being the mainstay of the southern economy at the time. Hepworth and West (1988) also found that the worse the economy, the greater the number of lynchings. More important, they found that almost all of the additional lynchings during tough economic times were of blacks. Lynching of whites increased little or not at all when whites were threatened. Another study found that more blacks were legally executed when whites felt threatened (Tolnay, Beck, & Massey 1992). Not only do threat and fear trigger prejudice, but prejudiced responses can be severe.

Most of us like to think that we would help anyone we could during an emergency. I certainly did not want to think that I would hesitate to help a black person in trouble when I would rush to help a white person. But I probably would hesitate. I would not consciously decide to hesitate. It would just take me longer to get there.

Gaertner and Dovidio (1977) wanted to know if white bystanders would hesitate in helping a black person during an emergency. The researchers thought that even though people believe that they would help everyone equally, white people would be more likely to help a white person than a black person. A subtle process might occur in white people's minds to prevent them from coming to the aid of a black person as quickly as they would a white person. A white person who believes in racial equality might spring to the aid of a black person whenever the white person thought that delay might appear racist. However, Gaertner and Dovidio predicted that when there was something in the situation *other than racism* that might explain a delay, whites would hesitate to help a black person.

Gaertner and Dovidio (1977) designed a study where white people had the opportunity to help a black or a white accident victim. The researchers also designed their study so that white people would have either more or less accountability for their helping behavior. To make people feel more or less accountable for helping an accident victim, they either worked alone with a person who had the accident or worked with three other people. Recall from Chapter 1 that bystanders who witness an emergency are more likely to help if other people are not available. Often, when several people witness an emergency, no one helps because everyone thinks that someone else will probably do it. For example, when I see an accident on the freeway I usually think, Why should I call 911, they probably have five calls about the accident already. Gaertner and Dovidio used this "bystander effect" to give people a reason to hesitate in helping an accident victim. If white people are concerned about appearing racist, they would help quickly when they are the only witness to a black person's accident. However, when there are several witnesses to a black person's accident, a white person might worry less about appearing racist and hesitate to help.

In the study, Gaertner and Dovidio (1977) brought people into the laboratory to work in groups of either one or three people. People were seated alone in single-person rooms. Their task was to try to transmit their thoughts to a person who was trying to show that she had extrasensory perception. People could listen to the person who spoke to them using a microphone connected to speakers in the individual lab rooms. Sometimes people thought they were the only person who was listening. Sometimes they thought that two other people were listening at the same time in different rooms. People saw the ID card of the person they were listening to. Some people saw a picture of a black woman; others saw a picture of a white woman. They were also shown the room where the woman would be working, right across the hall from their own room. People then worked on the task. They tried to send their thoughts to the woman whose picture they had seen. She reported her guesses to them through the speakers. In the middle of the task, however, the women suddenly commented that there was a stack of chairs that looked like it would fall over. Through the speakers, people could hear her get up to try to straighten the chairs. People then heard her scream. She said, "They're falling on me. . . ." followed by more screams, then silence. You would rush across the hall to help, wouldn't you? Gaertner and Dovidio wanted to know whether white people in the study would help a black victim less often than they would help a white victim when there were other bystanders around to help.

The results were interesting. Gaertner and Dovidio (1977) found that white people helped the black woman somewhat more often and more quickly when they thought they were the only witness to the accident. When a white person was the only witness to the accident, the person rushed to help the black woman 94 percent of the time. When the victim was white, the white witness tried to help only 81 percent of the time. On the surface, it seems that whites overcompensate in helping blacks to avoid appearing racist. However, Gaertner and Dovidio predicted quite different results when people thought there were other witnesses available to help. When other witnesses were available, would white people then be less willing to help a black person than they would a white person?

Gaertner and Dovidio (1977) were right. When there were other witnesses available to help, white people came to the aid of the black woman less than 38 percent of the time. White people helped the white woman twice as often, 75 percent of the time. When something in the situation gives me an excuse not to help a black person, I will be less likely to help. My prejudice, it seems, is alive and well. It just gets harder to see as I try to do the right thing. Now that I know I have a tendency to hesitate when helping people who are different from me, maybe I will come to their aid faster in an emergency. I hope so. The truth might set me free, but it usually makes me uncomfortable first.

BEYOND PREJUDICE

Now we know that our best intentions regarding racial equality will not solve the problem. But we can still make progress, and we have. On questionnaires designed to measure prejudice, Americans have shown less and less conscious prejudice against African Americans over the last 40 years.[3] Our automatic prejudiced reactions might be a different story. Have our automatic prejudiced reactions also diminished over the years? Some indirect evidence suggests improvement in our automatic reactions as well.

Wittenbrink, Judd, and Park (1997) designed a way to measure automatic prejudice. They tested people with their automatic prejudice technique and also gave them a questionnaire designed to measure prejudice. They found that people who scored high on automatic prejudice also usually scored high on the standard prejudice questionnaire. And people who scored low on automatic prejudice usually scored low on the standard prejudice questionnaire. It did not happen all the time. However, the two measures of prejudice were similar for enough people that it hints at progress. If automatic prejudice and standard prejudice are related, then when standard prejudice goes down, automatic prejudice might go down also. Because we know that standard measures of prejudice have been declining for 40 years,

[3]For example, see Schuman, Steeh, and Bobo, 1985.

maybe automatic prejudice has been declining also. We cannot be sure because ways to measure automatic prejudice have only recently been developed. So we do not know what the automatic prejudice level was 20 or 30 years ago. Still, there is reason to hope that at least some progress has been made.

Social psychological research has also shown that some of the social policies of the last 40 years can be effective in changing prejudiced attitudes. Recall from Chapter 1 that Martin Luther King Jr. brushed aside the argument that to obtain racial equality, people's hearts and minds would have to change first. In the 1950s, popular opinion on civil rights maintained that "you can't legislate morality." Martin Luther King wanted to change the laws first. He hoped that hearts and minds would follow, but he was not going to wait for them. Now we know that he was right. Popular opinion about African Americans is more positive since civil rights legislation was passed in the 1960s. Recent research suggests that people's hearts and minds may have followed their new behavior as they obey civil rights laws.

Leippe and Eisenstadt (1994) set up a situation to force a change in people's behavior. They then looked to see if their general beliefs changed to agree with their new behavior. In the study, white people first completed questionnaires that determined their attitudes toward affirmative action and African Americans in general. As you would expect, people's personal opinions about affirmative action varied widely, ranging from strongly for affirmative action to strongly against it. Then half of them were asked to write an essay strongly favoring affirmative action. By writing the essay, people were acting as if they were in favor of affirmative action regardless of what they originally believed. The other half of the people in the study did not write an essay. They simply waited in a room for 15 minutes.

After people had finished their essays or waited in the room, they all completed another questionnaire that measured their attitudes toward affirmative action and African Americans in general. Leippe and Eisenstadt (1994) had two research questions. First, would people who had been asked to write an essay favoring affirmative action have more positive attitudes toward African Americans at the end of the study than people who had waited in a room? Second, would the attitudes of people who had been asked to write an essay favoring affirmative action be more positive on the questionnaire at the end of the study than they were on the questionnaire at the beginning of the study?

Leippe and Eisenstadt (1994) first checked to see if people who waited in a room had the same attitudes toward African Americans as people asked to write the pro–affirmative action essay. They did. At the beginning of the study there was no difference in attitudes toward African Americans between the essay writers and the group that waited in a room. When researchers got people to act as if they were in favor of affirmative action, would that also change their attitudes toward African Americans in general? Leippe and Eisenstadt found that attitudes did change. People who wrote the essay favoring affirmative action, whether they wanted to or not, were more in favor of affirmative action at the end of the study than were people who waited in a room. That is, people who acted as if they were in favor of something actually came to believe more in it. Changing people's behavior is an effective way to change their attitudes. Not only were people who wrote the essay more in favor of affirmative action; at the end of the study, they were also more positive about

African Americans in general. Prejudice had been reduced. Perhaps most interest-ing, Leippe and Eisenstadt found that people who started the study with the most negative feelings about blacks changed their attitudes the most after writing the es-say. Having to write the essay had the biggest positive effect on the people who dis-agreed with it the most. Progress can be made in our personal struggles against prejudice, and we are making progress slowly.

Notice that what people did in the Leippe and Eisenstadt (1994) study is simi-lar to what you do when you write affirmations. Remember affirmations from Chapter 1? Affirmations are positive statements that people write about themselves. The idea is that by writing about myself in a positive way, I will grow to become more like the person in the affirmation. The first affirmations I wrote were about honesty. I wanted to stop lying. But I resisted writing those first affirmations. It did not feel right. I did not believe I was honest. How was it going to help to write that I was honest when I wasn't? It did not make sense. I made myself write those first affirmations anyway. No better plan came to mind, I guess, and I was miserable. Still those simple sentences of less than 10 words were extremely difficult to write. My writing arm cramped. I felt sick to my stomach. Social psychologists call that sick feeling *cognitive dissonance.*

Cognitive dissonance (or now usually just *dissonance*) refers to psychological discomfort that occurs when our behavior threatens our beliefs about ourselves.[4] Because I thought of myself as dishonest, writing about myself as if I were honest caused me to feel uncomfortable. That uncomfortable feeling is dissonance. Most people might not feel any dissonance after writing they were honest because most people consider themselves reasonably honest. Unless our behavior somehow be-trays our beliefs about ourselves, we do not feel dissonance.

Imagine for a minute that you have just woken up feeling a little disoriented. You are in somebody else's bed. You remember that you had gone to a party the night before and had a few drinks. You were separated from your friends. Still, you decided to stay and have another drink. You remember feeling good and meeting people who seemed interesting. The rest of the night is a blank. Now you realize that you do not know where your clothes are. Just then a naked man walks into the bedroom, smiling. Dissonance is what you feel as you try to remember if you have ever seen him before.

Most people would feel uncomfortable because they do not think of themselves as people who go to bed with strangers. To reduce that uncomfortable feeling of dissonance, we can change the troublesome behavior or we can change our attitude toward that behavior. For example, you could behave very carefully in the future to make sure it never happens again. The dissonance would fade as you try to forget about the unfortunate incident. Or you could change your attitude toward sleeping

---

[4]In the 40 years since Festinger (1957) first proposed the theory of cognitive dissonance, the theory has moti-vated much good research and just as much controversy. It seems that some part of the theory bothers almost everyone. For more on the development of cognitive dissonance research see Aronson (1969) and Cooper and Fazio (1984). Steele (1988) relates dissonance research to self-affirmation. Tesser and Cornell (1991) relate dissonance research to the wider field of social psychological research on the self that was described in Chap-ters 3 and 4.

He probably doesn't feel cognitive dissonance because smoking has yet to contradict his self-image

with strangers. You might decide that he seems like a nice guy. Maybe things aren't so bad.

The theory of cognitive dissonance says that when we feel uncomfortable because our behavior has betrayed our beliefs, we are motivated to reduce the conflict between behavior and belief. We likely will try to change one or the other. Either we change our behavior to agree with our beliefs about ourselves, or we change our beliefs about ourselves to conform to our behavior. In my case, I could stop writing affirmations about honesty so I could continue to think of myself as dishonest. Or I could stop lying so my affirmations about my honesty would become true. Similarly, people may behave as if they are not prejudiced to conform to law or social pressure regardless of their true beliefs. Dissonance research suggests that when people behave as if they are not prejudiced, their beliefs about African Americans become more positive.

RACE AS A STATUS CHARACTERISTIC

While it is a relief to know that we are making progress in racial relations, it would also help to know why progress is so slow. The problem is complicated because race is not just a stereotype. Race is also a status characteristic. Chapter 7 described how status characteristics work in the business world. When we work in groups, we use status characteristics to guess who will help us get the job done. We often have little real knowledge of the capabilities of the people we work with, especially if the task at hand is new or complicated. So we fall back on traditional rules of thumb, guidelines to help us work together. Often, especially in modern work groups, the status characteristics we use make little sense.

Chapter 7 focused on another status characteristic, gender. Before modern machinery, upper body strength was crucial to performing many agricultural tasks. It made sense to expect that men would be better than women at wrestling a heavy plow through rocky soil. Now, however, important work tasks can be performed at least as competently by women as by men. The important work we do today requires mental ability and networking with diverse people. Yet we still expect that men will perform better than women will in a wide variety of situations. The process is largely nonconscious. Even people who believe strongly in equal treatment for men and women behave as if they expect men to contribute more to the success of a work group.

The effect of status characteristics on our behavior is even more widespread than the effect of stereotypes. Stereotypes affect our behavior toward members of other groups. Status characteristics affect our behavior toward members of our own group as well. Not only do men behave as if they expect men to contribute more; women also behave as if men are more important to group success (Pugh & Wahrman 1983).

Webster and Driskell (1978) set up a situation to see if race is a status characteristic. Researchers brought people into the laboratory and put them in separate rooms. They worked together with a partner who they saw on a television monitor. Sometimes, the two partners disagreed as they worked together. When partners disagree, each has to decide whether to insist on her own opinion or change her mind to go along with what her partner thinks is right. If a person usually changes her mind to go along with her partner, then she expects that her partner is highly capable and has much to contribute. In contrast, if she usually insists on her own opinion, then she probably expects that her partner is less capable and has little to contribute.

In work situations where partners disagreed, people were strongly motivated to get the right answer to the problems they faced (Webster & Driskell 1978). If they thought that their partner had the right answer, then they would want to change their minds. Researchers assigned people to one partner who was African American. Webster and Driskell predicted that people would stick with their own opinions most of the time when they disagreed with a black partner. Earlier studies had shown that when people expected their partner to contribute little to the group's success, they stuck with their own opinion about 65 percent to 75 percent of the time.

Would white people behave as if a black person has little to contribute to the group? They did. When people disagreed with a black partner, they stuck with their own opinion 68 percent of the time. People may not be aware of it, but they behave as if they expect black people to be less competent and contribute less than white people do.

Webster and Driskell (1978) also wanted to find out if race was the overriding factor rather than how competent people expected the partner to be. Maybe people would ignore the opinions of the black partner even when they thought she was highly competent. Researchers repeated the study. This time, however, they showed people that their black partner was actually more competent than they were. Researchers gave people two ability tests and showed them that they had scored poorly while their black partner scored well, showing very high ability. If race were all that mattered to people, then they would ignore the opinions of the black partner just as often when they knew that the black partner was more competent than they were. However, Webster and Driskell thought people were behaving according to their expectations for their partner's competence. The stereotype of African Americans leads people to believe that black people will be less competent than white people are. Because African Americans are expected to be less competent, their opinions are ignored. Webster and Driskell predicted that when people expected a black partner to be more competent, they would stick with their own opinions less often.

The prediction was correct (Webster & Driskell 1978). When people were given ability tests and shown that their black partner had higher ability than they had, they changed their mind to go along with their black partner more often. When white people disagreed with their black partner, they stuck with their opinion 58 percent of the time compared to 68 percent of the time in the first study. Race is not everything to people, but it does make a difference. Notice that even when people had strong evidence that a black partner was more competent than they were, they still ignored the black partner's opinion more than half the time.

Status characteristics also tell us who is more deserving of high rewards. In this society, most of us believe that people who contribute more on the job should be paid more. We expect that people with valued status characteristic will contribute more. Thus we expect people with valued status characteristics (for example, men and European Americans) to be rewarded more highly than others.

Ayres (1991) used status characteristics theory to predict how much people will pay for a new car. It might seem reasonable that white men, for example, would pay the most for cars because they are more highly rewarded and can afford to pay more. However, that is not the way the world works. Ayres predicted that because white men are thought to be more deserving, car dealers would make them the lowest offers. More precisely, he predicted that a white man would pay the least, a black man or a white woman would pay more, and a black woman would pay the most *for the same car.*

Research assistants went out shopping for cars at 90 different car dealerships. One shopper was a black woman, one was a white woman, one was a black man, and three were white men. All of the shoppers were similar in age, education, and style of dress. Shoppers were trained to give people exactly the same information. For example, they all told salespeople that they would finance the car themselves. Shoppers were also trained to bargain for the best price in exactly the same way. Then shoppers individually went to car dealers and bargained for the same cars. The shoppers then recorded two pieces of information that allowed Ayres (1991) to test his predictions. Shoppers recorded the salesperson's response to their initial question, "How much would I have to pay to buy this car?" They also recorded the salesperson's final offer at the end of bargaining.

Who gets the best deals when buying cars? White men do. Not because of their skill at bargaining but because of who they are. Ayres (1991) found that when white men shopped for cars, the initial offer made by the salesperson would give the dealer $818 in profit. When the shopper was a white woman, the salesperson's initial offer was slightly higher, giving $829 profit to the dealer. For a black man, the salesperson's initial offer was much higher, $1,534 profit to the dealer. The salesperson's initial offer to a black woman was higher still, $2,169 profit to the dealer. Research results dramatically supported Ayres's predictions. The effects of race and gender combine, allowing white men to pay the least for cars. Black women pay the most, while white women and black men pay amounts in between.

At the end of bargaining, the combined effects of race and gender were still strong. Men got the best offers, leaving the dealer with only $139 in profit on average. Black women got the worst offers, giving the dealer a profit of $1,185. White women and black men received offers in between, $806 in dealer profit for white women and $1,051 for black men. Even though different shoppers bargained the same way for the same cars, race and gender determined the price people would pay.

Because race is a status characteristic, people expect African Americans to be less competent than European Americans. Because people expect blacks to be less competent, blacks are considered less deserving than whites. Along with hostility, then, the stereotype that African Americans are less competent causes serious problems. For most fields other than entertainment and athletics, African Americans are expected to be less competent than European Americans are. Because we value competence so highly in modern society, we think that highly competent people are more deserving than are others. Thus we freely discriminate against people we expect to be less competent. The growing use of intelligence testing and college entrance examinations highlights the problem. People can argue that if African Americans are less intelligent than are European Americans, then perhaps African Americans should not be professionals and leaders. When some medical and law schools discontinued affirmative action policies, the number of new African-American students dropped dramatically, sometimes to near zero. But admission was based on standardized tests. So it was fair, right? Should African Americans be allowed to attend college even though they do not score as high as European Americans do on college entrance exams? Are African Americans less intelligent than European Americans are? These are explosive questions.

PREJUDICE AND INTELLIGENCE

On average, African Americans score lower than European Americans on a wide variety of intelligence and ability tests. While the gap has gotten smaller in recent years, a substantial difference in ability test scores remains between races. It will not go away by itself. We cannot ignore it. It is one scientific finding that has no trouble attracting a wide audience.[5] What we have to do now is explain it. Why do African Americans score lower than European Americans do on those standardized tests?

Because of the peculiar way that social psychologists look at the world, they seem especially well suited to explain the troubling gap in test scores between African Americans and European Americans. Recall the fundamental lesson of social psychology from Chapter 1. Individual character and ability play less of a role in events than people usually think they do. Social forces and other factors outside the individual often play a greater role than people think. When we see a person be-

---

[5]Hernnstein and Murray's (1994) best-seller, *The Bell Curve: Intelliegence and Class Structure in American Life,* is an example.

having in a certain way, we attribute that behavior to the inner qualities of the person. Even when that person's behavior has been virtually dictated by circumstances outside her control, we explain it as the result of the kind of person she is. Attributing behavior to an individual's character is such a basic part of thinking in Western societies that social psychologists call it the fundamental attribution error. When a person does well in school, we think it is because she is a good student. She has high academic ability. When a person gets a very high score on an intelligence test, we think it is because she is very smart. It seems so obvious. Few people would question that explanation unless they were social psychologists. A social psychologist would wonder whether the fundamental attribution error was making the explanation seem obvious (Meyers 1996). Is there an explanation for a high score on an intelligence test other than intelligence? What else might affect the score a person gets on a test?

Scientists are as prone to the fundamental attribution error as anyone else is. The development of scientific testing for individual ability rests on a reasonable assumption: A person scores high on an ability test because of high ability or scores low because of low ability. That would mean that African Americans score lower on ability tests because they have lower ability. Scientists, then, have looked for explanations for the lower ability of African Americans. Biologically oriented scientists look for genetic explanations. Social scientists look at the social conditions in which African Americans live. For example, because African Americans face poverty and discrimination, perhaps they do not develop to their full intellectual potential. Much research has been done in these areas, but neither genetic nor social explanations have received much support. After scientists sort out all the known factors that contribute to intelligence, a sizable unexplained gap between black and white intelligence remains.[6]

Social psychologists, however, wonder whether the assumption that blacks are less intelligent is wrong. What if the fundamental attribution error fools us into believing that blacks are less intelligent? Maybe African Americans score lower on ability tests for some reason other than lower intelligence. What if African Americans are just as smart as European Americans are? Given this quite different assumption, social psychologists try to explain why blacks might score lower on ability tests even when they are just as capable as whites are.

While my own prejudice against African Americans has become painfully apparent, the belief that African Americans were less intelligent was never part of my thinking. I missed that part of the stereotype. A lucky accident allowed me to grow up with the opposite impression. I had little contact with African Americans while I grew up. Segregation was not legal, but it existed all the same. The exception was a friend of my father named Paul Byrd. He was a professor of mathematics at San Jose State University, one of the few African Americans on the faculty at the time. My father and mother both taught mathematics, so I thought that mathematics professors were pretty smart. Professor Byrd would come to our house for dinner and I would listen to the conversation of the adults. My father seemed to place great weight on Professor Byrd's opinions. After one of these evenings, my father told

[6]For a good overview of research on the topic see Neisser and colleagues (1996).

me that Paul Byrd was brilliant. Because I am a human being who easily forms stereotypes, I started to think that African Americans must be really smart.

When I was eight or nine years old, my father started to teach me to play chess. I read about great chess masters. Chess playing became the true test of intelligence for me. My impression of Paul Byrd's intelligence was confirmed when he regularly beat my father at chess. Then one afternoon my parents held a party for faculty members in the backyard. I wandered aimlessly among the adults, not knowing quite what to do with myself. Paul Byrd noticed my plight. He left the group of adults, came over to me, and asked if I wanted to play chess. We sat down at the chessboard for 15 minutes or so while he showed me chess strategy. He was more interested in me for a little while than all the important adults at the party. After that, I thought that Paul Byrd must be the smartest person in the world. Later, when I started to look at the research that tried to explain why blacks were less intelligent than whites, something felt wrong. I could not accept the assumption that blacks were less intelligent. There must be some other explanation for those lower ability test scores. In a few years, I would find out what that explanation was.

Society has made some progress since I played chess with Professor Byrd. There are a few more black professors at San Jose State University than there were. Professor Shelby Steele is one of them. He is an English professor whose popular book, *The Content of Our Character,* caused controversy because it points out problems with affirmative action. Steele (1990) also tries to explain why so many bright African Americans do not perform up to their potential in school. His experience as a black man and as a teacher has led him to believe that blacks are afraid of ambition. They are especially afraid of competing with whites. But blacks are only selectively afraid to compete. In two areas, entertainment and athletics, blacks stand out and are highly successful. For example, Steele writes about how black high school students compete to be the best dancers and pride themselves on dancing better than whites. Blacks, however, avoid competition with whites in academic areas that lead to real power in society. It is as if blacks fear that success in school will bring rejection. Fear of ambition causes black students to belittle those who do well in school, to think that studying is foolish and school a waste of time. Black children get a double message from parents, teachers, and society: "Go to school but don't really apply yourself. The risk is too high" (Steele 1990, p. 51).

Shelby Steele's brother, Professor Claude Steele of Stanford University, is a social psychologist. Claude Steele wanted to find out whether the fear that black students felt when competing with whites in school could really lower their scores on an ability test. Claude Steele and Joshua Aronson (1995) brought students into the laboratory and gave them a standard ability test. Researchers gave students difficult problems from the Graduate Record Examination (GRE). The GRE is the standard examination for entrance to many university graduate school programs. Both black and white university students completed the problems that researchers had taken from the GRE. Researchers told students that their performance would be a "genuine test of your verbal abilities and limitations." Black students then believed that test results would be used to compare their abilities with the abilities of whites who also took the test. Steele and Aronson thought that black students would do worse than whites on the test if they were afraid of academic competition with whites.

All the students who took the test were from the same prestigious university, Stanford. Still, it was not surprising that Steele and Aronson (1995) were correct. Black students scored lower on the test of academic ability when they thought their scores would allow them to be compared to white students. However, black students score lower than white students in many test situations. How could researchers be sure that fear of academic competition with whites produced the low test scores of blacks? Steele and Aronson wanted to know whether black students would score higher when they did not think their scores competed with those of white students. For example, if students thought they were just answering questions to familiarize themselves with different kinds of test problems, then would black students score as well as white students do? If a simple change in the wording of test instructions caused blacks to score as well as whites, then differences in intelligence could *not* be responsible for the low scores of blacks on the first test.

Steele and Aronson (1995) repeated their study. This time, however, researchers made no reference to verbal ability. They told students that the questions were to familiarize them "with the kinds of problems that appear on tests you may encounter in the future." After this simple change in instructions, would black students score as high as white students on the same test? They did. When test instructions made no reference to testing students' ability, black students scored just as high on the standard test questions as white students did. It is clear that black students were as capable of doing well on the test as white students were. However, when black students thought their ability was being tested and their ability scores would be compared to those of white students, black students scored lower. Steele and Aronson showed that black students do hesitate to show how smart they are.

Why are blacks reluctant to show their intellectual ability? The writing of Professor Shelby Steele and the research of Professor Claude Steele suggest an answer: Blacks fear the consequences of academic success. Here we have the kind of explanation that I was looking for. It explains why African Americans score lower than European Americans on standard ability tests without assuming that African Americans are any less intelligent. Nonetheless, I was skeptical. What is it about success that blacks are so afraid of? And why are blacks afraid of academic success but not athletic success? The "fear of success" theory implies that African Americans expect to be punished in some way for academic success but not for athletic success. In other words, society allows African Americans to be athletes and entertainers, but punishes them when they try to be scholars. At least it means that African Americans *expect* to be punished for academic success. But why would blacks expect to be punished for doing what everyone seems to be pushing them to do?

By 1990, many universities and large corporations had affirmative action programs. Universities were competing with each other for the small pool of top black students. Corporations desperately sought black college graduates for management positions to deflect charges of bias in hiring and promotion. Universities scrambled for African Americans with Ph.D.s to fill choice faculty positions. What is there to fear about a tenured faculty position as a professor at a prestigious university? After all, tenure means that even if your white coworkers hate you, no one can fire you. I had thought that with affirmative action, blacks would be doing everything possible to do well in school. But black male enrollment in college has decreased during the

Calvin and Hobbes   by Bill Watterson

In some situations it might be safer not to do too well in school

years of affirmative action. Being white, I had difficulty seeing what African Americans had to fear from academic success.

Professor Lois Benjamin, a black sociologist at Hampton University in Virginia, interviewed successful black Americans to examine the problems they had overcome in reaching success. In one of the interviews, black physicist John Lamont tells a story from his childhood that shows how black children might expect trouble to come from showing how smart they are (Benjamin 1991). Lamont's father was a self-taught aeronautical engineer who invented devices for airplanes during the 1930s and 1940s. The best job he could get, however, was as a janitor at a gas company in Washington, D.C. He struggled through the economic depression of the 1930s trying to support a family on a janitor's wages. When the economy improved during the 1940s, Lamont's father decided to try for a better job. He asked his white foreman if he could apply to be a machinist at the gas company. The engineering work Lamont's father had done made him extremely well qualified to work as a machinist. The foreman, however, was skeptical that a black man could operate complicated machinery. Lamont's father offered to demonstrate his ability and handled the various machines easily. Lamont tells how, instead of winning a promotion, his father's display of technical competence cost him a job. The foreman was enraged by the obvious competence of a black man. He immediately fired Lamont's father from his job as a *janitor*. Black children learn to be careful when showing white people how smart they are. For example, Arroyo and Zigler (1995) found that black students who had positive attitudes toward academic success were also extremely concerned about losing the approval of others.

Rubovits and Maehr (1973) wanted to see if black children had reason to avoid academic success. Researchers recruited undergraduate women who were enrolled in a teacher training course. Teacher trainees volunteered for the project to gain teaching experience. In the study, each teacher trainee would lead a class discussion for a group of four students. Students were seventh and eighth graders. In each class, two students were black and two were white. Before the class began, each teacher trainee was given a seating chart with the names and IQ scores of each student. Researchers had randomly assigned IQ scores to students so that teachers thought one black student and one white student in her class had high IQs (about 130).[7] These students were labeled "gifted." Teachers thought the other black student and the other white student in her class had average IQs (about 100). These students were labeled "nongifted." Researchers thought that teachers would treat gifted students differently from nongifted students. As you might expect, researchers thought that gifted students would get more teacher praise and attention than would nongifted students. Researchers also thought that teachers would treat white students differently from black students. Again as you might expect, researchers thought that white students would get more teacher praise and attention than would black students. The teacher trainees were, after all, white.

What Rubovits and Maehr (1973) found was much more surprising and a bit shocking. Just as they had predicted, gifted *white* students were praised most often, criticized the least, and given the most attention. However, teachers treated black students exactly the opposite. Gifted black students were praised the least and given the least attention. Almost all the criticism of gifted students was directed at black gifted students. Teachers criticized gifted black students more than nongifted white students and more than nongifted black students. The results are especially surprising because these were young teacher trainees. They had grown up with civil rights and attended a university in the northern Midwest. They were not older teachers who might have been accustomed to segregated classrooms and the expectation that blacks should not be educated. Nonetheless, teachers punished black students for being smart.

The theory that African Americans fear the consequences of academic success has solid support. Steele and Aronson's (1995) research showed that black students were hesitant to show their intelligence when competing with white students. Rubovits and Maehr's (1973) research showed that black students actually are punished for showing their academic ability to white teachers. Black students, then, have good reason to fear academic success. Still, something about the fear of success theory bothered me. I had trouble seeing myself responding the way the African Americans apparently were. I felt that if I were being treated the way African Americans are, then I would try twice as hard to show people they could not push me around that way. I would do better in school, not worse. I would ace those tests, then throw them in the faces of people who said I was not smart. What if African Americans had some sort of weakness that prevents them from performing when it counts? That would explain why intelligence did not lead to success in school for African Americans.

One advantage of a good theory is that it makes predictions for the behavior of a wide variety of people, not just those of one particular group. One day, a graduate student of mine, Jeffrey Lucas, told me some ideas he had about how status characteristics theory related to self-esteem. Recall that people use status characteristics like race to get some idea of how much ability people have. When a person has a

---

[7]The IQ scale is a way to compare intelligence test scores from different tests. The average IQ score is 100. Most people will score within 15 IQ points of the average. So an IQ score of 115 represents above-average intelligence while an IQ score of 85 represents below-average intelligence. Less than 5 percent of people have an IQ of 130 or higher.

Calvin and Hobbes

by Bill Watterson

Calvin considers the consequences of success

highly valued status characteristic, such as being white in this society, people expect him to be very competent. They also expect him to contribute a lot to the group and to deserve high rewards for his contributions. People then treat him better and reward him more. So Jeff thought that having a highly valued status characteristic would lead to higher self-efficacy.

Self-efficacy is like self-esteem in that it deals with how highly people regard themselves. However, self-efficacy is more specific than self-esteem. Self-efficacy looks at how much a person thinks she is capable of accomplishing (Bandura 1986). A person with high self-efficacy should work harder and stay with a task longer than a person with low self-efficacy. High self-efficacy, then, is related to better academic performance (Multon, Brown, & Lent 1991).

As Jeff and I talked about status characteristics and self-efficacy, we realized that status characteristics theory said something very clearly about the gap between black and white intelligence test scores. First, by increasing self-efficacy, having a highly valued status characteristic (being white, for example) should lead to a small increase in intelligence test scores. Perhaps more important, however, were the expectations people would have for the *consequences* of those intelligence test scores. According to status characteristics theory, performances by high-status people are honored and rewarded. However, even very successful performances by low-status people are devalued and ignored. Thus European Americans, as high-status people in this society, have great incentive to perform at a high level. In contrast, African Americans have little incentive to perform because they expect their efforts to go unrewarded. Recent work in status characteristics theory goes further still. Strong performances by low-status people are also considered selfish and illegitimate (Berger, Ridgeway, Fisek, & Norman 1998; Ridgeway 1982). Rather than a valued contribution to the group, a strong performance by a low-status person is seen as a selfish grab for power. Thus status characteristics theory explains why African Americans would be punished for a strong academic performance. African Americans, then, have good reason to be wary of showing how smart they are.

Status characteristics theory does not apply only to African Americans. The theory implies that any low-status person whose accomplishments are punished rather than rewarded will perform poorly. It means that if white people suddenly found themselves to be low status, then they would perform poorly too. If high-status people suddenly became low status, then they would do poorly in school. But the most surprising prediction is that if white people were low status, then they would score lower on intelligence tests, just as black people now do.

By the time Jeff and I finished talking, I was excited. What had begun as a casual conversation had become a research agenda. When a scientific theory makes predictions that contradict what people feel strongly to be true, then a social psychologist jumps at the chance to test it. I had felt, as many white people would, that I would behave differently than African Americans do. I thought that if I were discriminated against, then I would work harder. I would do better on an intelligence test than I otherwise would, not worse. Status characteristics theory, however, was telling us the opposite. When placed in low-status positions and expecting punishment for success, white people would score lower on an intelligence test than they otherwise would. The theory said that by changing people's social position, *we could change their IQ.*

Jeff and I put our other projects aside and set out to test the prediction that white people's intelligence test scores would drop if they were treated the way low-status people are. It would be complicated. We would need help. Jeffrey Houser, then a professor at Bowling Green State University, signed onto the project, as did Shane Thye, who became a professor at the University of South Carolina. A friend and colleague at the University of Iowa, Professor Barry Markovsky, also agreed to help.

The first thing we had to do was figure out how to change people's social status. We had to turn high-status white college students into low-status people. Then we could give them a standard intelligence test to see if they scored lower than white college students usually do. Luckily for us, Cecilia Ridgeway at Stanford University had been working for several years to develop a technique for creating a status characteristic. We adapted her technique for bringing people into the laboratory and convincing them that they were either high status or low status.[8]

Handedness—whether people are right- or left-handed—is part of their identities. However, people now do not expect right-handers to be any smarter than left-handers or vice versa. Handedness, then, is not a status characteristic. It is status neutral. That made it ideal for our use. We thought we could make it into a status characteristic for people. We decided to bring people into the lab and provide them with evidence that being right-handed helped people a great deal in performing a particular group task. We could provide other people with evidence that being right-handed would hurt them when working with others on the task. Then we could compare how people performed when they thought being right-handed was a social asset with how they performed when they thought it was a social liability.

Almost everyone considers herself or himself either right- or left-handed. We could bring people into the lab and convince them that their handedness would make them either high status or low status. For example, we could show people scientific evidence that right-handers made better team leaders in the particular kind of work they were about to do for our study. We could show other people that

[8]For details of Ridgeway's technique see Ridgeway, Boyle, Kuipers, and Robinson (1995 and 1998).

right-handers made poor team leaders in the work to be done by their team. We could flip a coin and make people believe they were either high status or low status based on their handedness.

Having convinced people that their handedness was a status characteristic, we could set up a situation where low-status people would expect ability test scores to have consequences similar to those faced by African Americans. Half the people in the study were randomly assigned to be low status. We explained to them that they would probably not be assigned to be high-paid leaders. They would have more menial jobs with the group because low-status people had little leadership ability. We also told people that other group members resented low-status leaders. In the study rooms, a sign on the wall warned people not to harass low-status group members. The sign urged people to "support weaker group members." The sign let people know that researchers did not approve of people being mistreated because they were low status. It also reminded low-status people that their handedness could put them in jeopardy. Then we told people that they would be assigned to a job based on their score on an aptitude test. Good jobs would go to people who scored high on the test. Less desirable jobs would go to those who did not do as well.

People competed for three job levels in the work group by taking the aptitude test. "Supervisors" would be paid $17.00 an hour, "analysts" would be paid $8.00 an hour, and "menials" would be paid $4.50 an hour. While low-status people were told that they would probably not be supervisors, they could still be analysts. Everyone in the study had an incentive to do her or his best on the test. People, whether low status or high status, would make substantially more money and have a more interesting job if they scored high on the aptitude test.

For the aptitude test, we chose a standard test of mental ability, the Raven Progressive Matrices Test. The Raven test has been used for more than 50 years. It is considered one of the least biased tests of intelligence. We predicted that people who were made low status in our study would score lower on the intelligence test than those who had been high status. Would 15 minutes of being convinced they were low status actually lower the IQs of privileged white university students?

The people we had made low status did score lower on the standard intelligence test than the people we had made high status. On average, low-status people had IQ scores on the Progressive Matrices Test that were 7 to 8 points lower than those of high-status people (Lovaglia, Lucas, Houser, Thye, & Markovsky 1998). To give you an idea of how big that 7 IQ point difference is, the difference between the average high school graduate and the average college graduate is about 15 IQ points. In general, African Americans score about 10 IQ points lower than do European Americans. Keep in mind that African Americans taking an IQ test have been discriminated against for years. In our study, the IQ of white students dropped by 7 points after they had been discriminated against for about 15 minutes.

We redid the study and included an affirmative action program (Lovaglia et al. 1998).[9] We told people in the study that we wanted low-status people to have a fair

---

[9]Crocker, Voelkl, Testa, and Major (1991) showed how affirmative action programs can hurt African Americans, who have greater reason to attribute their successes as well as their failures to racism rather than to their personal talents and abilities.

chance at being a supervisor and earning $17 an hour. Low-status people who scored high on the aptitude test could write a brief speech and present it to a committee composed of a professor and two graduate students. Low-status people who did well on the speech would become supervisors. This gave low-status people additional incentive to do well on the aptitude test. It also increased their exposure to criticism. We predicted that despite the additional incentive of the affirmative action program, low-status people would continue to score lower than high-status people do on the standard intelligence test. We were right. Just as before, low-status people scored about seven IQ points lower than did high-status people.

We talked to people after the study to make sure they understood what had happened. We had to correct the misimpression we had given people that being left-handed or right-handed had something to do with talent for working with people. Talking to people who participate in studies is also a good way to find out if people's experiences in the study match what researchers expect them to experience. All the people in our study were satisfied with their experience. After we had explained the study to them, they said they understood why we conducted the study the way we had. We found that the study was highly believable to people who participated in it. One person who was made high status said that she became so upset by the discrimination against low-status people that she could not concentrate on the aptitude test. The most frequent comment by people who had been low status was that they knew they were being discriminated against. Because they were being discriminated against, low-status people said that they tried extra hard on the aptitude test. They said they wanted to show researchers that such discrimination would not lower their performance. They said they knew they had done very well on the test. However, despite their determination to do well, all of the low-status people who made these comments scored below average on the intelligence test. They had made the same fundamental attribution error that I had made. They believed their personal ability alone determined their test performance. In fact, their test performance depended quite a bit on their social status.[10]

The discovery that I am prejudiced led to some good research. The research showed how the belief in the low intelligence of African Americans stems from a fundamental attribution error. Scores on intelligence tests do not depend only on the intelligence of the test taker. Intelligence test scores also depend on the consequences people expect from those scores. Yet knowing why I'm prejudiced is only a start. The roots of racial prejudice run deep. Our primate ancestors probably broke into subgroups that tried to annihilate one another. Primate researchers found that when a chimpanzee population became too large in one area, a subgroup split off to live in a neighboring area (Wrangham & Peterson 1996). Once the separate groups had formed, however, hostility developed between them. Researchers watched as the stronger group formed raiding parties to patrol the border area between the two chimpanzee territories. A raiding party would patrol until it happened upon an isolated member of the other group foraging for food. Then the raiding party would

---

[10]Results of two excellent recent studies further support the idea that the expected consequences of a test score, rather than test content alone, determine how well people perform on standardized mental ability tests. See Brown and Josephs (1999) and Shih, Pitinsky and Ambady (1999).

attack, often killing the other group member. It was a natural experiment in forming groups with minimal distinctions between them. A clear boundary between us and them was all that was needed between groups of chimpanzees to produce lethal consequences. If prejudice is that deeply ingrained in our evolutionary history, then prejudice is not going away despite our best intentions. Prejudice is at least in part an automatic reaction triggered by our fears. In that sense, all prejudice is cowardice. Fear is part of being human, as is prejudice. We fight the battle against our own fear and prejudice every day. We will never completely win, but we lose only when we stop fighting.

Further Reading

Of General Interest

Benjamin, L. (1991). *The black elite: Facing the color line in the twilight of the twentieth century.* Chicago: Nelson-Hall.

Brannigan, G. G., & Merrens, M. R. (Eds.). (1995). *The social psychologists: Research adventures.* New York: McGraw-Hill.

Jones, J. M. (1996). *The psychology of racism and prejudice.* New York: McGraw-Hill.

Rosenthal, R., & Jacobsen, L. (1992). *Pygmalion in the classroom: Teacher expectation and pupils' intellectual development.* New York: Irvington.

Schuman, H., Bobo, L., & Steeh, C. (1985). *Racial attitudes in America: Trends and Interpretations.* Cambridge, MA: Harvard University Press.

Shipler, D K. (1997). *Country of strangers: Blacks and whites in America.* New York: Alfred A. Knopf.

Steele, S. (1990). *The content of our character.* New York: St. Martin's Press.

Turner, J. C. (1991). *Social influence.* Pacific Grove, CA: Brooks/Cole.

Recent and Technical Issues

Bargh, J. A., Chaiken, S., Govender, R., & Pratto, F. (1992). The generality of the automatic attitude activation effect. *Journal of Personality and Social Psychology, 62,* 893–912.

Brown, R. P. and Josephs, R. A. (1999). A burden of proof: Stereotype relevance and gender differences in math performance. *Journal of Personality and Social Psychology, 76,* 246–257.

Crocker, J., & Luhtanen, R. (1990). Collective self-esteem and ingroup bias. *Journal of Personality and Social Psychology, 58,* 60–67.

Crocker, J., Thompson, L. L., McGraw, K. M., & Ingerman, C. (1987). Downward comparison, prejudice, and evaluation of others: Effects of self-esteem and threat. *Journal of Personality and Social Psychology, 52,* 907–916.

Epstein, J., & Harackiewicz, J. M. (1992). Winning is not enough: The effects of competition and achievement orientation on intrinsic interest. *Personality and Social Psychology Bulletin, 18,* 128–138.

Ethier, K. A., & Deaux, K. (1994). Negotiating social identity when contexts change: Maintaining identification and responding to threat. *Journal of Personality and Social Psychology, 67,* 243–251.

Gilbert, D. T., & Hixon, J. G. (1991). The trouble of thinking: Activation and application of stereotypic beliefs. *Journal of Personality and Social Psychology, 60,* 509–517.

Hughes, M., and Thomas, M. E. (1998). The continuing significance of race revisited: A study of race, class, and quality of life in America, 1972–1996. *American Sociological Review, 63,* 785–795.

Jussim, L., & Eccles, J. S. (1992). Teacher expectations II: Construction and reflection of student achievement. *Journal of Personality and Social Psychology, 63,* 947–961.

Lord, C. G., & Saenz, D. S. (1985). Memory deficits and memory surfeits: Differential cognitive consequences of tokenism for tokens and observers. *Journal of Personality and Social Psychology, 49,* 918–926.

Madon, S., Jussim, L., & Eccles, J. (1997). In search of the powerful self-fulfilling prophecy. *Journal of Personality and Social Psychology, 72,* 791–809.

Ruggiero, K. M., & Taylor, D. M. (1997). Why minority group members perceive or do not perceive the discrimination that confronts them: The role of self-esteem and perceived control. *Journal of Personality and Social Psychology, 72,* 373–389.

Schulman, K. A., Berlin, J. A., Harless, W., Kerner, J. F., Sistrunk, S., Gersh, B. J., Dube, R., Taleghani, C. K., Burke, J. E., Williams, S., Eisenberg, J. M., and Escarce, J. J. (1999). The effect of race and sex on physicians' recommendations for cardiac catheterization. *New England Journal of Medicine, 340,* 618–626.

Shih, M., Pittinsky, T. L., & Ambady, N. (1999). Stereotype susceptibility: Identity salience and shifts in quantitative performance. *Psychological Science, 10,* 80–83.

Steele, C. M. (1997). A threat in the air: How stereotypes shape intellectual identity and performance. *American Psychologist, 52,* 613–629.

Taylor, D. M., Wright, S. C., Moghaddam, F. M., & Lalonde, R. N. (1990). The personal/group discrimination discrepancy: Perceiving my group, but not myself, to be a target for discrimination. *Personality and Social Psychology Bulletin, 16,* 254–262.

CHAPTER 9

The Power In and Out of Love

Love is powerful to the extent that it allows people to accomplish things that they otherwise would not be able to accomplish. When we work for a larger purpose than merely our own survival or well-being, we accomplish more than we do when focused narrowly on our own success in a self-interested way. Recall that Chapter 4 talked about getting outside yourself and your own problems to get on with your life. Certainly parents work harder and with more focus to provide for their children than they did before the children arrived. When we think of the power of romantic love, we think of two people working together to overcome great obstacles, bound together as one by their love. While romantic love may well have that kind of power, social psychologists have yet to study it. Instead, social psychologists have taken a less romantic approach to the way that people use power in romantic love.

For two people in a romantic relationship, love gives each power over the other. That power is rarely equally divided between two people in a relationship. One usually has more power than the other does. The more in love with someone you are, the more dependent you are on him. His approval matters to you. You may watch anxiously for any sign that he is losing interest in the relationship. Emerson (1962) noticed that dependence is the opposite of power. The more dependent you are on someone, the more power he has over you.

When he is more in love than you are, power in the situation is reversed. He is dependent on you for approval. He caters to your needs. You have the power to make him miserable by making yourself unavailable. He is more dependent on the relationship than you are. That is, he is more interested in seeing the relationship continue than you are, while you are less dependent on it. The more interested someone is in seeing a relationship continue, the less power she has in it. Within a romantic relationship, love makes people vulnerable. The more in love you are, the less power you have. Social psychologists call this the principle of least interest (Homans 1971, 1974; Thibaut & Kelley 1959).

> **Principle of least interest:** *The person who has the least interest in continuing a relationship has the most power in it.*

cathy®

by Cathy Guisewite

Cathy knows about power in romantic relationships

While it may be true that love empowers people when their love is returned, love also makes people vulnerable. Falling in love puts people at risk. That is why love can produce feelings of intense joy as well as terrible anxiety.

In the seventh grade, I fell hopelessly in love with a girl at school, Christine, lots of freckles and a turned-up nose. I spent every spare minute with Chris. All I wanted was to be close to her. I was late to everything that term, late to class, late to track practice, late to dinner. I constantly daydreamed of our future together. We would be married. Christine seemed to feel the same about me at first. Then she gradually lost interest. She found reasons why it would not be convenient for me to walk her home. She wanted to hang out with her girlfriends instead of me. My anxiety increased. I tried harder to please her. Still, we spent a lot of time together until the end of the term. When school let out for summer it was harder for me to see her—or perhaps easier for her to avoid me. I was frantic. Then I heard that she had gotten together with an older boy, a high school student who was the lifeguard at her neighborhood pool. It was over. I knew that I could never compete with those qualifications. Despite the strength of my love for her, I was powerless. Losing Christine was a shock similar to that experienced by victims of traffic accidents. The pain was actually physical as well as psychological and emotional. Worse still, I knew that Chris did not hate me or even dislike me. She just didn't care. She was not interested in me. Her lack of interest gave her the power to hurt me.

The end of my relationship with Christine gave me a glimpse of the principle of least interest. During the weeks that followed the breakup, I went over and over our relationship in my mind. I wanted desperately to know what went wrong. What could I have done differently? However, I was not interested in learning how to develop a loving, stable relationship. Rather, I wanted to guarantee that nobody would have the power to hurt me that way again. At the age of 13, my solution to the problem of love was simple but effective: If you don't care much about someone, then she can't hurt you. In my next romantic relationship, the girl would have to be more interested in me than I was in her. Otherwise, I would stay single. Not surprisingly, for a while after that my relationships were unsuccessful. I eventually was able to open up to romantic love again. However, the lesson of that lost love was clear because it was so surprising to me: Love gives people power over you. Be careful.

The most comprehensive, scientific study of human sexual behavior shows how vulnerable love can make people. When women fall in love, they risk more than their emotional wellbeing; they also increase the chance that they will be physically assaulted. Sexual assault, rape, is a large problem in the United States. More than five times as many rapes were reported in the 1990s as were reported in the 1970s. Because people are reluctant to talk about sexual matters and many sexual assaults are not reported to the police, we do not know if the number of sexual assaults is really growing so rapidly, or if more of the rapes that have occurred all along are now being reported. However, it is clear that sexual assault is frighteningly common, disrupting the lives and health of millions of women in the United States. Lately, more attention has been paid to sexual assaults committed by a person whom the victim knows or is related to. It turns out that complete strangers commit relatively few rapes.

University of Chicago researchers (Laumann, Gagnon, Michael, & Michaels 1994) surveyed sexual behavior in the United States. They used the best scientific methods to ensure that the information they gathered was as accurate as possible. People will always be reluctant to talk about their sexual behavior. Nonetheless, the information from the University of Chicago survey is the best available. One question researchers wanted to answer was, Who commits sexual assault? That is, how are victims of sexual assault related to their attacker?

Almost a quarter (22 percent) of the women who were surveyed reported that they had been forced to commit a sexual act by a man at some time in their lives. Researchers then asked for more information from women who said they had been forced to have sex. Researchers asked women whether they knew their attacker and if so, what their relationship was to him. As earlier studies had already found, only a small percentage (4 percent) of women who had been assaulted reported being forced by a stranger. Some 19 percent were forced by an acquaintance to commit a sexual act, and 22 percent were forced by someone they knew well. But in the biggest category by far, in almost half of the cases of forced sex reported (46 percent), victims were forced to commit a sexual act by someone they were in love with (Laumann et al. 1994). Being in love gives your partner power over you. The more in love you are, the more power your partner has. Misplaced love can have serious consequences by giving power to someone who cares little about you.

THE POWER OF ALTERNATIVES

A romantic couple does not exist in a vacuum. Partners in a relationship are part of a larger network of potential partners and interested observers. The power a person has within a romantic relationship depends in part on the people in the network other than her partner in romance. When Emerson (1962) pointed out that the dependence of one partner meant power for the other, he also suggested two ways to create power in a relationship. We have already seen the first way to create power.

cathy®

by Cathy Guisewite

Cathy's power comes from having an alternative to Irving

Christine's power over me came from my overwhelming desire to continue the relationship. Her relative indifference to our relationship gave her power over me. Power in a relationship comes from the greater psychological dependence that one partner has on continuing the relationship. The second way to create power is more social in nature. It involves people outside the romantic relationship as well as the psychological states of the romantic partners.

If people outside the romantic relationship can substitute for one of the partners, then the other partner has more power. That is, if one of the partners has a suitable romantic alternative, then the other partner can be left out, powerless. One reason that Christine became less interested in continuing our relationship was that she had an alternative to it. Rather than spend time with me, she could spend time with the lifeguard. Because I had no alternative partner, I was powerless within that relationship. In networks of romantic partners and potential romantic partners, greater access to alternative partners gives some people power over others.

When people are directly connected to some people but only indirectly connected to other people, then all of those direct and indirect connections form a social network. For example, your extended family is a network. If your sister moves to Sweden and marries a person whom you have never met, your new brother-in-law becomes part of your family. However, you have no direct connection to him. He is connected to you only through your sister, with whom you have a direct connection.

In a similar way, groups of people who are romantic partners or potential romantic partners form a social network. I had a direct romantic relationship to Christine. The lifeguard, however, was also part of my network because I was indirectly tied to him through his relationship with Christine. His presence in the network and his behavior could change the balance of power in my relationship with Christine. He could have a big effect on my life, although we had never met.

Networks composed of dating partners and potential dating partners are good examples of what social psychologists call *exchange networks*. Exchange networks easily develop power differences. The primary reason that people stay in an exchange network is that they receive something of value to them. For example, when you work at a job you become part of an exchange network. You exchange your time and skill for a paycheck. On a date, two people may exchange a variety of valued resources, for example, gifts, affection, intimacy, jokes, and laughter if the date goes well.

People also may date more than one person over a period of time, so a network forms. People are directly connected to people they are dating and they are indirectly connected to other people who are interested in dating the same person. The reason that power differences develop so easily in dating networks is that a date generally consists of only two people. Other people who may have been interested in dating one of them may be left out. When the pattern of potential dating partners is such that some people may be left out without a date that they really wanted to go on, then the people who stay home alone have little power in their relationship with a person who is out on a date with someone else. Power develops in exchange networks when some people can be excluded from a relationship that they value (Markovsky, Willer, & Patton 1988).

For example, suppose that you are attracted to Kelly. If Kelly is also attracted to you, then the two of you can get together and both benefit.[1] But suppose that Toby becomes attracted to Kelly. You are now on the end of a simple network with Kelly in the middle between you and Toby. If Kelly goes out with Toby, then you will be excluded. You spend the evening alone. If Kelly goes out with you, then Toby will be excluded. Either way, Kelly is out on a date and either you or Toby is home alone. Kelly, then, has power over you and Toby. On subsequent dates, you may offer Kelly more than you otherwise would. To reduce the possibility that you will be excluded from a date, you might spend more money and wait more patiently if Kelly is late. You might go to a basketball game because Kelly is a fan when you would rather have gone to the ballet.

Power in the dating network changes dramatically if Toby has an alternative to dating Kelly. (We can probably add one more person to the network and still keep the names straight.) Suppose Lee arrives and becomes interested in Toby, creating a somewhat more complicated network.

YOU——KELLY——TOBY——LEE

The lines connecting the names mean that two people have some interest in dating each other. For example, you are interested in dating Kelly. Lee is interested in dating Toby. However, you and Lee have no romantic interest in each other, possibly because you have yet to meet Lee. By joining the dating network, Lee increases Toby's power because now Toby has an alternative date. Toby can go out with Lee if Kelly is not interested. But Lee's interest in Toby affects more than just Toby's power. A more subtle and interesting result is that Lee's interest in Toby reduces Kelly's power over *you*. Kelly no longer has the power to play you and Toby against each other. Your relationship with Kelly will be much more equal. Perhaps on the next date you can go to the ballet if you want. You may not even know Lee and be only vaguely aware of Toby, but their interests and behavior influence your relationship with Kelly. Changes in a network that are only distantly and indirectly re-

[1]This example is taken from Lovaglia (in press).

lated to you can change the amount of power you have in your relationships with those close to you.[2]

MAKING CONTACT

The first approach in a romantic relationship is often not verbal or even physical. Remember that being in love with someone makes people vulnerable. Approaching someone you are romantically attracted to is risky. A rejection can be not just disappointing but painfully embarrassing as well. One of the first things that people do when they are attracted to someone is look at that person—a lot. One reason that people spend so much time looking at the person who attracts them is to see if she or he will look back. It is a clue that maybe the attraction is mutual.

A number of eye contact strategies are possible. For example, staring too long and hard at a person could make you look desperate. It may too obviously advertise your interest, giving the other person power over you. And people don't like to be stared at. The trick is to look quickly but often enough that the other person notices, yet, not so often that she or he is certain that you are interested. Then, if the other person is curious, she or he may start looking back, checking to see if you really are interested. Your goal, then, is to play hard to get. Keep yourself from looking as much as you would like. As long as the other person is not certain that you are romantically interested, curiosity will keep her or him checking on your romantic signals. If two people keep looking at each other—a lot—a romantic relationship may well bloom.

Kellerman, Lewis, and Laird (1989) wanted to know what happens when two people gaze into each other's eyes. Would their attraction for each other increase just because they looked at each other's eyes? To find out, researchers brought young men and women into the laboratory. Researchers paired men and women who did not know each other. Before the new couples met, researchers took each man and woman aside and asked them to look at the person they were about to meet in a certain way. Half of the people were to sit quietly in a room with the other person and gaze at their partner's eyes. The rest of the people were also told to sit quietly in a room with the other person, but to gaze at their partner's hands.

Researchers randomly picked people to gaze at their partner's eyes or hands. It would be like flipping a coin for each person. When the coin comes up heads, people are told to gaze at their partner's eyes. When it comes up tails, people are told to gaze at their partner's hands. The result is that some couples gaze into each other's eyes. Some couples gaze at each other's hands. For other couples, one person gazes at the other's hands while the partner gazes at her or his eyes. After people had looked at their partners for two minutes, researchers separated the couples and

[2]Exchange networks can become large and complicated. A growing area of research attempts to predict exactly how much power each person in an exchange network will have. Major research developments in this area include Cook and Emerson (1978), Cook, Emerson, Gillmore, and Yamagishi (1983), Markovsky, Willer, and Patton (1988), Markovsky, Skvoretz, Willer, Lovaglia, and Erger (1993), Lovaglia, Skvoretz, Willer, and Markovsky (1995).

asked people to fill out a survey. The survey contained a series of questions to see how much attraction and passion people felt for the person they had looked at. Kellerman, Lewis, and Laird (1989) predicted that couples who gazed into each other's eyes would feel more attraction and passion for their partner than would couples where one or both partners gazed at the other's hands.

Kellerman, Lewis, and Laird (1989) were correct. When members of a couple gaze into each other's eyes, their passion and attraction for each other actually do increase. Researchers found that strangers who had been asked to gaze into each other's eyes reported more attraction and passion for their partner than was the case when one or both partners gazed at the other's hands. Looking at a person—a lot—and getting the person to look back at you can lead to romance.

PASSIONATE EMOTIONS CONFLICT

Passionate love creates intense joy and equally intense anxiety for people in love. Conflicting emotions may be necessary for passionate love to develop. For a couple to become passionately involved, it almost seems that something has to get in the way first, as if frustration is necessary to get love going. Sigmund Freud thought that all of the barriers that society puts up to prevent young couples from getting together serve to increase passion. Society develops customs and rules to prevent romantic relationships from forming too easily. Custom may require that young couples be chaperoned. They may be given almost no privacy. A young woman's male relatives may chase off men who are interested in her. According to Freud, when society increases the frustration level of romantic partners, their passion increases as well. Passion requires emotional arousal. Surprisingly, negative emotions work as well or better than positive emotions to spark romantic love.

Conflicting emotions are a staple of romance novels. Our heroine, Vivica, has flashing violet eyes. She is in the executive training program for a large international corporation controlled by the dashing and ruthless Brock. Brock has steely gray eyes. (Brown or blue eyes are rare in romance novels.) Although destined for passionate romance, Vivica and Brock begin their relationship by confronting each other. Brock and Vivica first meet in the mailroom, where Vivica is personally seeing that important documents are sent by express courier. At the same time, Brock leads a group of major stockholders on a tour of the facility. When Brock sees the ravishing Vivica in the mailroom, he tries to impress the stockholders by asking her to get them all coffee. Vivica's violet eyes flare as she informs Brock that she is an executive trainee, not a receptionist. Brock's jaw muscles clench while he fights to control himself. He suggests that she continue her duties in the mailroom where she is likely to stay for the remainder of her career.

Infuriated, Vivica sets out to change the way that the corporation treats women, both as employees and as customers. She believes that Brock and men like him are responsible for most of what is wrong with the corporation and the world. An international consumer boycott of corporation products develops. Brock blames Vivica for the boycott but cannot fire her because she may sue. They must work together in a series of increasingly heated confrontations. The boycott reduces corporate income to the point where bankruptcy looms. All unnecessary personnel are laid off. A skeleton crew of the most talented executives works through the weekend to come up with a strategy to save the company. Vivica and Brock are thrown together, working frantically. Late Sunday night, they finish a proposal that they will take to the bank the next morning. They have saved the corporation. Suddenly the lights go out. The building has lost electrical power as a storm rages. Vivica and Brock, trapped in his palatial office on the sixty-second floor of the corporate headquarters building, are dazzled by the lights of the city below them, flickering in the wind. He finds candles and an old bottle of wine. As he grapples with the cork, she reaches to help him. Their eyes meet. Suddenly, they are locked in a frenzied kiss as they struggle to get each other out of their clothes. They make passionate love on Brock's massive executive desk. The negative emotion that Vivica and Brock felt toward each other as their relationship began increased their passion when they eventually fell in love. Social psychologists have found that this common plot line in popular fiction has a sound basis.

It seems that any kind of arousal can intensify sexual attraction, whether it is emotional excitement or simple physical activity. White, Fishbein, and Rutstein (1981) brought male college students into the laboratory and asked them to run in place for two minutes, long enough that they were breathing hard. Other male college students were asked to run in place for only a few seconds. After the men had exercised, researchers asked them to watch a brief videotape of an attractive woman being interviewed. After watching the attractive woman, the men answered a series of questions about how romantically attracted they were to the woman. For example, men were asked how physically attractive she was, how sexy, and how much they would like to kiss her. Researchers predicted that men who had run in place for two minutes would find the woman more attractive than would men who had exercised for only a few seconds. Researchers thought that the physical arousal produced by exercise would increase the men's romantic interest in the woman. It worked. Men who had run in place for two minutes found the woman much more attractive and sexy than did men who had run for only a few seconds.

White, Fishbein, and Rutstein (1981) also tried the experiment using emotional rather than physical arousal. Researchers brought men into the laboratory and asked them to watch one of three videotapes. Some of the men saw an unpleasant but exciting tape about gruesome murders. Others saw a boring tape about frog anatomy. Still others saw a videotape of a funny comedy routine that provided positive excitement. Then the men watched another videotape, the interview with the attractive woman. After watching the attractive woman, all the men answered the questions about how attractive they found her.

Researchers made the interesting prediction that men who had been negatively excited by the videotape about gruesome murders would find the woman more attractive than would men who watched the boring tape about frog anatomy. Researchers also predicted that men who had been positively excited by watching a funny comedy routine would find the woman more attractive than would men who watched the boring tape. That is, the men's emotional excitement would increase their attraction to the woman. It would not matter whether the emotions were positive or negative. Again researchers were correct. Men who had watched the grisly murders and men who had watched the funny comedy routine were more attracted to the woman than were men who had watched the boring tape about frog anatomy (White, Fishbein & Rutstein 1981).

Social psychologists confirm that increased emotional arousal makes men and women more attractive to each other. Further, negative emotions seem especially effective at sparking romance. Donald Dutton and Arthur Aron (1974), researchers at the University of British Columbia, wanted to see if men would be more attracted to a beautiful woman when they were anxious or afraid. They proposed that the kind of emotional arousal men felt would not matter much. Anxiety or fear would make a woman more attractive to them.

Dutton and Aron (1974) found a setting that produced anxiety in a large number of men. An attractive female research assistant approached the anxious men. She asked them to complete a psychological questionnaire. Then she gave the men her name and phone number in case the men wanted further information about the study. The psychological questionnaire gave researchers information about the sexual content of the men's thoughts just after meeting the attractive woman. Researchers could also tell how likely the men would be to act on their sexual attraction. If anxious men were attracted to the woman, then they would be especially likely to call her afterward. To see if anxiety really did produce any sound results, researchers repeated the experiment with a similar group of men who were not anxious. Would the attractive woman prompt more sexually oriented thoughts in anxious men than she did in men who were not anxious? Would anxious men be more likely to phone her afterward?

Dutton and Aron (1974) found anxious men at a suspension bridge that crossed a canyon in a park in British Columbia. A popular tourist attraction, the suspension bridge was a footbridge only a few feet wide but hundreds of feet long. The bridge was suspended on thin steel cables and swayed precariously when people walked across it. The bridge had only a low wire as a guardrail, making it difficult to walk across and maintain balance while holding onto the safety wire. The bridge crossed a rocky canyon more than 200 feet deep. A fall would be deadly. Most men who crossed the bridge reported that it made them anxious. For comparison, researchers found similar men who were not anxious at another bridge upriver from the suspension bridge. The comparison bridge was a solid wood bridge that did not sway when people crossed it. It was wider than the suspension bridge and was only 10 feet above a small creek. Most men who crossed the comparison bridge reported little or no anxiety.

The same attractive woman approached men at both bridges. She asked them to fill out the psychological questionnaire and gave them her phone number. At the suspension bridge where men were anxious, she wrote down the name, Gloria, along with her phone number. At the comparison bridge where men were not anxious, she wrote down the name Donna. That way when men called, researchers could easily tell if they had been on the suspension bridge or the comparison bridge. Men who had been on the suspension bridge would ask for Gloria. Men who had been on the comparison bridge would ask for Donna. Researchers could thus see if they had been right in predicting that anxious men would report more sexually oriented thoughts after meeting an attractive woman than would men who were not anxious.

The psychological questionnaire was quite simple. Men were shown a picture of a young woman covering her face with one hand and reaching out with the other hand. The picture was not sexually suggestive at all. The attractive research assistant then asked the men to write a "brief, dramatic story" based on the picture. Later people who did not know why the men wrote the stories would rate how much sexual content each story contained. For example, if a man described the young woman in the picture as a "girlfriend," then the story was given a sexual imagery rating of 2. If sexual intercourse was mentioned, the story was given a sexual imagery rating of 5. Mention of a kiss would be rated 3. Different people were asked to rate the stories and they generally agreed with each other on the sexual imagery ratings that the stories received. Would anxious men really use more sexual imagery in their stories than men who were not anxious?

They did. Dutton and Aron (1974) found that men who had anxiously crossed the wobbly suspension bridge wrote stories with quite a bit of sexual imagery. The average rating was 2.5 for anxious men. That is, most anxious men wrote stories that mentioned at least a girlfriend or some romantic behavior such as a kiss. In comparison, men who had calmly crossed the solid wood bridge wrote stories with little sexual imagery. The average rating was 1.4 for men who were not anxious. That is, most men who were not anxious did not go so far as to mention a girlfriend or any romantic behavior at all. Researchers concluded that anxiety from crossing a swaying suspension bridge increased the sexual content of men's thoughts upon meeting an attractive woman.

In addition to the stories that the men wrote, their behavior afterward also suggests that anxious men were more attracted to the research assistant than were men who were not anxious. Half of the anxious men later phoned the research assistant to ask Gloria for "more information." In contrast, only about 10 percent of the men who were not anxious phoned to talk to Donna. Why would so many more of the anxious men call than would the men who were not anxious? Dutton and Aron (1974) concluded that the men who had been anxious were more sexually interested in the attractive research assistant than were men who had not been anxious.

Although Dutton and Aron (1974) felt they had strong evidence that anxiety could produce sexual attraction in men, their study had a weakness. (For more on the strengths and weaknesses of various research methods see the appendix.) Because researchers found men for their study who were already anxious, researchers could not be sure that their anxiety was what increased their sexual attraction to the research assistant. It could have been something else. For example, what if men who went to the suspension bridge were thrill-seekers who had more sexually oriented personalities than did men who went to the solid wood bridge? The results that researchers found would not be due to different levels of anxiety but to different personalities of men who chose different kinds of recreation. Dutton and Aron decided to test their idea again in a different kind of study. If both studies produced the same results, then researchers could be confident that it was the men's anxiety that increased their sexual attraction to the research assistant.

For their second study, Dutton and Aron (1974) brought men into their laboratory and made some of them anxious. Researchers told the men that they would receive electric shocks as part of the experiment. Half of the men in the experiment were told to expect electric shocks that were "quite painful." The rest of the men in the experiment were told to expect a "mere tingle," which some people actually enjoyed. Men who expected painful electric shocks were more anxious and fearful than were men who expected only a tingle. As each man waited for the experiment to begin, anticipating either a painful shock or a mild tingle, he was joined by an attractive female research assistant who waited with him. Then researchers sent the man off by himself to complete the experiment. Alone in a room, each man in the experiment filled out a questionnaire that included questions about how attractive he had found the woman in the waiting room. For example, "How much would you like to ask her out on a date?" and "How much would you like to kiss her?" Men answered on a five-point scale where 5 would be a strong desire to ask her out on a date or kiss her. Men who answered 1 had no desire to ask her out or kiss her. Dutton and Aron predicted that men who had been made anxious expecting painful electric shocks would be more attracted to the woman that they sat next to in the waiting room than would men who expected a "mere tingle." That is, researchers expected anxious men to give higher desire ratings in response to how much they would like to ask out or kiss the woman in the waiting room.

Dutton and Aron (1974) were correct. Men who expected a strong shock rated their desire for the woman at 3.5. In contrast, men who expected only a mild tingle rated their desire for the woman at only 2.8. Statistical analysis shows a substantial difference in sexual desire between anxious men and men who were not anxious. Researchers concluded that the results from their laboratory experiment confirmed the earlier results from the study at the suspension bridge. Anxious, frightened men found a woman more sexually attractive than did men who were not anxious or frightened.

These results explain some interesting romantic behavior (Dutton & Aron 1974). Horror movies and slasher films have long been favorites of teenagers on dates. It may be that the anxiety and fear produced by the movie heighten the sexual attraction felt by the dating couple. We could do a quick study to find out. Ask young people what kind of movie they would choose for a date with someone they were just getting to know—for example, on a third or fourth date. Then ask young people what kind of movie they would choose for a date with a person they had been romantically involved with for a long time—for example, someone who they

cathy®   **by Cathy Guisewite**

Cathy overlooks a safe bet

had dated exclusively for six months. Do you think that people would be more likely to choose a slasher film when they were beginning a relationship with someone than they would after the relationship had matured? If so, then maybe they are using the excitement produced by the movie to heighten their sexual attraction to each other at the beginning of the relationship. It would be interesting to find out.

In popular fiction, women are usually attracted to somewhat dangerous men. Stable, safe, considerate men usually get left out. You may know women—and men too—who go from one disastrous relationship to another, always seeming to choose the same kind of lover. When introduced to someone you think would be perfect for them, they show no interest at all. In the standard TV plot, mom and dad are pushing their daughter into a relationship with Mr. Right. He is studying to be a doctor, comes from a wealthy family, has beautiful manners. Mr. Right falls for the daughter, takes her out on expensive dates, and buys her thoughtful gifts. She responds by running off with the local garage mechanic who has dropped out of high school and parks his Harley-Davidson on the parents' front lawn when he arrives to take her away. Why is he so attractive? He has little to offer except that he is wild, a little dangerous. In short, exciting.

THE ROMEO AND JULIET EFFECT

Parents often disapprove of the people their children become romantically involved with. It seems that the more parents object, the more committed to the romance their children become. Could it be that parental interference intensifies the child's romantic relationship? Do the parents' objections push the young couple together? Researchers named this the "Romeo and Juliet effect" and tried to find out if it exists.

Driscoll, Davis, and Lipetz (1972) wanted to see whether romance grows stronger when parents interfere. Researchers used two questionnaires in surveying couples who were romantically involved. The first questionnaire asked about the extent of the romantic involvement. For example, people rated how much they loved and needed their partners. Other questions asked about how much a person's parents objected to the romantic partner. For example, people rated how much their parents interfered with the romantic relationship, hurt the relationship, and tried to make the partner look bad. Six to ten months later researchers went back to the same couples and asked the same questions again. Researchers could now tell whether parental interference increased romantic love. By comparing how much in love people said they were on the first and second questionnaires, researchers could tell whether their love had increased, decreased, or stayed the same in the months between the two questionnaires. Researchers also could tell from the first questionnaire how much the couple's parents were interfering in their relationship. Would couples who said their parents interfered more on the first questionnaire also say they were more in love on the second questionnaire than they had on the first one? They did. People whose parents interfered in their relationship reported being more in love on the second questionnaire than they had on the first one. In contrast, when parents interfered less in the relationship, couples reported little increase in love on the second survey compared to the first one. Driscoll, Davis, and Lipetz confirmed what Shakespeare knew: A couple's love grows when parents interfere.

Wegner and Gold (1995) demonstrated the difficulty of trying to derail a passionate romance. When people actively try not to think about a romantic partner, the opposite occurs. People who try to avoid thinking about a romantic partner actually think about the partner more. Trying to repress romantic desire creates obsessive thoughts and desires for the person that you are trying to banish from your thoughts.

Investigating further, Wegner and Gold (1995) predicted a rebound effect when people try to suppress thoughts of an old romance. They wanted to determine whether thoughts about an old romance would become increasingly obtrusive when a person tried to suppress them. Researchers brought people into the laboratory and asked them to think about an old flame, a "significant past romantic relationship." People then completed a questionnaire about the relationship. People were hooked up to a machine that measured physical changes in their bodies, like a lie detector. Researchers could then tell if people became emotionally excited. Sometimes people's emotions conflict with their thoughts. Even if people could suppress their romantic thoughts, researchers predicted that their emotional feelings about the person might get stronger in response to the attempt at suppression.

After people had thought about their old flame and were hooked up to the machine that measured physical changes in their bodies, they were asked to "free associate," to think aloud about the old flame they had just described. Then, for two minutes, people were told to "think aloud about anything at all." During the two-minute think-about-anything period, half the people were also specifically told to try *not* to think about the old flame, but to mention it if they did. The rest of the people were told to try not to think about a neutral topic, the Statue of Liberty, but to mention it if they did. Wegner and Gold (1995) predicted that when people tried not to think about their old flame, they would mention their old flame *more* during the two minute think-about-anything period. In contrast, when people were not trying suppress their romantic thoughts, they would mention their old flame *less* during the think-about-anything period. Researchers also predicted that people who tried to suppress their romantic thoughts would become more emotionally excited.

Both of Wegner and Gold's (1995) predictions were correct. People who tried to suppress romantic thoughts talked about their old flames more during the think-about-anything period than did people who did not try to suppress romantic thoughts. Also, people who tried to suppress romantic thoughts became more emotionally excited than did people who had not tried to suppress romantic thoughts. Trying to get past an old love by putting him or her out of your mind may not be the best advice. Not only is it unlikely to work, but it may backfire.

WHY LOVERS KEEP SECRETS

Lovers sometimes try to keep their romance secret for a variety of reasons. Like Romeo and Juliet, their families may disapprove. Lovers may be married or committed to another when the new relationship begins. Or lovers may simply want privacy, knowing that their friends and families will be interested in the new relationship. Bring that special person in your life home to meet your parents and soon Mom steers the conversation toward the wedding. Secrecy is a way to protect an intimate relationship from social pressure.

Secrecy, however, might have a more direct effect on romance. Wegner, Lane, and Dimitri (1994) proposed that secrecy might increase passion in a romantic relationship. Researchers thought that keeping a relationship secret would require people to spend more time thinking about their secret love. Earlier research had shown that trying to keep a word secret made it easier for people to remember that word (Wegner & Lane 1995). Somehow, keeping something secret makes it seem more important. Tesser and Paulhus (1976) had found that the more people thought about a person they had dated, the more their love for that person grew. Similarly Wegner, Lane, and Dimitri (1994) thought that the more time people spent thinking about their romantic relationship, the more compelling the relationship would seem. Thus when a relationship was secret, people would spend more time thinking about it. It would become more important to them and more passionate.

Wegner, Lane, and Dimitri (1994) investigated whether people would think about past relationships more when the relationship had been secret than they would when it had not been secret. They began with a survey. Sometimes science is simple. One way to find out what people are thinking is to ask them. Questions on the survey asked people about their romantic histories. People were asked to list their past romances. People then ranked their past romances from the romance they thought about most down to the romance they thought about least. Then people were asked to evaluate the relationships at the top and the bottom of their ranking. Questions about the most-thought-about and least-thought-about relationship asked how secret or open the romance was. Researchers predicted that the relationships that people thought about most would more often have been secret than relationships that people thought about least.

The prediction was correct: People who completed the survey did think more about secret relationships than they did about open relationships (Wegner, Lane, & Dimitri 1994). The relationships that people put at the top of their lists, the ones they thought most about, were more likely to be secret ones than the ones at the bottom of the list, the ones people thought least about. Survey results supported the idea that secrecy increases the amount of thought people give to a relationship. However, researchers could not be confident, based on the survey results alone, that secrecy causes people to think about a relationship more. Other explanations are possible. For example, when a romantic relationship is very important to people, they may try to keep it secret. Experiments provide better evidence than surveys do about whether one thing causes another. (See the appendix on methods.) The trick is to create a romantic relationship in the laboratory, then see if people are more attracted to their partner when the relationship is secret than they are when the relationship is not secret.

Wegner, Lane, and Dimitri (1994) brought groups of four young people together to play cards, two men and two women who were unacquainted. The card game was played with two teams, each composed of a man and a woman. Team members sat across from each other at a card table. Researchers asked one team to play cards with their feet touching under the table. Some of the couples who were to play with their feet touching were asked to do so secretly. That is, the couple was to try not to let their opponents in the card game know that their feet were touching. The rest of the couples who played with their feet touching were told that it was OK to let their opponents know that the couples' feet were touching under the table. After the card game, people completed a questionnaire in which they rated the attractiveness of their partner. Would couples who had secretly played with their feet touching be more attracted to each other than couples whose touching feet had not been a secret?

Surprisingly, yes. When newly created couples tried to keep their touching a secret, they were more attracted to each other than were couples who did not try to keep their touching a secret. Thus secrecy does seem to promote romance.

IS LOVE BLIND?

People in love seem to see particular things in peculiar ways. They seem oblivious to the most obvious faults of the person they love. Many of us know people who stay in a relationship long after it becomes clear that the relationship is harmful. Often people will fall in love with someone whose attitudes they would normally find unattractive. For example, how could Vivica fall for Brock, knowing his primitive attitudes toward women? Did she think he would change? How could love be that blind?

Researchers at Baylor Medical School and the University of Maine investigated how people in love could overlook attitudes that they would normally find objectionable (McClanahan, Gold, Lenney, Ryckman, & Kulberg 1990). If love were truly blind, then people would not see that a person they were attracted to had attitudes different from their own. Or perhaps people simply become more tolerant of differences in a person they are attracted to. People may still see the differences but minimize their importance. To find out, researchers brought young men into the laboratory and asked them to answer survey questions about their attitudes on various subjects. While each young man answered the survey questions, a researcher brought in an attractive female research assistant who pretended to be another participant in the study. The researcher then told the young man that he might be working with the attractive woman later in the study. Later, researchers showed each young man his attractive partner's completed survey. Her survey had been filled out so that her attitudes disagreed with his attitudes in several important ways. Such dissimilar attitudes usually mean that people will dislike each other at least a little. After the young man had found out how different his partner's attitudes were, the attractive research assistant and the young man were again brought together in a room. For half the young men, the attractive research assistant spent five minutes talking and flirting with the young man after he completed the survey. For the rest of the young men, the research assistant was busy with her own work and did not talk to the young man. Then, young men were taken to a room by themselves and asked a series of questions about how attractive they found their partner and how similar her attitudes were to their own. In addition, young men were asked if they would volunteer to work with the attractive research assistant on another project. Young men had the choice of volunteering for up to six hours of additional work with the attractive woman.

Would a young man who was attracted to a woman because she flirted with him forget that her attitudes were different from his own? Is love that blind? In some ways, it is. As expected, researchers found that young men were more attracted to the young woman when she flirted with them than they were when she did not flirt. Also, when the attractive woman flirted with them, the men volunteered to work with her later for an average of almost two and a half hours. In contrast, when she did not flirt with them, they volunteered to work with her for an average of less than half an hour. Clearly, the men were more attracted to a woman who flirted (McClanahan et al. 1990).

But was love blind? Would young men forget that the woman's attitudes were different from their own after she flirted with them? Apparently they did. Young men rated their attitudes as very similar to the young woman's attitudes when she flirted with them. In contrast, young men rated their attitudes as quite different from the young woman's attitudes when she had not flirted (McClanahan et al. 1990). However, when asked to recall the woman's attitudes toward individual topics, men were just as accurate when they were attracted to the woman as they were when they were not attracted to her. It was not that love is blind so much as tolerant. When young men were attracted to the woman, they knew how different their attitudes were from hers. They just minimized the importance of those differences.

It is easy to see how infatuated people become involved with incompatible partners. Love is blind. Those important differences that make people incompatible don't seem to matter much when people fall in love. But what keeps people together in unhappy relationships, sometimes for years? Rusbult and Martz (1995) investigated why women stay in abusive relationships. What factors make it easier for a woman to break away from a man who abuses her? Researchers proposed that women stay in abusive relationships because of three factors: (1) satisfaction gained from the relationship, (2) the quality of alternative support they expect if they leave the relationship, and (3) the size of the investment they have in the relationship. A woman who is less satisfied, has alternative sources of support, and has invested relatively little in a relationship will find it easier to leave.

To find out if they were right, researchers surveyed women at a shelter for battered women. Women at the shelter answered a series of questions about how committed they were to the relationship they had escaped, at least temporarily. Women also answered questions related to the three factors researchers thought were important in determining whether women would leave an abusive relationship. First, they answered questions about how dissatisfied they were—for example, questions about the duration and severity of abuse. Second, they answered questions about their alternatives—for example, their education and income. Third, they answered questions about their investment in the relationship—for example, how long the relationship had lasted and whether they were married to the person who had abused them. Rusbult and Martz (1995) predicted that women who were less dissatisfied, who had fewer alternatives, and who had a greater investment in the relationship would be more committed to the relationship. Perhaps more important, they predicted that such women would be more likely to return to the abusive relationship after leaving the shelter.

Survey results from the women at the shelter for battered women supported Rusbult and Martz's (1995) ideas. Women were more committed to abusive relationships when the abuse was less severe, when their low income and education restricted their alternative resources outside the relationship, and when they were married to the man who abused them. In addition, researchers could also predict correctly which women would return to the abusive relationship based on their satisfaction with the relationship, their alternatives to the relationship, and their investment in the relationship.

Rusbult and Martz's (1995) work underscores the point that women do not get trapped in abusive relationships because of a character flaw. It is comforting to think that women are in abusive relationships because of a psychological need to be abused. If that were true, then it would be unlikely that you would ever find yourself in an abusive relationship, as long as you are a strong, independent-minded woman. Recall from Chapter 1 that this is another example of the fundamental attribution error. We blame individuals for events that may actually be caused by wider social factors. We blame the victims for their misfortune because that makes us more comfortable. We think that since we are not like them, we could not possibly be in an abusive relationship ourselves. Unfortunately, reality is less comforting. Virtually any woman can be trapped in an abusive relationship. Rusbult and Martz's work reinforces the advice that women leave a relationship at the first sign of abuse. It is easier to leave earlier rather than later. Women should strive to maintain their alternatives to a relationship. Remember that alternatives are a source of power. If women have an independent income, they are less likely to find themselves trapped.

Many people have satisfying relationships that they would like to continue. How can people protect their relationships from the competition of alternative potential partners? In modern society, we are thrown together with a wide variety of people, some of them very attractive. Many of us travel because of our work. We are separated from our romantic partners regularly. Some people seem to find it easy to stay committed to one person despite tempting alternatives. Others cannot resist and have one affair after another. How do people resist temptation and ward off infatuation with someone new?

Johnson and Rusbult (1989) thought that once attracted to someone, most people would find it difficult to resist temptation. Researchers thought that people who were committed to a relationship must have some way to keep themselves from becoming attracted to other people. It isn't that people who are committed to a relationship have stronger character. Rather, committed people do not see the new people they meet as attractive.

To test their ideas, Johnson and Rusbult (1989) began by using surveys. They asked people involved in romantic relationships how committed they were to their current relationship and how attractive they found any potential alternative partners. People who participated in the study completed a survey about every week for a number of weeks. Researchers could then tell whether people were becoming more committed to their partners and whether they found potential new partners less attractive. As researchers had predicted, when people became more committed to their partners, they found the available alternative less attractive.

Recall, however, that surveys are not as good as experiments at pinning down the causes of results. To find out whether it was the commitment to the relationship that caused people to find alternative partners less attractive, Johnson and Rusbult (1989) also conducted an experiment. Researchers brought people into the laboratory and asked them to play a role. In the role, people were in a romantic relationship. They then met an attractive alternative partner. How attractive would they find the new partner? Women were given the role of Sarah, a 21-year-old college student:

> For the past 3 months, Sarah has been dating Robert. However, at a social gathering Sarah notices an extremely attractive man looking at her from across the room. From the way he's looking at her, Sarah assumes that he's attracted to her. What does Sarah think about this situation? Does she want to approach the stranger? Does she want him to approach her? (p. 975)

Men in the study had the same role with genders reversed.

Half the people in the study were in highly committed roles. For example, Sarah would enjoy being in this exclusive relationship and find it fulfilling in many ways. The rest of the people in the study were in less committed roles. For example, Sarah would not really want to be involved in an exclusive relationship and would want to date other people. After playing their roles, people answered questions about how committed they were to their relationship and how attractive they found the new alternative partner. Would people who played the role of a person committed to a relationship find an alternative partner less attractive? They did. Johnson and Rusbult (1989) found that people who had played the role of a person committed to a relationship said that they were less attracted to an alternative partner than had people who played the role of a person less committed to a relationship.

People who are committed to stable, exclusive relationships find potential alternative partners less attractive. It is one way to protect a valuable relationship when we are in daily contact with attractive people who might threaten that relationship. Rather than be strong and resist temptation, it is easier to avoid temptation in the first place. While we cannot in most cases remove the source of temptation, we can reduce temptation by seeing alternative partners as less attractive. In other words, people are more likely to stay in a satisfying romantic relationship if they stop looking for romantic partners after they have found one.

Love is a difficult subject to study in a systematic way. Many of the topics that social psychologists study resist scientific analysis. Nonetheless, the research reviewed in this chapter shows that social psychologists can provide useful knowledge about how romantic relationships work or do not work. Similarly, other chapters have directed social psychological research at important problems such as warding off depression, getting along with other people, working more effectively, and prejudice. Social psychologists have found that people look at the world in ways that sometimes lead them astray. For example, we commit the fundamental attribution error. We think that situations result from individual personality or character when they are often caused by wider social factors. We are prone to a number of such biases that reduce our effectiveness as human beings. Social psychological research produces knowledge we can use to overcome some of our limitations, to improve our lives and the lives of those around us.

Science is effective at increasing our knowledge of the world around us because it uses a social system to correct the biases of individual scientists. The appendix describes how science works to compensate for some of the biases to which we are all prone. Many people think that scientists must be more objective or rational or intelligent than other people to produce valid scientific knowledge. However, that idea is one more example of the fundamental attribution error. It is easy to think that the personal characteristics of scientists—their objectivity, rationality, and intelligence—are responsible for producing scientific knowledge. We overlook the fact that science is a social process that requires many people working together to produce knowledge that we hope will benefit us all.

Further Reading

Of General Interest

Clark, M. S., & Pataki, S. P. (1995). Interpersonal processes influencing attraction and relationships. In Abraham Tesser (Ed.), *Advanced social psychology* (pp. 283–331). New York: McGraw-Hill.

Hendrick, S. S., & Hendrick, C. (1992). *Romantic love*. Newbury Park, CA: Sage.

Homans, G. C. (1974). *Social behavior: Its elementary forms.* New York: Harcourt Brace Jovanovich.

Michael, R. T., Gagnon, J. H., Laumann, E. O., & Kolata, G. (1995). *Sex in America: A definitive study.* New York: Warner Books.

Sternberg, R. J. (1998). *Love is a story: A new theory of relationships.* New York: Oxford University Press.

Sternberg, Robert, J. & Barnes, M. L. (Eds.). (1988). *The psychology of love.* New Haven, CT: Yale University Press.

Walsh, A. (1991). *The science of love: Understanding love and its effects on mind and body.* Buffalo, NY: Prometheus.

Recent and Technical Issues

Agnew, C. R., Van Lange, P. A. M., Rusbult, C. E., & Langston, C. A. (1998). Cognitive interdependence: Commitment and the mental representation of close relationships. *Journal of Personality and Social Psychology, 74,* 939–954.

Beach, S. R., Tesser, A., Fincham, F. D., Jones, D. J., Johnson, D., & Whitaker, D. J. (1998). Pleasure and pain in doing well, together: An investigation of performance-related affect in close relationships. *Journal of Personality and Social Psychology, 74,* 923–938.

De Munck, V. C. (Ed.). 1998. *Romantic love and sexual behavior.* Westport, CT: Praeger.

Dion, K. K., & Dion, K. L. (1991). Psychological individualism and romantic love. *Journal of Social Behavior and Personality, 6,* 17–33.

Drigotas, S. M., & Rusbult, C. E. (1992). Should I stay or should I go? A dependence model of breakups. *Journal of Personality and Social Psychology, 62,* 62–87.

Hayashi, G. M. & Strickland, B. R. (1998). Long-term effects of parental divorce on love relationships: Divorce as attachment disruption. *Journal of Social and Personal Relationships, 15,* 23–38.

Hazan, C. & Shaver, P. (1987). Romantic love conceptualized as an attachment process. *Journal of Personality and Social Psychology, 52,* 511–524.

Lovaglia, M. J. (in press). Understanding network exchange theory. *Advances in group processes.* Greenwich, CT: JAI Press.

Mikulincer, M., & Erev, I. (1992). Attachment style and structure of romantic love. *British Journal of Social Psychology, 30,* 273–291.

Rusbult, C. E., Verette, J., Whitney, G. A., Slovik, L. F., & Lipkus, I. (1991). Accommodation processes in close relationships: Theory and preliminary empirical evidence. *Journal of Personality and Social Psychology, 60,* 53–78.

Singelis, T., Choo, P., & Hatfield, E. (1995). Love schemas and romantic love. *Journal of Social Behavior and Personality, 10,* 15–36.

Sprecher, S. (1998). The effect of exchange orientation on close relationships. *Social Psychology Quarterly, 61,* 220–231.

Van Lange, P. A. M., Rusbilt, C. E., Drigotas, S. M., Arriaga, X. B., Witcher, B. S., & Cox, C. L. (1997). Willingness to sacrifice in close relationships. *Journal of Personality and Social Psychology, 72,* 1373–1395.

Willer, D., Lovaglia, M. J., & Markovsky, B. (1997). Power and influence: A theoretical bridge. *Social Forces, 76,* 571–603.

Appendix: How Do We Know?

There is an advertising campaign for a pain reliever in which a person says that he does not pay much attention to what doctors and scientific studies have to say about its effectiveness. Instead, he says, he tried it on his own tough headaches. Only when it worked for him was he convinced.

The advertisement illustrates both how hardheaded and practical people can be and how easily we fool ourselves into accepting all sorts of nonsense. "Don't trust the experts. Check it out for yourself." Sound advice. To be worth your time and money, a remedy should both have strong scientific support and work for you. All the medical research in the world is no good unless your head stops hurting. But the person in the advertisement also implies that the scientific studies are not worth much. Only his own experience counts. It seems like every few weeks a new scientific study comes out. Eat oats. Don't drink coffee. Coffee is OK. Eat fish. Don't eat too much fish. All the studies are scientific yet one study seems to contradict another. What good is science anyway? It allows us to be certain about so little.

THE PHILOSOPHICAL QUESTION

The question—How do we know something is true?—is philosophical. A big part of modern philosophy wrestles with exactly how science goes about helping discover what is true. Perhaps the most commonly accepted version of how science works comes from the famous philosopher Sir Karl Popper, who emigrated to England from his native Germany before World War II to escape the Nazis. Popper (1968) proposed that science works because scientists state their ideas in ways that make it possible to prove them wrong. For example, a scientist might analyze stress in fault lines in the earth's crust and predict that a major earthquake will occur in a certain location within five years. If no major earthquakes occur in that area, then the scientist will have to admit that her analysis was wrong. A less scientific idea would be that earthquakes occur because planets and stars are inharmonious. A major earthquake is then seen as evidence that the idea is correct because the planets and stars must have been inharmonious. Lack of an earthquake is also evidence that the idea is correct because, obviously, the planets and stars must be in harmony. The scientist's prediction is more precise, and therefore easier to prove wrong. Then if a major earthquake does occur exactly where the scientist said it would, we can have more confidence that the scientist's analysis was correct. Every time the scientist makes a precise prediction that turns out to be correct, her idea passes another test. The more tests that a scientific idea passes, the more confident we are that it is correct. However, if the idea fails to pass a test, then according to Karl Popper it must be discarded and a better idea found.

There is no doubt that Karl Popper's ideas capture a good deal of how science is done. Scientists do make guesses then try to see if those guesses were right. However, science is more complicated than the picture of it painted by Popper. A good scientist does not give up on her ideas just because they fail to pass a few early tests. Maybe she did not have the experiment set up properly. Maybe the guess she made was inconsistent with her theoretical ideas. Good scientists sometimes work for years to show that their ideas are correct even though the evidence consistently proves them wrong. Then some breakthrough in technique shows that the idea was right all along. Had scientists followed Popper's advice and discarded their ideas when they failed to pass a test, much of what we know today as scientific fact would never have been discovered.

Other scientific ideas become widely accepted before passing any real tests at all. Einstein's Theory of Relativity is a good example. The Theory of Relativity passed its first test only years after it was accepted as correct by most physicists. When an interviewer asked Einstein if he was relieved that evidence now showed his theory to be correct, Einstein replied with one of his most famous lines. Einstein said that God, while subtle, was not malicious. Einstein and most established physicists were confident that the theory was correct and would be shown to be correct eventually. Evidence supporting the theory of relativity is still coming in more than 90 years later. Scientists also grow fond of their own ideas. They can easily fool themselves into thinking those ideas are passing tests when the evidence for them is minimal or clearly refutes them.

How then do scientists decide what is true?

Philosopher Ian Hacking sees scientists as more practical than did Karl Popper. Hacking (1983) proposes that scientists work with whatever they find useful. If an idea proves useful, allowing a scientist to accomplish some more immediate goal, then the idea is valid. As long as the idea continues to be useful, it is regarded as sound. A scientific idea is abandoned only if it stops working entirely or if a more useful idea replaces it.

Microwaves are a good example. How do you know that microwaves are real? You can look up the theory and research in the physics library and convince yourself that you know how microwaves are supposed to work. But it will still seem abstract and theoretical, won't it? It won't be part of your real world. Then go home and cook dinner in a few minutes in your microwave oven. Now the reality of microwaves is easy to see. Microwaves are real to us because they can be used to accomplish some practical goal.

Scientists use unproven ideas to work on their immediate problems. Good science requires faith that mistaken ideas will eventually be discovered when the work built on them collapses.

THE SOCIAL PSYCHOLOGY OF SCIENTISTS

Scientists had produced such monumental wonders that they were placed on a high pedestal during the first half of the twentieth century. Scientists were seen as more rational and smarter than were other people. Much of what scientists said was believed, even when scientists spoke on topics outside of their scientific expertise. For example, William Shockley, famous for inventing the transistor, took to speaking out on the genetic inferiority of black people. Shockley had no training or expertise in the biological and social research necessary to decide the question. (See Chapter 8 for current research which shows that differences in mental ability test scores for different racial and ethnic groups result from social conditions.) However, Shockley's views were widely quoted in the media. People listened to him because he was a successful scientist.

James D. Watson cracked the pedestal on which scientists stood when he published a hugely entertaining book about his discovery of the structure of the DNA molecule, *The Double Helix*, in 1968. *The Double Helix* was a best seller that showed scientists as they really are, human. People began to realize that scientists were prone to all of the limitations and errors that plague everybody else.

Some of the biases that get in the way of finding out how things really work have been described in this book. Scientists commit the fundamental attribution error. They may mistakenly believe that things happen in society because of personal characteristics when they are actually produced by social factors. The scientific approach to intelligence testing is a good example. It is as easy for scientists as for anyone else to assume that people's intelligence must determine their scores on intelligence tests. The social factors noted in Chapter 8 that have recently been shown to make a difference in those test scores are overlooked.

In *An Enquiry Concerning Human Understanding,* first published in the 1700s, the philosopher David Hume noticed the human tendency to assume that one thing causes another (Hume 1748/1966). He said that whenever two things happen at about the same time, people immediately conclude that one of them caused the other. But that is often not the case. For example, consider two common events. First, a teenager is late getting home at night. Second, his worried parents hear a siren from an ambulance going by on the highway. Because the late child is on their mind when they hear the siren, parents are likely to assume that the ambulance has something to do with the child being late. They will leap to the conclusion that their child has had an accident. In most cases, parents are wrong about the connection between the siren and their child. However, no matter how many times we notice that we are wrong, that two things happening at about the same time are just coincidence, we continue to assume that two things happening together must be connected. For example, police detectives commonly say that they do not believe coincidence. Are they wrong? Certainly coincidence is common. But assuming coincidence will not help a detective solve a case. Our human biases are often useful even though they can cloud reality.

We give too much weight to first impressions. We jump to conclusions. Then we cling to our beliefs when new evidence should show us that we are wrong (Ross, Lepper, & Hubbard 1975). In addition, people commonly look for evidence that confirms what they already believe and ignore evidence that contradicts their beliefs (Lord, Lepper & Preston 1984). When we try to estimate how big or small something is, we measure it against some mental standard. We try to judge how much bigger or smaller it is than something similar that we have experienced. For example, if you drive an older inexpensive car, then you might estimate that most people's cars are worth less than $10,000. If you drive a new luxury car, then you might estimate that most people's cars are worth more than $20,000. Our estimates of reality are anchored to our personal experiences, distorting our judgment (Tversky & Kahneman 1974). We are likely to make generalizations from one or two examples without considering how representative those examples might be (Hamill, Wilson, & Nisbett 1980). Science is a way to correct for these and other biases that cloud human judgment.

In science, researchers check each other's work for accuracy. The biases of one scientist tend to balance out those of another, unless most scientists have the same biases. That is why it is important for scientists to come from as many diverse backgrounds as possible. For example, if all or most scientists are white men from upper-class backgrounds, then some "scientific" results will inevitably reflect the biases shared by upper-class white men.

Attempts to more accurately see reality by correcting for human biases led to the experimental approach.

THE EXPERIMENTAL APPROACH

Most of the research described in this book used experiments. As a research method, experiments have the advantage of pinning down what causes what. Here is how experiments work.

Experimenters want to keep a situation exactly the same, then change only one thing and observe the result. Suppose you want to see if a light switch really causes a light to turn on and off. You conduct an experiment. You stand by the light switch and see that nothing else in the room is changing. You flip the switch. The light goes out. Nothing changed except that you flipped the switch. You now have evidence that your flipping the switch caused the light to turn off. But what if the bulb burned out? Maybe the switch did not cause the light to go out after all. How can you tell? You flip the switch again. (Researchers call this *replicating* the experiment.) If the light goes on, you have more evidence that it was the switch and not some other unknown factor that causes the light to turn on or off. If you still are not convinced, you try the light switch again. The light goes out. You try it at different times of the day. Eventually you are convinced that the light switch causes the light to turn on or off. Then, when you need additional light to solve some practical problem—reading a book, for example—you look for a light switch to flip. As Ian Hacking (1983) suggested, the results of experiments become real when they are used successfully to solve some practical problem.

Experiments that investigate how people think and behave are more complicated. Experimenters want to do something to different people, then see if people respond in a particular way to what happened to them. The problem is that individual people are all different from each other. Are they responding differently because of what the experimenter did or because they are different kinds of people? Social psychology experiments would be easier to do if people were exact clones of each other.

Experimenters handle the problem of individual differences in the people they study by trying out their experiment on a lot of people and dividing those people into two groups. In a good experiment, those two groups will be as similar at the beginning of the experiment as it is possible to make them. If, on average, people in one group respond differently to what the experimenter did than do people in the other group, then the experimenter has evidence that what she did caused people to respond a certain way. The trick is to make the two groups of people in the experiment as similar as possible.

When people are brought into a laboratory, researchers can separate them into two similar groups by randomly assigning people to one group or the other. Random assignment means that researchers pick people to be in Group 1 or in Group 2 purely by chance. They flip a coin or blindly draw numbers out of a box. If the coin comes up heads, then the person goes to Group 1. If the coin comes up tails, then the person goes to Group 2. Individual differences will average out in the two groups. For example, there would be about the same number of left-handers in both groups. Researchers, then, would not have to worry that whether a person was left-handed made a difference in how she responded to the experiment. However, the system of randomly assigning people to different groups so that both groups will be similar is not foolproof.

People have so many individual differences that the two groups could still be very different for some unknown reason, purely by chance. Researchers use statistics to tell how likely that is to happen. Using statistics, researchers can tell how strong the evidence from any given experiment is. Also, researchers know that if they keep doing the experiment over and over—if there are enough people randomly assigned to Group 1 and Group 2—then the two groups will be identical for all practical purposes.

If the two groups of people in the experiment are similar, then a social psychology experiment is not much different from the light switch experiment. The experimenter does something to one group then sees how people in that group respond. The experimenter does something else to people in the other group then sees how they respond. If people in the two groups respond differently, then the experimenter has evidence that what she did to people caused them to respond in a certain way.

The experiment described in Chapter 8 is a good example. Lovaglia, Lucas, Houser, Thye, and Markovsky (1998) showed how social factors cause changes in mental ability test scores, even when everyone takes a the same unbiased test under identical conditions. Researchers brought people into the laboratory and randomly assigned them to two groups. People in Group 1 were treated like members of a disadvantaged minority. Group 1 people were led to expect some problems to arise if they scored high on the IQ test. For example, their coworkers might resent them; they might be accused of cheating. People in Group 2 were treated like members of an advantaged majority. People in Group 2 got the same instructions as the people in Group 1. That is, Group 2 people were led to expect that Group 1 people (those in the disadvantaged minority) would expect problems to arise if Group 1 people scored high on the IQ test. A large number of people were randomly assigned to Group 1 and Group 2 to increase the similarity between the two groups. The two groups were similar, received the same instructions, and took the same unbiased IQ test. The only significant difference between the two groups was that Group 1 was treated as a disadvantaged minority while Group 2 was treated as an advantaged majority. Because Group 1 being treated as a disadvantaged minority was the only significant difference between the groups, researchers were confident that membership in Group 1 caused the low IQ scores of the Group 1 people. Then researchers replicated the study. That is, researchers repeated the study in different ways to see if they would get the same results. They did.

THE ETHICS OF EXPERIMENTS

Experiments provide solid evidence that what the experimenter did caused people to respond in a certain way. Experimenters cause people to do things they otherwise would not have done. Thus experimenters must be careful not to harm the people that they work with. Because of the risk that experiments pose, proposed research is now reviewed by committees whose job it is to protect the safety and well-being of research participants.

Medical experiments have perhaps the greatest potential for harm. When risky medical procedures are tested, all too often the people chosen for the test are poor or disadvantaged. An extreme example is the experiment conducted on syphilis patients around Tuskegee, Alabama (Jones 1993). Medical researchers wanted to investigate the damage caused by syphilis in its later stages. To do that meant researchers would have to watch syphilis patients without treating them while the disease slowly killed them. How could normal human beings withhold care while watching for years as other people died? It was no coincidence that the people chosen for the study were poor black men. Doctors would be unlikely to consider such a study on rich professionals like themselves. Researchers are human, too, subject to all the biases that plague the rest of us. Discovering how syphilis progresses in the human body was a worthwhile goal. Researchers judged that the knowledge gained from the study would offset the cost in human life, but only because they did not consider the particular lives in question to be worth much.

Every experiment intervenes in people's lives to some extent. Thus experimenters must judge whether the knowledge gained will be worth enough to offset any disruption to the lives of people who participate in it. For example, Philip Zimbardo and his colleagues conducted one of the most famous social psychology experiments at Stanford University (Haney, Banks, & Zimbardo 1973). The knowledge gained from the experiment was profound. It changed the way that people look at the question of good and evil. You decide whether the knowledge gained was worth the cost to the people who participated in it.

Zimbardo wanted to find out if evil acts could be caused by social conditions rather than by the character defects of evil people. Recall from Chapter 1 that Zimbardo's idea was another way to show how we commit the fundamental attribution error. Most people who do not know about Zimbardo's experiment continue to believe that evil is caused by the character defects in evil people rather than by social conditions.

To find out if social conditions could produce antisocial behavior in normal, mentally healthy people, Zimbardo and his colleagues set up their own prison. Researchers randomly assigned people to be either prison guards or prisoners. That is, a coin was flipped for each person to decide whether he would be a prisoner or a prison guard. Zimbardo paid student volunteers to take two weeks out of their lives to participate in a full-time, 24-hour-a-day experiment. He did not tell them what would happen to them.

Researchers set up a prison in a few rooms in the basement of the psychology department at Stanford University (Zimbardo 1979). On the day the experiment began, Stanford students who had been randomly assigned to be prison guards reported for duty at the prison. They were issued guard uniforms and told to maintain order among prisoners. Guards were issued sunglasses so prisoners could not see their eyes. Guards carried billy clubs, whistles, and handcuffs. They were warned not to use physical violence.

Stanford students randomly assigned to be prisoners had a different experience. Zimbardo had contracted the local police department to go to each prisoner's home and arrest him. You can imagine the law-abiding college students' surprise as police led them in handcuffs to police cars. At the police station, prisoners were booked as suspected felons. They were then blindfolded and driven to the prison. At the prison, each prisoner was stripped and given a full-body search before being issued a prisoner's uniform, a towel, and some bedding. Unable to absorb how much their lives had changed, most prisoners sat dazed on cots in their barren cells. The "Stanford County Prison" had become their life.

Serious abuses of prisoners began appearing the first day. At first some prisoners resisted the guards' orders. Guards reacted harshly, forcefully restoring order. From then on, guards increasingly behaved like the stereotype of brutal prison guards and prisoners behaved like passive victims. Every prison guard engaged in abusive behavior toward the prisoners. Many seemed to enjoy the power they held over the prisoners. Normal, mentally healthy Stanford students became evil within a day after given power over people just like themselves in a coercive social situation. Nothing about the individual character of the students caused their abusive behavior. Totally by chance, they found themselves in a social situation that had corrupted them.

Due to the guards' abusive behavior, the first prisoner had to be released on the second day. He alternated between crying and rage. His thinking was disorganized and he showed symptoms of severe depression. Three more prisoners were released soon after with similar symptoms. One prisoner developed a rash over his entire body caused by the stress of the guards' abusive treatment.

On a TV interview in 1998, Philip Zimbardo said that he too was caught up in the fascination with power. Although troubled by what he saw, he was so excited by the experiment that he let the guards' abusive behavior continue. Toward the end of the first week of the experiment, he invited a colleague down to the basement to watch the abnormal behavior that prison conditions had created. Zimbardo's colleague was horrified when she saw how guards were treating prisoners and how prisoners were behaving. She told Zimbardo that he must stop it. In the interview, Zimbardo said that only then did he realize that something evil was happening—to the prisoners, to the guards, and to himself. He stopped the experiment.

The Stanford prison experiment was extremely important. Not only did it teach us the power of social situations to produce evil in normal human beings, but it also had a positive impact on our society. Knowledge gained from Zimbardo's research has been used to devise procedures in real prisons that decrease abuses of power by prison guards. Given the important knowledge and social benefits that the study produced, was it ethical for Zimbardo to allow students to be mistreated as prisoners? To turn normal students into brutal guards? Do you think it should have been conducted?

Another social benefit of Zimbardo's study is that universities set up committees to oversee research. The Stanford prison experiment made it clear that a single researcher should not have the power to set up experiments that could harm people who participate in them. Social situations that give people power over others will corrupt even highly moral people. The power that experimenters hold over people who participate in their experiment may cloud experimenters' judgment. Now, before an experiment begins, experimenters must get approval from a committee of other researchers and concerned community members such as ministers. It is unlikely that a researcher could get approval to conduct the Stanford prison experiment today.

CAN YOU REACH GENERAL CONCLUSIONS FROM THE BEHAVIOR OF COLLEGE SOPHOMORES?

Experiments are usually done on small samples of people. A typical experiment might have less than a hundred participants, often college students. How can experimenters be so confident that they have found out something about the way people behave in general? Would people who are not college students have responded differently to the experiment? A social psychology laboratory is an artificial environment. How do you know that people would not respond differently in the "real world"?

The value of experiments lies in the researcher's ability to use them to test a theory by obtaining one small piece of reliable information at a time. In an experiment, the artificial nature of the research setting becomes an advantage (Webster & Kervin 1971). Because the laboratory setting is artificial, the experimenter can make sure that two groups are essentially identical. Then the experimenter can change one thing in the situation. She does something to one of the groups that she does not do to the other. If the groups respond differently, then she has evidence that what she did caused the difference in behavior between the two groups.

While it is true that people may respond quite differently outside the laboratory, experimenters can conclude that their results are valid whenever key conditions exist that produced the laboratory results. The problem is knowing which conditions are key. After all, social psychology laboratories resemble situations outside the laboratory very little. Zelditch (1980) put it this way: "Can you really study an army in the laboratory?" He concluded that you can study complex social situations using artificial laboratory experiments. However, he cautioned that generalizing the results of an experiment is a mistake. It is true that real soldiers on a real battlefield may respond differently than do college students in a makeshift "war" in the basement of a psychology building. So what do the results of experiments tell us if we cannot generalize them to other situations? Zelditch concludes that experiments are useful because they test theories. A theory explains how some social factor causes another. It lists the key elements necessary to produce a specific response from people. Then the experiment is set up using those key elements. The results of the experiment either support or contradict the researcher's theory. Just as in the light switch experiment, if repeated experiments in different settings support a theory, then researchers can be confident that it is valid.

Experiments, then, test a theory. The theory tells which key elements are needed to produce the results it predicts. A well-tested theory can be used to predict events and human behavior in any situation—no matter how distant from the laboratory—that contains the key elements specified by the theory.

Mook (1983) makes the same point in a different way. According to Mook, experiments need not resemble naturally occurring situations in order to generalize to them. All studies have limits on how much their results can be generalized. Again, it is not the results that should be generalized, but the conclusions made from a valid theory. We know that a theory is valid when it has been tested by a series of experiments.

Experiments have several advantages, but conducting them is not always possible or even desirable. Many research methods have been developed that contribute to the growth of scientific knowledge. Science works by systematically organizing the work of diverse researchers using many different methods (Szmatka & Lovaglia 1996).

Further Reading

Of General Interest

Diesing, P. (1991). *How does social science work? Reflections on practice.* Pittsburgh: University of Pittsburgh Press.

Hacking, I. (1983). *Representing and intervening.* Cambridge: Cambridge University Press.

Kuhn, T. S. (1970). *The structure of scientific revolutions* (2nd ed.). Chicago: University of Chicago Press.

Mahoney, M. J. (1976). *Scientist as subject: The psychological imperative.* Cambridge, MA: Ballinger.

Medawar, P. (1984). *The limits of science.* Oxford: Oxford University Press.

Watson, J. D. (1968). *The Double Helix.* New York: Atheneum.

Zimbardo, P. G. (1973). On the ethics of intervention in human psychological research: With special reference to the Stanford prison experiment. *Cognition, 2,* 243–256.

More Difficult Yet Worth the Effort

Bloor, D. (1991). *Knowledge and social imagery.* Chicago: University of Chicago Press.

Bordeau, P. (1977). *Outline of a theory of practice.* Cambridge: Cambridge University Press.

Cohen, B. P. (1989). *Developing sociological knowledge: Theory and method.* Chicago: Nelson-Hall.

Feynman, R. (1994). *The character of physical law.* New York: Modern Library.

Habermas, J. (1988). *On the logic of the social sciences.* Cambridge: MIT Press.

Hume, D. (1966). *An enquiry concerning human understanding.* La Salle, IL: Open Court. (Original work published 1748)

Lakatos, I., & Musgrave, A. (Eds.). (1970). *Criticism and the growth of knowledge.* Cambridge: Cambridge University Press.

Latour, B. (1987). *Science in action.* Cambridge, MA: Harvard University Press.

Popper, K. R. (1968). *Conjectures and refutations: The growth of scientific knowledge.* New York: Harper and Row.

References

Aderman, D. (1972). Elation, depression, and helping behavior. *Journal of Personality and Social Psychology, 24,* 91–101.

Agnew, C. R., Van Lange, P. A. M., Rusbult, C. E., & Langston, C. A. (1998). Cognitive interdependence: Commitment and the mental representation of close relationships. *Journal of Personality and Social Psychology, 74,* 939–954.

Allen, V. L., & Wilder, D. A. (1975). Categorization, belief similarity, and intergroup discrimination. *Journal of Personality and Social Psychology, 32,* 971–977.

Alloy, L. B., & Abramson, L. Y. (1979). Judgment of contingency in depressed and nondepressed studnts: Sadder but wiser? *Journal of Experimental Psychology: General, 108,* 441–485.

Alloy, L. B., Abramson, L. Y., & Viscusi, D. (1981). Induced mood and the illusion of control. *Journal of Personality and Social Psychology, 41,* 1129–1140.

Alloy, L. B., & Ahrens, A. H. (1987). Depression and pessimism for the future: Biased use of statistically relevant information in predictions for self versus others. *Journal of Personality and Social Psychology, 52,* 366–378.

Ambady, N., Hallahan, M., & Rosenthal, R. (1995). On judging and being judged accurately in zero-acquaintance situations. *Journal of Personality and Social Psychology, 69,* 518–529.

American Psychiatric Association. (1994). *Diagnostic and statistical manual of mental disorders* (4th ed.). Washington, DC: Author.

Anderson, C. A., Miller, R. S., Riger, A. L., Dill, J. C., & Sedikides, C. (1994). Behavioral and characterological attributional styles as predictors of depression and loneliness: Review, refinement, and test. *Journal of Personality and Social Psychology, 66,* 549–558.

Archer, R. L., & Burleson, J. A. (1980). The effects of timing of self-disclosure on attraction and reciprocity. *Journal of Personality and Social Psychology, 38,* 120–130.

Archer, R. L., & Cook, C. E. (1986). Personalistic self-disclosure and attraction: basis for relationship or scarce resource. *Social Psychology Quarterly, 49,* 268–272.

Arkin, R. M., & Maruyama, G. M. (1979). Attribution, affect, and college exam performance. *Journal of Educational Psychology, 71,* 85–93.

Aronson, E. (1969). The theory of cognitive dissonance: A current perspective. In L. Berkowitz (Ed.), *Advances in experimental social psychology* (vol. 4, pp. 1–34). San Diego: Academic Press.

Arroyo, C. G., & Zigler, E. (1995). Racial identity, academic achievement, and the psychological well-being of economically disadvantaged adolescents. *Journal of Personality and Social Psychology, 69,* 903–914.

Axsom, D., Yates, S., & Chaiken, S. (1987). Audience response as a heuristic cue in persuasion. *Journal of Personality and Social Psychology, 53,* 30–40.

Ayres, I. (1991). Fair driving: Gender and race discrimination in retail car negotiations. *Harvard Law Review,* 104, 817–872.

Bandura, A. (1986). *Foundations of thought and action.* Englewood Cliffs, NJ: Prentice-Hall.

Bargh, J. A., Chaiken, S., Govender, R., & Pratto, F. (1992). The generality of the automatic attitude activation effect. *Journal of Personality and Social Psychology, 62,* 893–912.

Bargh, J. A., Chen, M., & Burrows, L. (1996). Automaticity of social behavior: Direct effects of trait construct and stereotype activation on action. *Journal of Personality and Social Psychology, 71,* 230–244.

Bargh, J. A., & Pietromonaco, P. (1982). Automatic information processing and social perception: The influence of trait information presented outside of conscious awareness on impression formation. *Journal of Personality and Social Psychology, 43,* 437–449.

Baron, R. A. (1987). Interviewer's moods and reactions to job applicants: The influence of affective states on applied social judgments. *Journal of Applied Social Psychology, 17,* 911–926.

Baron, R. A. (1990). Environmentally induced positive affect: Its impact on self-efficacy, task performance, negotiation, and conflict. *Journal of Applied Social Psychology, 20,* 368–384.

Baron, R. S., Vandello, J. A., & Brunsman, B. (1996). The forgotten variable in conformity research: Impact of task importance on social influence. *Journal of Personality and Social Psychology, 71,* 915–927.

Baumeister, R. F. (1986). *Identity: Cultural change and the struggle for self.* New York: Oxford University Press.

Baumeister, R. F., & Cairns, K. J. (1992). Repression and self-presentation: When audiences interfere with self-deceptive strategies. *Journal of Personality and Social Psychology, 62,* 851–862.

Beach, S. R., Tesser, A., Fincham, F. D., Jones, D. J., Johnson, D., & Whitaker, D.J. (1998). Pleasure and pain in doing well, together: An investigation of performance-related affect in close relationships. *Journal of Personality and Social Psychology, 74,* 923–938.

Beck, E. M., & Tolnay, S. E. (1990). The killing fields of the deep south: The market for cotton and the lynching of blacks, 1882–1930. *American Sociological Review, 55,* 526–539.

Becker, H. S. (1963). *Outsiders: Studies in the sociology of deviance.* New York: Free Press.

Bem, D. J. (1965). An experimental analysis of self-persuasion. *Journal of Experimental Social Psychology, 1,* 199–218.

Bem, D. J. (1967). Self-perception: An alternative interpretation of cognitive dissonance phenomena. *Psychological Review, 74,* 183–200.

Benjamin, L. (1991). *The black elite: Facing the color line in the twilight of the twentieth century.* Chicago: Nelson-Hall.

Berger, J., Cohen, B. P., & Zelditch, M., Jr. (1972). Status characteristics and social interaction. *American Sociological Review, 37,* 241–255.

Berger, J., Fisek, M. H., Norman, R. Z., & Zelditch, M., Jr. (1977). *Status characteristics and social interaction.* New York: Elsevier.

Berger, J., Norman, R. Z., Balkwell, J. M., & Smith, R. F. (1992). Status inconsistency in task situations: A test of four status processing principles. *American Sociological Review, 57,* 843–855.

Berger, J., Ridgeway, C., Fisek, M. H., & Norman, R. Z. (1998). The legitimation and delegitimation of power and prestige orders. *American Sociological Review, 63,* 379–405.

Berger, J., & Zelditch, M., Jr. (Eds.). (1985). *Status, rewards and influence: How expectations Organize behavior.* San Francisco: Jossey-Bass.

Berger, J., & Zelditch, M., Jr. (Eds.). (1993). *Theoretical research programs: Studies in theory growth.* Stanford, CA: Stanford University Press.

Berger, J., Zelditch, M., Jr., & Anderson, B. (1989). *Sociological theories in progress: New formulations.* Newbury Park, CA: Sage.

Berger, P. L., & Luckmann, T. (1966). *The social construction of reality.* New York: Doubleday.

Berglas, S., & Jones, E. E. (1978). Drug choice as a self-handicapping strategy in response to noncontingent success. *Journal of Personality and Social Psychology, 36,* 405–417.

Berkowitz, L. (1987). Mood, self-awareness, and willingness to help. *Journal of Personality and Social Psychology, 52,* 721–729.

Berkowitz, L., & Frodi, A. (1979). Reactions to a child's mistakes affected by her/his looks and speech. *Social Psychology Quarterly, 42,* 420–425.

Biernat, M., & Kobrynowicz, D. (1997). Gender- and race-based standards of competence: Lower minimum standards but higher ability standards for devalued groups. *Journal of Personality and Social Psychology, 72,* 544–557.

Billig, M. G., & Tajfel, H. (1973). Social categorization and similarity in intergroup behavior. *European Journal of Social Psychology, 3,* 7–52.

Bloor, D. (1991). *Knowledge and social imagery.* Chicago: University of Chicago Press.

Bootzin, R. R. (1997). Examining the theory and clinical utility of writing about emotional experiences. *Psychological Science, 8,* 167–169.

Bordeau, P. (1977). *Outline of a theory of practice.* Cambridge: Cambridge University Press.

Branch, T. (1988). *Parting the waters: America in the King years, 1954–63.* New York: Simon & Schuster.

Brannigan, G. G., & Merrens, M. R. (Eds.). (1995). *The social psychologists: Research adventures.* New York: McGraw-Hill.

Brewer, M. B., & Silver, M. (1978). Ingroup bias as a function of task characteristics. *European Journal of Social Psychology, 8,* 393–400.

Brown, R. P., & Josephs, R. A. (1999). A burden of proof: Stereotype relevance and gender differences in math performance. *Journal of Personality and Social Psychology, 76,* 246–257.

Burke, P. J. (1991). Identity processes and social stress. *American Sociological Review, 56,* 836–849.

Burke, P. J. (1997). An identity model for network exchange. *American Sociological Review, 62,* 134–150.

Burke, P. J., & Reitzes, D. C. (1991). An identity theory approach to commitment. *Social Psychology Quarterly, 54,* 239–251.

Butler, D., & Geis, F. L. (1990). Nonverbal affect responses to male and female leaders: Implications for leadership evaluations. *Journal of Personality and Social Psychology, 58,* 48–59.

Byrne, R. (1995). *The thinking ape: Evolutionary origins of intelligence.* Oxford: Oxford University Press.

Card, A. L., Jackson, L. A., Stollak, G. E., & Ialongo, N. S. (1986). Gender role and person-perception accuracy. *Sex Roles, 15,* 159–171.

Carnegie, D. (1932). *Lincoln, the unknown.* New York: Century.

Carnegie, D. (1936). *How to win friends and influence people.* Garden City, NY: Dale Carnegie and Associates.

Chaiken, S. (1980). Heuristic versus systematic information processing and the use of source versus message cues in persuasion. *Journal of Personality and Social Psychology, 39,* 752–766.

Chaiken, S., & Eagly, A. H. (1983). Communication modality as a determinant of persuasion: The role of communicator salience. *Journal of Personality and Social Psychology, 45,* 241–256.

Chaiken, S., & Maheswaran, D. (1994). Heuristic processing can bias systematic processing: Effects of source credibility, argument ambiguity, and task importance on attitude judgment. *Journal of Personality and Social Psychology, 66,* 460–473.

Chelune, G. J. (1976). Reactions to male and female disclosure at two levels. *Journal of Personality and Social Psychology, 34,* 1000–1003.

Cialdini, R. B. (1978). Low-ball procedure for producing compliance: Commitment then cost. *Journal of Personality and Social Psychology, 36,* 463–476.

Cialdini, R. B. (1993). *Influence: Science and practice.* New York: HarperCollins.

Cialdini, R. B., Cacioppo, J. T., Bassett, R., & Miller, J. A. (1978). Lowball procedure for producing compliance: Commitment then cost. *Journal of Personality and Social Psychology, 36,* 463–476.

Cialdini, R. B., & De Nicholas, M. E. (1989). Self-presentation by association. *Journal of Personality and Social Psychology, 57,* 626–631.

Cialdini, R. B., Green, B. L., & Rusch, A. J. (1992). When tactical pronouncements of change become real change: The case of reciprocal persuasion. *Journal of Personality and Social Psychology, 63,* 30–40.

Cialdini, R. B., & Schroeder, D. A. (1976). Increasing compliance by legitimizing paltry contributions: When even a penny helps. *Journal of Personality and Social Psychology, 34,* 599–604.

Clark, M. S., & Pataki, S. P. (1995). Interpersonal processes influencing attraction and relationships. In A. Tesser (Ed.), *Advanced social psychology* (pp. 283–331). New York: McGraw-Hill.

Cohen, B. P. (1989). *Developing sociological knowledge: Theory and method.* Chicago: Nelson-Hall.

Cohen, E. (1993). From theory to practice: The development of an applied research program. In J. Berger & M. Zelditch Jr. (Eds.), *Theoretical research programs: Studies in the growth of theory* (pp. 385–414). Stanford, CA: Stanford University Press.

Collins, N. L. & Miller, L. C. (1994). Self-disclosure and liking: a meta-analytic review. *Psychological Bulletin, 116,* 457–475.

Conley, F. K. (1998). *Walking out on the boys.* New York: Farrar, Straus and Giroux.

Cook, K. S., & Emerson, R. M. (1978). Power, equity and commitment in exchange networks. *American Sociological Review, 43,* 721–739.

Cook, K. S., Emerson, R. M., Gillmore, M. R., & Yamagishi, T. (1983). The distribution of power in exchange networks: Theory and experimental results. *American Journal of Sociology, 89,* 275–305.

Cook, K. S., Fine, G. A., & House, J. S. (1995). *Sociological perspectives on social psychology.* Boston: Allyn and Bacon.

Cooley, C. H. (1902). *Human nature and the social order.* New York: Scribner.

Cooper, J., & Fazio, R. H. (1984). A new look at dissonance theory. In L. Berkowitz (Ed.), *Advances in experimental social psychology* (vol. 17, pp. 229–266). New York: Academic Press.

Crocker, J., & Luhtanen, R. (1990). Collective self-esteem and ingroup bias. *Journal of Personality and Social Psychology, 58,* 60–67.

Crocker, J., Thompson, L. L., McGraw, K. M., & Ingerman, C. (1987). Downward comparison, prejudice, and evaluation of others: Effects of self-esteem and threat. *Journal of Personality and Social Psychology, 52,* 907–916.

Crocker, J., Voelkl, K., Testa, M., & Major, B. (1991). Social stigma: The affective consequences of attributional ambiguity. *Journal of Personality and Social Psychology, 60,* 218–228.

Damasio, A. R. (1994). *Descarte's error: Emotion, reason, and the human brain.* New York: Grosset/Putnam.

Darby, B. W., & Schlenker, B. R. (1982). Children's reactions to apologies. *Journal of Personality and Social Psychology, 43,* 742–753.

Darley, J. M., & Batson, C. D. (1973). From Jerusalem to Jericho: A study of situational and dispositional variables in helping behavior. *Journal of Personality and Social Psychology, 27,* 100–108.

Darley, J. M., & Latane, B. (1968). Bystander intervention in emergencies: Diffusion of responsibility. *Journal of Personality and Social Psychology, 8,* 377–383.

de Munck, V. C. (Ed.). (1998). *Romantic love and sexual behavior.* Westport, CT: Praeger.

de Waal, F. (1996). *Good natured.* Cambridge, MA: Harvard University Press.

Deaux, K. (1984). From individual differences to social categories: Analysis of a decade's research on gender. *American Psychologist, 39,* 105–116.

DePaulo, B. M., Kenny, D. A., Hoover, C. W., Webb, W., & Oliver, P. V. (1987). Accuracy of person perception: Do people know what kinds of impressions they convey? *Journal of Personality and Social Psychology, 52,* 303–315.

Deppe, R. K., & Harackiewicz, J. M. (1996). Self-handicapping and intrinsic motivation: Buffering intrinsic motivation from the threat of failure. *Journal of Personality and Social Psychology, 70,* 868–876.

Derlega, V. J., & Chaikin, A. L. (1976). Norms affecting self-disclosure in men and women. *Journal of Consulting and Clinical Psychology, 44,* 376–380.

Devine, P. (1989). Stereotypes and prejudice: Their automatic and controlled components. *Journal of Personality and Social Psychology, 56,* 5–18.

Diesing, P. (1991). *How does social science work? Reflections on practice.* Pittsburgh: University of Pittsburgh Press.

Dion, K. K., & Dion, K. L. (1991). Psychological individualism and romantic love. *Journal of Social Behavior and Personality, 6,* 17–33.

Drigotas, S. M., & Rusbult, C. E. (1992). Should I stay or should I go? A dependence model of breakups. *Journal of Personality and Social Psychology, 62,* 62–87.

Driscoll, R., Davis, K. E., & Lipetz, M. E. (1972). Parental interference and romantic love: The Romeo and Juliet effect. *Journal of Personality and Social Psychology, 24,* 1–10.

Duncan, B. L. (1976). Differential social perception and attribution of intergroup violence: Testing the lower limits of stereotyping blacks. *Journal of Personality and Social Psychology, 34,* 590–598.

Dutton, D. G., & Aron, A. P. Some evidence for heightened sexual attraction under conditions of high anxiety. *Journal of Personality and Social Psychology, 30,* 510–517.

Eagly, A. H., Karau, S. J., & Makhijani, M. G. (1995). Gender and the effectiveness of leaders: A meta-analysis. *Psychological Bulletin, 117,* 125–145.

Eagly, A. H., Makhijani, M. G., & Klonsky, B. G. (1992). Gender and the evaluation of leaders: A meta-analysis. *Psychological Bulletin, 111,* 3–22.

Emerson, R. M. (1962). Power-dependence relations. *American Sociological Review, 27,* 31–41.

Epstein, J., & Harackiewicz, J. M. (1992). Winning is not enough: The effects of competition and achievement orientation on intrinsic interest. *Personality and Social Psychology Bulletin, 18,* 128–138.

Ethier, K. A., & Deaux, K. (1994). Negotiating social identity when contexts change: Maintaining identification and responding to threat. *Journal of Personality and Social Psychology, 67,* 243–251.

Evans, J. St. B. T. (1972). Reasoning with negatives. *British Journal of Psychology, 63,* 213–219.

Fein, S. (1996). Effects of suspicion on attributional thinking and the correspondence bias. *Journal of Personality and Social Psychology, 70,* 1164–1184.

Feingold, A. (1992). Good-looking people are not what we think. *Psychological Bulletin, 111,* 304–341.

Fenigstein, A., & Levine, M. P. (1984). Self-attention, concept activation and the causal self. *Journal of Experimental Social Psychology, 20,* 231–245.

Festinger, L. (1957). *A theory of cognitive dissonance.* Stanford, CA: Stanford University Press.

Feynman, R. (1994). *The character of physical law*. New York: Modern Library.

Fleming, J. H., Darley, J. M., Hilton, J. L., & Kojetin, B. A. (1990). Multiple audience problem: A strategic communication perspective on social perception. *Journal of Personality and Social Psychology, 58,* 593–609.

Forgas, J. P. (1998). On feeling good and getting your way: Mood effects on negotiator cognition and bargaining strategies. *Journal of Personality and Social Psychology, 74,* 565–577.

Forsyth, D. R., Berger, R. E., & Mitchell, T. (1981). The effects of self-serving vs. other-serving claims of responsibility on attraction and attribution in groups. *Social Psychology Quarterly, 44,* 59–64.

Foschi, M., & Foddy, M. (1988). Standards, performances, and the formation of self-other expectations. In M. A. Webster, Jr., & M. Foschi (Eds.), *Status generalization* (pp. 248–260). Stanford, CA: Stanford University Press.

Foschi, M., Lai, L., & Sigerson, K. (1994). Gender and double standards in the assessment of job applicants. *Social Psychology Quarterly, 57,* 326–339.

Foschi, M., & Lawler, E. J. (1994). *Group processes: Sociological analyses*. Chicago: Nelson-Hall.

Fouts, R. (1997). *Next of kin*. New York: Morrow.

Fox, M. F., & Ferri, V. C. (1992). Women, men and their attributions for success in academe. *Social Psychology Quarterly, 55,* 257–271.

Frazier, P. A. (1990). Victim attributions and post-rape trauma. *Journal of Personality and Social Psychology, 59,* 298–304.

Freedman, J. L., & Fraser, S. C. (1966). Compliance without pressure: The foot in the door technique. *Journal of Personality and Social Psychology, 4,* 195–202.

Frey, K. P., & Eagly, A. H. (1993). Vividness can undermine the persuasiveness of messages. *Journal of Personality and Social Psychology, 65,* 32–44.

Frodi, A. M., & Lamb, M. E. (1980). Child abusers' responses to infant smiles and cries. *Child Development, 51,* 238–241.

Gaertner, S. L., & Dovidio, J. F. (1977). The subtlety of white racism, arousal, and helping behavior. *Journal of Personality and Social Psychology, 35,* 691–707.

Gallup, G. G., Jr. (1970). Chimpanzees: Self-recognition. *Science, 167,* 86–87.

Gallup, G. G., Jr. (1998). Self-awareness and the evolution of social intelligence. *Behavioral Processes, 42,* 239–247.

Gecas, V., & Burke, P. J. (1995). Self and identity. In K. S. Cook, G. A. Fine, & J. S. House (Eds.), *Sociological perspectives on social psychology* (pp. 41–67). Boston: Allyn and Bacon.

Geisler, R. B., Josephs, R. A., & Swann, W. B., Jr. (1996). Self-verification in clinical depression: The desire for negative evaluation. *Journal of Abnormal Psychology, 105,* 358–368.

Gergen, K. J. (1991). *The saturated self*. New York: Basic Books.

Gibbins, K., & Walker, I. (1996). Social roles, social norms, and self-presentation in the quiz effect of Ross, Amabile and Steinmetz. *Journal of Social Psychology, 136,* 625–634.

Gilbert, D. T., & Hixon, J. G. (1991). The trouble of thinking: Activation and application of stereotypic beliefs. *Journal of Personality and Social Psychology, 60,* 509–517.

Gilbert, D. T., & Jones, E. E. (1986). Exemplification: The self-presentation of moral character. *Journal of Personality, 54,* 593–615.

Gilbert, D. T., Krull, D. S., & Malone, P. S. (1990). Unbelieving the unbelievable: Some problems in the rejection of false information. *Journal of Personality and Social Psychology, 59,* 601–613.

Gilbert, D. T., & Malone, P. S. (1995). The correspondence bias. *Psychological Bulletin, 117,* 21–38.

Gilbert, D. T., & Silvera, D. H. (1996). Overhelping. *Journal of Personality and Social Psychology, 70,* 678–690.

Gilbert, D. T., Tafarodi, R. W., & Malone, P. S. (1993). You can't not believe everything you read. *Journal of Personality and Social Psychology, 65,* 221–233.

Glass, D. C., McKnight, J. D., & Valdimasdottir, H. (1993). Depression, burnout, and perceptions of control in hospital nurses. *Journal of Consulting and Clinical Psychology, 61,* 147–155.

Godfrey, D. K., Jones, E. E., & Lord, C. G. (1986). Self-promotion is not ingratiating. *Journal of Personality and Social Psychology, 50,* 106–115.

Goffman, E. (1959). *The presentation of self in everyday life.* Garden City, NY: Doubleday.

Gonzales, M. H., Pederson, J. H., Manning, D. J., & Wetter, D. W. (1990). Pardon my gaffe: Effects of sex, status, and consequence severity on accounts. *Journal of Personality and Social Psychology, 58,* 610–621.

Gorassini, D. R., & Olson, J. M. (1995). Does self-perception change explain the foot-in-the-door effect? *Journal of Personality and Social Psychology, 69,* 91–105.

Gordon, R. A. (1996). Impact of ingratiation on judgments and evaluations: A meta-analytic investigation. *Journal of Personality and Social Psychology, 71,* 54–70.

Gotlib, I. H., & Lee, C. M. (1989). The social functioning of depressed patients: A longitudinal assessment. *Journal of Social and Clinical Psychology, 8,* 223–237.

Graziano, W. G., Jensen-Campbell, L. A., Shebilske, L. J., & Lundgren, S. R. (1993). Social influence, sex differences, and judgments of beauty: Putting the interpersonal back in interpersonal attraction. *Journal of Personality and Social Psychology, 65,* 522–531.

Greenberg, J. (1992). Depression, self-focused attention and the self-serving attributional bias. *Personality and Individual Differences, 13,* 959–965.

Habermas, J. (1988). *On the logic of the social sciences.* Cambridge: MIT Press.

Hacking, I. (1983). *Representing and intervening.* Cambridge: Cambridge University Press.

Hacking, I. (1995). *Rewriting the soul: Multiple personality and the sciences of memory.* Princeton, NJ: Princeton University Press.

Halberstadt, J. B., & Niedenthal, P. M. (1997). Emotional state and the use of stimulus dimensions in judgment. *Journal of Personality and Social Psychology, 72,* 1017–1033.

Hale, W. D., & Strickland, B. R. (1976). Induction of mood states and their effect on cognitive and social behaviors. *Journal of Social and Clinical Psychology, 44,* 155–159.

Hall, J. A. (1984). *Nonverbal sex differences: Communication accuracy and expressive styles.* Baltimore: Johns Hopkins University Press.

Hamill, R. C., Wilson, T. D., & Nisbett, R. E. (1980). Ignoring sample bias: Inferences about populations from atypical cases. *Journal of Personality and Social Psychology, 39,* 578–589.

Hamilton, V. L. (1980). Intuitive psychologist or intuitive lawyer? Alternative models of the attribution process. *Journal of Personality and Social Psychology, 39,* 767–772.

Haney, C., Banks, C., & Zimbardo, P. G. (1973). Interpersonal dynamics in a simulated prison. International *Journal of Criminology and Penology, 1,* 69–97.

Harber, K. D. (1998). Feedback to minorities: Evidence of a positive bias. *Journal of Personality and Social Psychology, 74,* 622–628.

Hart, A. J., & Morry, M. M. (1996). Nonverbal behavior, race, and attitude attributions. *Journal of Experimental Social Psychology, 32,* 165–179.

Hatfield, E., & Sprecher, S. (1986). *Mirror, mirror . . . : The importance of looks in everyday life.* Albany: State University of New York Press.

Hayashi, G. M., & Strickland, B. R. (1998). Long-term effects of parental divorce on love relationships: Divorce as attachment disruption. *Journal of Social and Personal Relationships, 15,* 23–38.

Hazan, C., & Shaver, P. (1987). Romantic love conceptualized as an attachment process. *Journal of Personality and Social Psychology, 52,* 511–524.

Heise, D. R. (1979). *Understanding events: Affect and the construction of social action.* New York: Cambridge University Press.

Henderson-King, E. I., & Nisbett, R. E. (1996). Anti-black prejudice as a function of exposure to the negative behavior of a single black person. *Journal of Personality and Social Psychology, 71,* 654–664.

Hendrick, S. S., & Hendrick, C. (1992). *Romantic love.* Newbury Park, CA: Sage.

Hepworth, J. T., & West, S. G. (1988). Lynchings and the economy: A time-series reanalysis of Hovland and Sears (1940). *Journal of Personality and Social Psychology, 55,* 239–247.

Hernnstein, R. J., & Murray, C. (1994). *The bell curve: Intelligence and class structure in American life.* New York: Free Press.

Higgins, E. T., Rholes, W. S., & Jones, C. R. (1977). Category accessibility and impression formation. *Journal of Experimental Social Psychology, 13,* 141–154.

Hirt, E. R., Zillman, D., Erickson, G. A., & Kennedy, C. (1992). Costs and benefits of allegience: Changes in fans' self-ascribed competencies after team victory versus defeat. *Journal of Personality and Social Psychology, 63,* 724–738.

Hochshild, A. R. (1989). *The second shift.* New York: Avon Books.

Hodgins, H. S., Liebeskind, E., & Schwartz, W. (1996). Getting out of hot water: Facework in social predicaments. *Journal of Personality and Social Psychology, 71,* 300–314.

Holtgraves, T. (1991). Interpreting questions and replies: Effects of face-threat, question form, and gender. *Social Psychology Quarterly, 54,* 15–24.

Homans, G. C. (1971). Attraction and power. In B. I. Murstein (Ed.), *Theories of attraction and love* (pp. 46–48). New York: Springer.

Homans, G. C. (1974). *Social behavior: Its elementary forms.* New York: Harcourt Brace Jovanovich.

Howard, J. W., & Rothbart, M. (1980). Social categorization and memory for in-group and out-group behavior. *Journal of Personality and Social Psychology, 38,* 301–310.

Hughes, M., & Thomas, M. E. (1998). The continuing significance of race revisited: A study of race, class, and quality of life in America, 1972–1996. *American Sociological Review, 63,* 785–795.

Hume, D. (1966). *An enquiry concerning human understanding.* La Salle, IL: Open Court. (Original work published 1748)

James, W. (1981). *The principles of psychology.* Cambridge, MA: Harvard University Press. (Original work published 1890)

Jamieson, K. H. (1995). *Beyond the double bind: Women and leadership.* New York: Oxford University Press.

Janoff-Bulman, R. (1979). Characterological versus behavioral self-blame: Inquiries into depression and rape. *Journal of Personality and Social Psychology, 37,* 1798–1809.

Johnson, D. J., & Rusbult, C. E. (1989). Resisting temptation: Devaluation of alternative partners as a means of maintaining commitment in close relationships. *Journal of Personality and Social Psychology, 57,* 967–980.

Joiner, T. E., Jr. (1994). Contagious depression: Existence, specificity to depressed symptoms, and the role of reassurance seeking. *Journal of Personality and Social Psychology, 67,* 287–296.

Joiner, T. E., Jr. (1995). The price of soliciting and receiving negative feedback: Self-verification theory as a vulnerability to depression theory. *Journal of Abnormal Psychology, 104,* 364–372.

Jones, E. E. (1986). Interpreting interpersonal behavior: The effects of expectancies. *Science, 234,* 41–46.

Jones, E. E. (1991). *Interpersonal perception.* New York: W. H. Freeman.

Jones, E. E., & Archer, R. L. (1976). Are there special effects of personalistic self-disclosure? *Journal of Experimental Social Psychology, 12,* 180–193.

Jones, E. E., & Gordon, E. M. (1972). Timing of self-disclosure and its effects on personal attraction. *Journal of Personality and Social Psychology, 24,* 358–365.

Jones, E. E., & Harris, V. A. (1967). The attribution of attitudes. *Journal of Experimental Social Psychology, 3,* 1–24.

Jones, E. E., Rock, L., Shaver, K. G., Goethals, G. G., & Ward, L. M. (1968). Pattern of performance and ability attribution: An unexpected primacy effect. *Journal of Personality and Social Psychology, 10,* 317–340.

Jones, J. H. (1993). *Bad blood: The Tuskegee syphilis experiment.* New York: Free Press.

Jones, J. M. (1996). *The psychology of racism and prejudice.* New York: McGraw-Hill.

Jussim, L., & Eccles, J. S.. (1992). Teacher expectations II: Construction and reflection of student achievement. *Journal of Personality and Social Psychology, 63,* 947–961.

Kanter, R. M. (1977). *Men and women of the corporation.* New York: Basic Books.

Kay, F. M., & Hagan, J. (1998). Raising the bar: The gender stratification of law-firm capital. *American Sociological Review, 63,* 728–743.

Kellerman, J., Lewis, J., & Laird, J. D. (1989). Looking and loving: The effects of mutual gaze on feelings of romantic love. *Journal of Research in Personality, 23,* 145–161.

Kluegel, J. R., & Smith, E. R. (1986). *Beliefs about inequality: Americans' view of what is and what ought to be.* New York: Aldine-de Gruyter.

Kruglanski, A., Webster, D. M., & Klem, A. (1993). Motivated resistance and openness to persuasion in the presence or absence of prior information. *Journal of Personality and Social Psychology, 65,* 861–876.

Kuhn, T. S. (1970). *The structure of scientific revolutions* (2nd ed.). Chicago: University of Chicago Press.

Lakatos, I., & Musgrave, A. (Eds.). (1970). *Criticism and the growth of knowledge.* Cambridge: Cambridge University Press.

Landy, D.. & Sigall, H. (1974). Beauty as talent: Task evaluation as a function of the performer's physical attractiveness. *Journal of Personality and Social Psychology, 29,* 299–304.

Langer, E. J., & Rodin, J. (1976). The effects of choice and enhanced personal responsibility for the aged: A field experiment in an institutional setting. *Journal of Personality and Social Psychology, 34,* 191–198.

Latané, B., & Nida, S. (1981). Ten years of research on group size and helping. *Psychological Bulletin, 89,* 308–324.

Latour, B. (1987). *Science in action.* Cambridge, MA: Harvard University Press.

Laumann, E. O., Gagnon, J. H., Michael, R. T., & Michaels, S. (1994). *The social organization of sexuality: Sexual practices in the United States.* Chicago: University of Chicago Press.

Leary, M. (1995). *Self-presentation: Impression management and interpersonal behavior.* Boulder, CO: Westview.

Leenaars, A. A., Bringmann, W. G., & Balance, W. D. G. (1978). The effects of positive vs. negative wording on subjects' validity ratings of "true" and "false" feedback statements. *Journal of Clinical Psychology, 34,* 369–370.

Leippe, M. R., & Eisenstadt, D. (1994). Generalization of dissonance reduction: Decreasing prejudice through-induced compliance. *Journal of Personality and Social Psychology, 67,* 395–413.

Leith, K. P., & Baumeister, R. F. (1996). Why do bad moods increase self-defeating behavior? Emotion, risk taking, and self-regulation. *Journal of Personality and Social Psychology, 71,* 1250–1267.

Lemert, E. M. (1951). *Social pathology.* New York: McGraw-Hill.

Lemert, E. M. (1962). Paranoia and the dynamics of exclusion. *Sociometry, 25,* 2–20.

Lemyre, L., & Smith, P. M. (1985). Intergroup discrimination and self-esteem in the minimal group paradigm. *Journal of Personality and Social Psychology, 49,* 660–670.

Lincoln, A. (1965). *Wit and Wisdom.* Mount Vernon, NY: Peter Pauper Press.

Lindenberg, V. (1959). *Meditation and mankind.* London: Rider.

Locksley, A., Ortiz, V., & Hepburn, C. (1980). Social catergorization and discriminatory behavior: Extinguishing the minimal intergroup discrimination effect. *Journal of Personality and Social Psychology, 39,* 773–783.

Lord, C. G., Lepper, M. R., & Preston, E. (1984). Considering the opposite: A corrective strategy for social judgment. *Journal of Personality and Social Psychology, 47,* 1231–1243.

Lord, C. G., & Saenz, D. S. (1985). Memory deficits and memory surfeits: Differential cognitive consequences of tokenism for tokens and observers. *Journal of Personality and Social Psychology, 49,* 918–926.

Lovaglia, M. J. (In press). Understanding network exchange theory. In *Advances in group processes.* Greenwich, CT: JAI Press.

Lovaglia, M. J. & Houser, J. A. (1996). Emotional reactions and status in groups. *American Sociological Review, 61,* 867–883.

Lovaglia, M. J., Lucas, J. W., Houser, J. A., Thye, S., & Markovsky, B. (1998). Status processes and mental ability test scores. *American Journal of Sociology, 104,* 195–228.

Lovaglia, M. J., Skvoretz, J., Willer, D., & Markovsky, B. (1995). Negotiated exchanges in social networks. *Social Forces, 74,* 123–155.

Luginbuhl, J. E. R., Crowe, D. H., & Kahan, J. P. (1975). Causal attributions for success and failure. *Journal of Personality and Social Psychology, 31,* 86–93.

Lyubomirsky, S., & Nolen-Hoeksema, S. (1995). Effects of self-focused rumination on negative thinking and interpersonal problem solving. *Journal of Personality and Social Psychology, 69,* 176–190.

Machiavelli, N. (1940). *The Prince and the Discourses.* New York: Modern Library. (Original works published 1532 and 1531, respectively)

Madon, S., Jussim, L., & Eccles, J. (1997). In search of the powerful self-fulfilling prophecy. *Journal of Personality and Social Psychology, 72,* 791–809.

Mahoney, M. J. (1976). *Scientist as subject:* The psychological imperative. Cambridge, MA: Ballinger.

Mantovani, G. (1995). Virtual reality as a communication environment: Consensual hallucination, fiction and possible selves. *Human Relations, 48,* 669–683.

Markovsky, B., Skvoretz, J., Willer, D., Lovaglia, M. J., & Erger, J. (1993). The seeds of weak power: An extension of network exchange theory. *American Sociological Review, 58,* 197–209.

Markovsky, B., Willer D., & Patton, T. (1988). Power relations in exchange networks. *American Sociological Review, 53,* 220–236.

McClanahan, K. K., Gold, J. A., Lenney, E., Ryckman, R. M., & Kulberg, G. E. (1990). Infatuation and attraction to a dissimilar other: Why is love blind? *Journal of Social Psychology, 130,* 433–445.

McDonald, H., & Hirt, E. R. (1997). When expectancy meets desire: Motivational effects in reconstructive memory. *Journal of Personality and Social Psychology, 72,* 5–23.

Mead, G. H. (1934). *Mind, self, and society.* Chicago: University of Chicago Press.

Medawar, P. (1984). *The limits of science.* Oxford: Oxford University Press.

Merton, R. K. (1948). The self-fulfilling prophecy. *Antioch Review, 8,* 193–210.

Metalsky, G. I., Joiner, T. E., Jr., Hardin, T. S., & Abramson, L. Y. (1993). Depressive reactions to failure in a naturalistic setting: A test of the hopelessness and self-esteem theories of depression. *Journal of Abnormal Psychology, 102,* 101–109.

Meyers, D. G. (1996). *Social psychology* (5th ed.). New York: McGraw-Hill.

Michael, R. T., Gagnon, J. H., Laumann, E. O., & Kolata, G. (1995). *Sex in America: A definitive study.* New York: Warner Books.

Michener, H. A., & DeLamater, J. D. (1994). *Social psychology* (3rd ed.). Fort Worth, TX: Harcourt Brace.

Midgley, C., Arunkumar, R., & Urdan, T. C. (1996). "If I don't do well tomorrow, there's a reason": Predictors of adolescents' use of academic self-handicapping strategies. *Journal of Educational Psychology, 88,* 423–434.

Mikulincer, M., & Erev, I. (1992). Attachment style and structure of romantic love. *British Journal of Social Psychology, 30,* 273–291.

Mikulincer, M., & Nachshon, O. (1991). Attachment styles and patterns of self-disclosure. *Journal of Personality and Social Psychology, 61,* 321–334.

Miller, A. G. (1976). Constraint and target effects in the attribution of attitudes. *Journal of Experimental Social Psychology, 12,* 325–339.

Miller, A. G., Ashton, W., & Mishal, M. (1990). Beliefs concerning the features of constrained behavior: A basis for the fundamental attribution error. *Journal of Personality and Social Psychology, 59,* 635–650.

Miller, N., Maruyama, G., Beaber, R. J., & Valone, K. (1976). Speed of speech and persuasion. *Journal of Personality and Social Psychology, 34,* 615–624.

Miller, R. L., Brickman, P., & Bolen, D. (1975). Attribution versus persuasion as a means for modifying behavior. *Journal of Personality and Social Psychology, 31,* 430–441.

Miller, W. R. & Seligman, M. E. P. (1975). Depression and learned helplessness in man. *Journal of Abnormal Psychology, 84,* 228–238.

Mook, D. G. (1983). In defense of external invalidity. *American Psychologist, 38,* 379–387.

Mori, D. A., Chaiken, S., & Pliner, P. (1987). "Eating lightly" and the self-presentation of femininity. *Journal of Personality and Social Psychology, 53,* 693–702.

Multon, K. D., Brown, S. D., & Lent, R. W. (1991). Relation of self-efficacy beliefs to academic outcomes: A meta-analytic investigation. *Journal of Counseling Psychology, 38,* 30–38.

Natale, M. (1977). Effects of induced elation-depression on speech in the initial interview. *Journal of Consulting and Clinical Psychology, 45,* 45–52.

Neisser, U., Boodoo, G., Bouchard, T. J., Jr., Boykin, A. W., Brody, N., Ceci, S. J., Halpern, D. F., Loehlin, J. C., Perloff, R., Sternberg, R. J., & Urbina, S. (1996). Intelligence: Knowns and unknowns. *American Psychologist, 51,* 77–101.

Nix, G., Watson, C., Pyszczynski, T., & Greenberg, J. (1995). Reducing depressive affect through external focus of attention. *Journal of Social and Clinical Psychology, 14,* 36–52.

Pegalis, L. J., Shaffer, D. R., Bazzini, D. G., & Greenier, K. (1994). On the ability to elicit self-disclosure: Are there gender-based and contextual limitations on the opener effect? *Personality and Social Psychology Bulletin, 20,* 412–420.

Pennebaker, J. W. (1990). *Opening up: The healing power of confiding in others.* New York: Morrow.

Pennebaker, J. W. (1997). Writing about emotional experiences as a therapeutic process. *Psychological Science, 8,* 162–166.

Pennebaker, J. W., Colder, M., & Sharp, L. K. (1990). Accelerating the coping process. *Journal of Personality and Social Psychology, 58,* 528–537.

Pennebaker, J. W., Hughes, C. F., & O'Heeron, R. C. (1987). The psychophysiology of confession: Linking inhibitory and psychosomatic processes. *Journal of Personality and Social Psychology, 52,* 781–793.

Pennebaker, J. W., & O'Heeron, R. C. (1984). Confiding in others and illness rate among spouses of suicide and accidental-death victims. *Journal of Abnormal Psychology, 93,* 473–476.

Peterson, C., & Bossio, L. M. (1991). *Health and optimism.* New York: Free Press.

Peterson, C., Seligman, M. E. P. and Vaillant, G. E. (1988). Pessimistic explanatory style is a risk factor for physical illness: A thirty-five-year longitudinal study. *Journal of Personality and Social Psychology, 55,* 23–27.

Petty, R. E., Schumann, D. W., Richman, S. A., & Strathman, A. J. (1993). Positive mood and persuasion: Different roles for affect under high- and low-elaboration conditions. *Journal of Personality and Social Psychology, 64,* 5–20.

Pfeffer, J. (1992). *Managing with power: Politics and influence in organizations.* Boston: Harvard Business School Press.

Phillips, J. (1995). *The magic daughter.* New York: Viking.

Popper, K. R. (1968). *Conjectures and refutations: The growth of scientific knowledge.* New York: Harper and Row.

Pugh, M. D., & Wahrman, R. (1983). Neutralizing sexism in mixed-sex groups: Do women have to be better than men? *American Journal of Sociology, 88,* 746–762.

Pyszczynski, T., & Greenberg, J. (1985). Depression and preference for self-focusing stimuli after success and failure. *Journal of Personality and Social Psychology, 49,* 1066–1075.

Pyszczynski, T., & Greenberg, J. (1987). Toward an integration of cognitive and motivational perspectives on social inference: A biased hypothesis-testing model. *Advances in Experimental Social Psychology, 20,* 297–340.

Pyszczynski, T., Hamilton, J. C., Herring, F. H., & Greenberg, J. (1989). Depression, self-focused attention, and the negative memory bias. *Journal of Personality and Social Psychology, 57,* 351–357.

Pyszczynski, T., Holt, K. & Greenberg, J. (1987). Depression, self-focused attention, and expectancies for positive and negative future life events for self and others. *Journal of Personality and Social Psychology, 52,* 994–1001.

Raps, C. S., Reinhard, K. E., & Seligman, M. E. P. (1980). Reversal of cognitive and affective deficits associated with depression and learned helplessness by mood elevation in patients. *Journal of Abnormal Psychology, 89,* 342–349.

Rhodewalt, F,. & Agustsdottir, S. (1986). Effects of self-presentation on the phenomenal self. *Journal of Personality and Social Psychology, 50,* 47–55.

Rhodewalt, F., Sanbonmatsu, D. M., Tschanz, B., Feick, D. L., & Waller, A. (1995). Self-handicapping and interpersonal trade-offs: The effects of claimed self-handicaps on observers' performance evaluations and feedback. *Personality and Social Psychology Bulletin, 21,* 1042–1050.

Ridgeway, C. (1982). Status in groups: The importance of motivation. *American Sociological Review, 47,* 76–88.

Ridgeway, C. L., Boyle, E., Kuipers, K. J., & Robinson, D. (1995, August). *Interaction and the construction of status beliefs.* Paper presented at the annual meeting of the American Sociological Association, Washington, D.C.

Ridgeway, C. L., Boyle, E. H., Kuipers, K. J., and Robinson, D. T. (1998). How do status beliefs develop? The role of resources ad interactional experience. *American Sociological Review, 63,* 331–350.

Riley, A., & Burke, P. J. (1995). Identities and self-verification in the small group. *Social Psychology Quarterly, 58,* 61–73.

Robinson, D., & Smith-Lovin, L. (1992). Selective interaction as a strategy for identity maintenance: An affect control model. *Social Psychology Quarterly, 55,* 12–28.

Rodin, J., & Langer, E. J. (1977). Long-term effects of a control-relevant intervention with the institutionalized aged. *Journal of Personality and Social Psychology, 35,* 897–902.

Rogers, R. W., & Prentice-Dunn, S. (1981). Deindividuating and anger-mediated interracial aggression: Unmasking regressive racism. *Journal of Personality and Social Psychology, 41,* 63–73.

Romero, G. J., & Garza, R. T. (1986). Attributions for the occupational success/failure of ethnic minority and nonminority women. *Sex Roles, 14,* 445–452.

Rosenhan, D. L. (1973). On being sane in insane places. *Science, 179,* 250–258.

Rosenhan, D. L. (1975). The contextual nature of psychiatric diagnosis. *Journal of Abnormal Psychology, 84,* 462–474.

Rosenthal, R., & Jacobsen, L. (1992). *Pygmalion in the classroom: Teacher expectation and pupils' intellectual development.* New York: Irvington.

Ross, L. (1977). The intuitive psychologist and his shortcomings: Distortions in the attribution process. In L. Berkowitz (Ed.), *Advances in experimental social psychology* (vol. 10, pp. 173–220). Orlando, FL: Academic Press.

Ross, L., Amabile, T. M., & Steinmetz, J. L. (1977). Social roles, social control, and biases in social-perception processes. *Journal of Personality and Social Psychology, 35,* 485–494.

Ross, L., Bierbauer, G., & Polly, S. (1974). Attribution of educational outcomes by professional and nonprofessional instructors. *Journal of Personality and Social Psychology, 29,* 609–618.

Ross, L., Lepper, M. R., & Hubbard, M. (1975). Perseverance in self perception and social perception: Biased attributional processes in the debriefing paradigm. *Journal of Personality and Social Psychology, 32,* 880–892.

Ross, L., & Nisbett, R. E., (1991). *The person and the situation: Perspectives of social psychology.* New York: McGraw-Hill.

Rotter, N. G., & Rotter, G. S. (1988). Sex differences in the encoding and decoding of negative facial emotions. *Journal of Nonverbal Behavior, 12,* 139–148.

Rubovits, P., & Maehr, M. L. (1973). Pygmalion in black and white. *Journal of Personality and Social Psychology, 25,* 210–218.

Rudman, L. A. (1998). Self-promotion as a risk factor for women: The costs and benefits of counterstereotypical impression management. *Journal of Personality and Social Psychology, 74,* 629–645.

Ruggiero, K. M., & Taylor, D. M. (1994). The personal/group discrimination discrepancy: Women talk about their experiences. *Journal of Applied Social Psychology, 24,* 1806–1826.

Ruggiero, K. M., & Taylor, D. M. (1997). Why minority group members perceive or do not perceive the discrimination that confronts them: The role of self-esteem and perceived control. *Journal of Personality and Social Psychology, 72,* 373–389.

Rusbult, C. E., & Martz, J. M. (1995). Remaining in an abusive relationship: An investment model analysis of nonvoluntary dependence. *Personality and Social Psychology Bulletin, 21,* 558–571.

Rusbult, C. E., Verette, J., Whitney, G. A., Slovik, L. F., & Lipkus, I. (1991). Accomodation processes in close relationships: Theory and preliminary empirical evidence. *Journal of Personality and Social Psychology, 60,* 53–78.

Savage-Rumbaugh, S., & Lewin, R. (1994). *Kanzi: The ape at the brink of the human mind.* New York: Wiley.

Schlenker, B. R., & Darby, B. W. (1981). The use of apologies in social predicaments. *Social Psychology Quarterly, 44,* 271–278.

Schuman, H., Bobo, L., & Steeh, C. (1985). *Racial attitudes in America: Trends and interpretations.* Cambridge, MA: Harvard University Press.

Schulman, K. A., Berlin, J. A., Harless, W., Kerner, J. F., Sistrunk, S., Gersh, B. J., Dube, R., Taleghani, C. K., Burke, J. E., Williams, S., Eisenberg, J. M., and Escarce, J. J. (1999). The effect of race and sex on physicians' recommendations for cardiac catheterization. *New England Journal of Medicine, 340,* 618–626.

Seligman, M. E. P. (1975). *Helplessness: On depression, development, and death.* San Francisco: W. H. Freeman.

Seligman, M. E. P. (1991). *Learned optimism: How to change your mind and your life.* New York: Pocket Books.

Seligman, M. E. P., Abramson, L. Y., Semmel, A., & von Baeyer, C. (1979). Depressive attributional style. *Journal of Abnormal Psychology, 88,* 242–247.

Shackelford, S., Wood, W., & Worchel, S. (1996). Behavioral styles and the influence of women in mixed-sex groups. *Social Psychology Quarterly, 59,* 284–293.

Shaffer, D. R., & Ogden, J. K. (1986). On sex differences in self-disclosure during the acquaintance process: The role of anticipated future interaction. *Journal of Personality and Social Psychology, 51,* 92–101.

Shepperd, J. A., & Arkin, R. M. (1991). Behavioral other-enhancement: Strategically obscuring the link between performance and evaluation. *Journal of Personality and Social Psychology, 60,* 79–88.

Shih, M., Pittinsky, T. L., & Ambady, N. (1999). Stereotype susceptibility: Identity salience and shifts in quantitative performance. *Psychological Science, 10,* 80–83.

Shimahara, N. (1984). Toward the equality of a Japanese minority: The case of the Burakumin. *Comparative Education, 20,* 339–353.

Shipler, D. K. (1997). *Country of strangers: Blacks and whites in America.* New York: Alfred A. Knopf.

Shulman, K. I., Tohen, M., & Kutcher, S. R. (1996). *Mood disorders across the life span.* New York: Wiley.

Simon, R. (1995). Gender, multiple roles, role meaning, and mental health. *Journal of Health and Social Behavior, 36,* 182–194.

Singelis, T., Choo, P., & Hatfield, E. (1995). Love schemas and romantic love. *Journal of Social Behavior and Personality, 10,* 15–36.

Skvoretz, J., & Willer, D. (1993). Exclusion and power: A test of four theories of power in exchange networks. *American Sociological Review, 58,* 801–818.

Smyth, J. M., Stone, A. A., Hurewitz, A., & Kaell, A. (1999). Effects of writing about stressful experiences on symptom reduction in patients with asthma or rheumatoid arthritis: A randomized trial. *Journal of the American Medical Association, 281,* 1304–1309.

Snyder, M., Decker Tanke, E., & Berscheid, E. (1977). Social perception and interpersonal behavior: On the self-fulfilling nature of social stereotypes. *Journal of Personality and Social Psychology, 35,* 656–666.

Sprecher, S. (1998). The effect of exchange orientation on close relationships. *Social Psychology Quarterly, 61,* 220–231.

Stangor, C., Lynch, L., Duan, C., & Glass, B. (1992). Categorization of individuals on the basis of multiple social features. *Journal of Personality and Social Psychology, 62,* 207–218.

Steele, C. M. (1988). The psychology of self-affirmation: Sustaining the integrity of the self. In L. Berkowitz (Ed.), *Advances in experimental social psychology* (vol. 21, pp. 261–302). San Diego, CA: Academic Press.

Steele, C. M. (1997). A threat in the air: How stereotypes shape intellectual identity and performance. *American Psychologist, 52,* 613–629.

Steele, C. M., & Aronson, J. (1995). Stereotype threat and the intellectual test performance of African Americans. *Journal of Personality and Social Psychology, 69,* 797–811.

Steele, S. (1990). *The content of our character.* New York: St. Martin's Press.

Sternberg, R. J. (1998). *Love is a story: A new theory of relationships.* New York: Oxford University Press.

Sternberg, R. J., & Barnes, M. L. (Eds.). (1988). *The psychology of love.* New Haven, CT: Yale University Press.

Stone, A. R. (1991). Will the real body please stand up? Boundary stories about virtual cultures. In M. Benedikt (Ed.), *Cyberspace: First steps* (pp. 81–118). Cambridge: MIT Press.

Storms, M. D. (1973). Videotape and the attribution process: Reversing actors' and observers" points of view. *Journal of Personality and Social Psychology, 27,* 165–175.

Strack, S., & Coyne, J. C. (1983). Social confirmation of dysphoria: Shared and private reactions to depression. *Journal of Personality and Social Psychology, 44,* 798–806.

Strickland, B. R., Hale, W. D., & Anderson, L. K. (1975). Effects of induced mood states on activity and self-reported affect. *Journal of Consulting and Clinical Psychology, 43,* 587–589.

Stryker, S. (1980). *Symbolic interactionism: A social structural version.* Menlo Park, CA: Benjamin-Cummings.

Swann, W. B., Jr. (1997). The trouble with change: Self-verification and allegiance to the self. *Psychological Science, 8,* 177–180.

Swann, W. B., Jr., Giuliano, T., & Wegner, D. M. (1982). Where leading questions can lead: The power of conjecture in social interaction. *Journal of Personality and Social Psychology, 42,* 1025–1035.

Swann, W. B., Jr., Griffin, J. J., Predmore, S. C., & Gaines, B. (1987). The cognitive affective crossfire: When self-consistency confronts self-enhancement. *Journal of Personality and Social Psychology, 52,* 881–889.

Swann, W. B., Jr., Pelham, B. W., & Krull, D. S. (1989). Agreeable fancy or disagreeable truth? Reconciling self-enhancement and self-verification. *Journal of Personality and Social Psychology, 57,* 782–791.

Swann, W. B., Jr., & Read, S. J. (1981). Acquiring self-knowledge: The search for feedback that fits. *Journal of Personality and Social Psychology, 41,* 1119–1128.

Swann, W. B., Jr., Stein-Seroussi, A., & McNulty, S. E. (1992). Outcasts in a white-lie society: The enigmatic worlds of people with negative self-conceptions. *Journal of Personality and Social Psychology, 62,* 618–624.

Swann, W. B., Jr., Wenzlaff, R. M., Krull, D. S., & Pelham, B. W. (1992). Allure of negative feedback: Self-verification strivings among depressed persons. *Journal of Abnormal Psychology, 101,* 293–306.

Swann, W. B., Jr., Wenzlaff, R. M., & Tafarodi, R. W. (1992). Depression and the search for negative evaluations: More evidence of the role of self-verification strivings. *Journal of Abnormal Psychology, 101,* 314–317.

Szmatka, J., & Lovaglia, M. J. (1996). The significance of method. *Sociological Perspectives, 39,* 393–415.

Szmatka, J., Skvoretz, J., & Berger, J. (1997). *Status, network, and structure: Theory development in group processes.* Stanford, CA: Stanford University Press.

Tajfel, H. (1970). Experiments in intergroup discrimination. *Scientific American, 23,* 96–102.

Tajfel, H., Billig, M. G., Bundy, R. P., & Flament., C. (1971). Social categorization and intergroup behaviour. *European Journal of Social Psychology, 1,* 149–179.

Taylor, D. A., Gould, R. J., & Brounstein, P. J. (1981). Effects of personalistic self-disclosure. *Personality and Social Psychology Bulletin, 7,* 487–492.

Taylor, D. M., Wright, S. C., Moghaddam, F. M., & Lalonde, R. N. (1990). The personal/group discrimination discrepancy: Perceiving my group, but not myself, to be a target for discrimination. *Personality and Social Psychology Bulletin, 16,* 254–262.

Taylor, S. E. (1983). Adjusting to threatening events: A theory of cognitive adaptation. *American Psychologist, 38,* 1161–1173.

Taylor, S. E. (1989). *Positive illusions: creative self-deception and the healthy mind.* New York: Basic Books.

Terry, D. (1997, April 28). 3 R's of 2 deaths: Romance, race, revenge. *New York Times,* p. A1.

Tesser, A. (1995). *Advanced social psychology.* New York: McGraw-Hill.

Tesser, A., & Cornell, D. P. (1991). On the confluence of self processes. *Journal of Experimental Social Psychology, 27,* 501–526.

Tesser, A., & Paulhus, D. L.. (1976). Toward a causal model of love. *Journal of Personality and Social Psychology, 34,* 1095–1105.

Thibaut, J. W., & Kelley, H. H. (1959). *The social psychology of groups.* New York: Wiley.

Thoits, P. A. (1986). Multiple identities: Examining gender and marital status differences in distress. *American Sociological Review, 51,* 259–272.

Thomas, W. I., & Thomas, D. S. (1928). *The child in America: Behavior problems and programs.* New York: Knopf.

Tidd, K. L., & Lockard, J. S. (1978). Monetary significance of the affiliative smile: A case for reciprocal altruism. *Bulletin of the Psychonomic Society, 11,* 344–346.

Tiger, L. (1979). *Optimism: The biology of hope.* New York: Simon & Schuster.

Tolnay, S. E., Beck, E. M., & Massey, J. L. (1992). Black competition and white vengeance: Legal execution of blacks as social control in the cotton south, 1890–1929. *Social Science Quarterly, 73,* 627–644.

Troyer, L., & Younts, C. W. (1997). Whose expectations matter? The relative power of first- and second-order expectations in determining social influence. *American Journal of Sociology, 103,* 692–732.

Turkle, S. (1995). *Life on the screen: Identity in the age of the Internet.* New York: Touchstone.

Turner, J. C. (1978). Social comparison and social identity: Some prospects for intergroup behavior. *European Journal of Social Psychology, 5,* 5–34.

Turner, J. C. (1991). *Social influence.* Pacific Grove, CA: Brooks/Cole.

Tversky, A., & Kahneman, D. (1974). Judgment and uncertainty: Heuristics and biases. *Science, 185,* 1124–1131.

Van Lange, P. A. M., Rusbilt, C. E., Drigotas, S. M., Arriaga, X. B., Witcher, B. S., & Cox, C. L. (1997). Willingness to sacrifice in close relationships. *Journal of Personality and Social Psychology, 72,* 1373–1395.

Velten, E., Jr. (1968). A laboratory task for induction of mood states. *Behaviour Research and Therapy, 6,* 473–482.

Vorauer, J. D., & Miller, D. T. (1997). Failure to recognize the effect of implicit social influence on the presentation of self. *Journal of Personality and Social Psychology, 73,* 281–295.

Walsh, A. (1991). *The science of love: Understanding love and its effects on mind and body.* Buffalo, NY: Prometheus.

Watson, J. D. (1968). *The double helix.* New York: Atheneum.

Webster, D. (1993). Motivated augmentation and reduction of the overattribution bias. *Journal of Personality and Social Psychology, 65,* 261–271.

Webster, M., Jr., & Driskell, J. E., Jr. (1978). Status generalization: A review and some new data. *American Sociological Review, 43,* 220–236.

Webster, M., Jr., & Driskell, J. E. (1983). Beauty as status. *American Journal of Sociology, 89,* 140–165.

Webster, M., Jr., & Foschi, M. (Eds.). (1988). *Status generalization: New theory and research.* Stanford, CA: Stanford University Press.

Webster, M., Jr., & Kervin, J. B. (1971). Artificiality in experimental sociology. *Canadian Review of Sociology and Anthropology, 8,* 263–272.

Wegner, D. M., & Gold, D. B. (1995). Fanning old flames: Emotional and cognitive effects of suppressing thoughts of a past relationship. *Journal of Personality and Social Psychology, 68,* 782–792.

Wegner, D. M., Lane, J. D. (1995). The cognitive consequences of secrecy. *Journal of Personality and Social Psychology, 69,* 237–253.

Wegner, D. M., Lane, J. D., & Dimitri, S. (1994). The allure of secret relationships. *Journal of Personality and Social Psychology, 66,* 287–300.

White, G. L., Fishbein, S., & Rutstein, J. (1981). Passionate love and the misattribution of arousal. *Journal of Personality and Social Psychology, 41,* 56–62.

Whiten, A., & Byrne, R. W. (1988). The Machiavellian intelligence hypotheses: Editorial. In R. W. Byrne & A. Whiten (Eds.), *Machiavellian intelligence: Social expertise and the evolution of intellect in monkeys, apes and humans* (pp. 1–9). Oxford: Clarendon Press.

Wiedenfeld, S. A., O'Leary, A., Bandura, A., Brown, S., Levine, S., & Raska, K. (1990). Impact of perceived self-efficacy in coping with stressors on components of the immune system. *Journal of Personality and Social Psychology, 59,* 1082–1094.

Willer, D., Lovaglia, M. J., & Markovsky, B. (1997). Power and influence: A theoretical bridge. *Social Forces, 76,* 571–603.

Wittenbrink, B., Judd, C. M., & Park, B. (1997). Evidence for racial prejudice at the implicit level and its relationship with questionnaire measures. *Journal of Personality and Social Psychology, 72,* 262–274.

Wood, J. V., Saltzberg, J. A., & Goldsamt, L. A. (1990). Does affect induce self-focused attention? *Journal of Personality and Social Psychology, 58,* 899–908.

Wood, J. V., Saltzberg, J. A., Neale, J. M., Stone, A. A., & Rachmiel, T. B. (1990). Self-focused attention, coping responses, and distressed mood in everyday life. *Journal of Personality and Social Psychology, 58,* 1027–1036.

Wood, W., & Eagly, A. H. (1981). Stages in the analysis of persuasive messages: The role of causal attributions and message comprehension. *Journal of Personality and Social Psychology, 40,* 246–259.

Wortman, C. B., Adesman, P., Herman, E., & Greenberg, R. (1976). Self-disclosure: An attributional perspective. *Journal of Personality and Social Psychology, 33,* 184–191.

Wrangham, R., & Peterson, D. (1996). *Demonic males: Apes and the origins of human violence.* Boston: Houghton Mifflin.

Zarnoth, P., & Sniezek, J. A. (1997). The social influence of confidence in group decision making. *Journal of Experimental Social Psychology, 33,* 345–366.

Zelditch, M., Jr. (1980). Can you really study an army in the laboratory? In A. Etzioni & E. W. Lehman (Eds.), *A sociological reader on complex organizations* (pp. 531–539). New York: Holt, Rinehart and Winston.

Zimbardo, P. G. (1973). On the ethics of intervention in human psychological research: With special reference to the Stanford prison experiment. *Cognition, 2,* 243–256.

Zimbardo, P. G. (1979). *Psychology and life.* Glenview, IL: Scott, Foresman.

Index